Culture Builders

Culture Builders

A HISTORICAL ANTHROPOLOGY OF

MIDDLE-CLASS LIFE

JONAS FRYKMAN

AND

ORVAR LÖFGREN

Translated by Alan Crozier

FOREWORD BY JOHN GILLIS

RUTGERS UNIVERSITY PRESS

New Brunswick and London

Library of Congress Cataloging-in-Publication Data

Frykman, Jonas, 1942–

Culture builders.

Translation of: Den kultiverade människan.

Bibliography: p.

1. Sweden—Social conditions.   2. Sweden—
Social life and customs.   3. Middle classes—
Sweden—History—19th century.   4. Middle classes—
Sweden—History—20th century.   I. Löfgren, Orvar.
II. Title.

HN573.F78   1987   305.5'5'09485   86–15459

ISBN 0–8135–1209–3

ISBN 0–8135–1239–5 (pbk.)

British Cataloging-in-Publication information available.

First published in Swedish by LiberFörlag in 1979;
reprinted in 1983.

Translation has been made possible through a grant from the
Swedish Research Council for the Humanities and the Social
Sciences.

· CONTENTS ·

CLEAN AND PROPER

BODY AND SOUL THROUGH PEASANT
AND BOURGEOIS EYES

Jonas Frykman

· F O R E W O R D ·

Outside the circle of folklorists, the work of Scandinavian ethnologists is not well known in the United States or Britain. This is a pity, for the revolution in the approach to folklore that has taken place there is as exciting as any of the developments in the "new history" occurring in the English-speaking world. It is, therefore, with great enthusiasm that I introduce the work of two of Sweden's leading younger ethnologists, Orvar Löfgren and Jonas Frykman, a book that, quite apart from its fascinating exploration of the formative period of the Swedish bourgeois culture, makes a marriage of folklore and history and provides a model for those social historians interested in exploring new and exciting terrains of culture.

In the United States and Britain, folklore and history have long been estranged in just the same way that anthropology and history have traditionally been separated. Beginning in the late nineteenth century, anthropologists focused their attentions on nonwestern "primitive" cultures, while the folklorists turned their attention largely to the peasantry as the bearers of the heritage of pure, unalloyed national culture. Both turned their backs on modern urban industrial society, and on the historical processes they regarded as destroying the supposedly timeless cultures that were their object of study. Anthropologists and folklorists have only recently begun to question this distinction between tradition and modernity, rural and urban, folk and contemporary cultures; but they are now beginning to turn in ever-larger numbers to the study of the contemporary city, the cultures of factory and office, and folklore of the media and mass entertainment. In the process, they have rediscovered history.

Anthropologists and folklorists are turning to the past, and, as the

Foreword

readers of this marvelous book will have the pleasure of discovering, opening up whole new areas of productive inquiry. Regrettably, most cultural historians have cut themselves off from whole regions of their chosen subject—including magic, ritual, food, animal lore, initiations, proverbial sayings, and gift giving—not only because they have been exclusively concerned with literate cultures, but also because they thought of all nonverbal forms as archaic survivals not worthy of serious treatment. The best historical anthropology to date has been concentrated on the medieval and early modern eras. When historians of the modern period have concerned themselves with ritual or symbol it has been in connection with the peasantry or marginal groups like gypsies, and certainly not with the upper classes.

It is here that Löfgren and Frykman make a splendidly original contribution. By turning their ethnological attention to the Swedish bourgeoisie at its most formative and triumphant moment, 1880 to 1910, they have achieved a tour de force that should capture the attention and admiration of every American and European historian. Löfgren and Frykman have brought folklore back home by investigating the very group that created the discipline in the first place. In doing so, they have created a radical reversal of perspective. By placing itself in the position of scientific observers, the late nineteenth-century middle class reinforced its sense of itself as representing a progressive, universal culture. It played the peasantry and proletariat off against each other. The former was defined as pure, but archaic; the latter degenerate, but reformable. Bourgeois culture itself was exempt from scrutiny, exempt even from history. By presenting itself as the culmination of human evolution, it created the myth of its own immortality.

This book deconstructs the myths that the Swedish bourgeoisie and its counterparts throughout the Western world created in the late nineteenth century and perpetuated for much of the twentieth. It allows us to appreciate the degree to which those things which we tend to think of as eternal and objective—time, sexuality, hygiene, even

Foreword

nature itself—are in fact subjective and changeable, serving the needs and interests of a particular class (and, it should be emphasized, a particular gender) at the expense of other competing groups, first the aristocracy and then the proletariat. This point has been made before, often by historians of ideas, but the originality of Löfgren and Frykman's achievement lies in the fact that they demonstrate so concretely and convincingly the way the bourgeoisie constructed its cultural dominion through the rituals and routines of everyday life. They use their insights as ethnologists to show the ways social reality was constructed, not just through words, but through ritual, taboo, gesture, and pilgrimage, all contributing in subtle and (to the anthropologically untrained eye) invisible ways to the reification of bourgeois values. They seat us at the dinner table, take us on vacations, invite us into the nursery, the bedroom, even the privy to show the way this culture institutionalized itself, and, through its myriad daily rituals and symbolic performances, created the illusion of its universality and therefore its claim to superiority.

To English readers familiar with Scandinavian culture only through Bergman films and the occasional novel, there is much here that will be of interest simply because of its "otherness." But the significant contribution of this innovative book lies in a rendering of the Swedish experience that can also tell us a great deal about our own mythologies and ritual reifications. In this sense, Löfgren and Frykman have done a double service by opening to liberating inspection not only their own culture but ours as well.

John Gillis

Culture Builders

· I N T R O D U C T I O N ·

What is culture? One answer to this question is to be found in a standard Swedish encyclopedia, where the genuine core of culture was defined in 1911 as:

> a moral and intellectual development, which manifests itself in milder manners, a purer concept of divinity, more rational laws, advanced forms for the organization of society and the state, acknowledged international law, peaceful coexistence between nations, the cultivation of science, literature, and art, an organized educational system, philanthropy, a greater regard for the right of the individual to attain full development, sensitivity and benevolence in interpersonal relations, insusceptibility to superstitions and mass suggestion, kind treatment of domestic animals and other living creatures, etc.
> (*Nordisk familjebok* 15.226)

This book tries to answer some of the questions raised by this rather self-assured definition of the good and proper life. Why is it important to be kind to animals, mild in manners, and respectful of the individual? In a way this is a study of the culture behind this definition of culture, a study of the making of a middle-class world view and life-style in nineteenth- and early twentieth-century Sweden. Our interest is focused on the ways in which this middle-class culture has been transformed into a mainstream way of life, a dominant culture in modern society.

The 1970s have seen the growth of a great scholarly interest in studying the cultural roots of our contemporary world view. To what

1

Introduction

extent has the reshaping of the modern person meant a complete reorganization of the ways in which we experience and perceive the world? Are our ways of thinking, feeling, and reacting fundamentally different from those of older, preindustrial or precapitalist cultures; and to what extent are the very categories and concepts with which we describe human thoughts, actions, ambitions, and needs also a product of this fundamental cultural change? How much do our own cultural ideas color notions such as nature, privacy, love, taste, power, and individuality?

Questions like these have been asked by scholars as diverse as Pierre Bourdieu, Norbert Elias, Michel Foucault, Richard Sennett, E. P. Thompson, and Raymond Williams. Thanks to the interdisciplinary efforts of these and many others, there exists today a rapidly expanding type of cultural research, which is located in the no-man's-land between the humanities and the social sciences, between history, anthropology, and sociology. These interdisciplinary approaches have different labels and different theoretical traditions. But whether they are called the history of mentalities, the study of the civilizing process, cultural sociology, or historical anthropology, they share an interest in the culture of everyday life and thought and a way of using history to challenge our standard views of the present.

Our study has drawn much of its inspiration from this interdisciplinary field, but our perspective comes from the tradition of European ethnology, which guides our approach, our conceptual framework, and the kinds of material we use as evidence.

Although it is an oversimplification, one can argue broadly that nineteenth-century European nations with colonies tended to develop an anthropological study of primitive societies, while the ethnographic interest in countries with few or no colonies was first directed toward "the primitives within," the rapidly disintegrating peasant culture. The latter approach dominated in the Scandinavian countries as well as in most of Central Europe, where folklorists and ethnologists

Introduction

salvaged the past and constructed an idealized picture of a traditional national peasant culture (Löfgren 1980:189ff.). Then came the time that the vanishing peasant culture could no longer be studied in the field but only in the ethnological archives, with their rich collections of material on peasant beliefs and ways of life. Gradually, European ethnologists also turned their interest to the study of modern industrial society, but retained a comparative, historical approach in which the present was profiled against a background of the past.

This research tradition is the background for the project of which this book is a part. It was started by ten of us in the Department of European Ethnology of the University of Lund, with the aim of studying cultural and social change in twentieth-century Sweden. We sought a different approach to the study of Swedish society and culture, based on an idea of looking at the totality rather than at local variations, and focusing on mainstream cultural formations. The problem was that the study of a subject like the dominant Swedish culture was defined as a more or less impossible or unsuitable task for an ethnologist. Back in the 1930s, European ethnologists had been busy generalizing about national character, popular mentalities, folk psychology, and the like. Some of these interests took the road toward *Blut und Boden* in Nazi Germany; others were abandoned because of their speculative nature. The failure of later attempts by cultural anthropologists schooled in the "culture and personality" tradition also acted as a deterrent. The pictures given, for example, of Japanese and German culture were very much reflections of an American middle-class culture. Insensitivity to class differences and an ahistorical approach gave the whole field of study of national cultures a bad reputation in the 1960s and 1970s. Cultural generalizations were definitely out (compare the discussion in Bock 1980).

Another problem was the realization that we lacked the tools to make contemporary everyday culture less self-evident. Our blindness to the familiar was marked, and the often trivial observations of many

Introduction

contemporary sociological studies of Swedish society underlined this dilemma. While students of more exotic settings have devised techniques for getting *into* a new culture, European ethnologists have struggled with the problem of getting *out*, of distancing themselves from far-too-familiar surroundings.

For us the historical perspective proved to be the tool we needed. Instead of starting in the 1970s, we decided to move back a century, to analyze the cultural roots of the present. How could a middle-class world view of today or working-class images of society, for example, be studied as cultural products, constructed over time? We decided to focus on the period of the last hundred years or so, when Sweden was transformed from an agrarian to an industrial and then to an urban society. This development was later and thus more compressed than in many other European countries.

We were interested in the extent to which class boundaries and cultural boundaries tended to overlap or be blurred by other factors such as gender, urban–rural polarities, and regional and occupational subcultures, as well as generational differences.

This focus on cultural differentiation was also a reaction against popular ideas of a national Swedish culture. Was that a meaningful analytical concept, and on what levels did such a form of collective consciousness exist? How had it been constructed over time, and by what processes had it become shared experience and identity? We felt the need first to deconstruct Swedishness before reconstructing it. This again brought up the question of cultural heterogenization or homogenization. Was the Sweden of 1980 a more homogeneous society that that of 1880, or had old forms of cultural differentiation been replaced by new ones?

The problem here was also one of choosing a level to study. Many observers of modern Swedish society have stressed its homogeneity. Economic differences were less marked than in most other European countries, and the language of class seemed rather muted. Similarities

Introduction

in consumption patterns and life-styles were striking, at least on a superficial level. The problem here was, of course, one of relations between form and meaning: shared forms of cultural expression may hide differences on the level of meaning. This problem is also evident in judging the extent of cultural change and continuity in society. Cultural forms can be carried through history, giving an impression of stability while being charged with new and different meanings and used in varying ways by different groups. In the same way, the rapid turnover of commodities, cultural fashions, and attitudes may hide a continuity on a deeper level. Old problems, old principles are dressed up in new forms.

These issues were also important for challenging some established views of modernization and change, which saw Swedish culture traveling the road from tradition to modernity, from distinct subcultures to shared mass culture. We wanted to approach the problem of social and cultural change in a less unilinear fashion.

Our research took as one of its starting points the popular stereotypes of Swedishness, common to outside observers and natives alike. These stereotypes portray the typical Swede as a nature-loving and conflict-avoiding person, obsessed with self-discipline, orderliness, punctuality, and the importance of living a rational life. One does not have to know much about Swedish society to realize that most of these are middle-class virtues. Trying to determine to what extent a middle-class life-style had become the mainstream Swedish culture in public discourse as well as in private life, we decided to look at the formation of a middle-class world view and everyday experience over the past hundred years.

This book is an attempt to analyze the culture of the bourgeoisie during the period from about 1880 to 1910. To profile this culture, from which we have inherited so many basic notions and ideas, we use our ethnological knowledge of nineteenth-century peasant life as an analytical contrast to the ways and views of the Oscarians (as these late

Introduction

Victorians are called in Sweden, from the reign of King Oscar II, 1872–1907). Orvar Löfgren contrasts the very different attitudes toward time and time keeping, as well as the uses and perceptions of nature; he compares gender constructs and patterns of child socialization in the two milieus and looks at the new polarizations between work and leisure, between public and private life, together with the new ideology of home and family life. Jonas Frykman studies notions of dirt, pollution, and orderliness, discussing the emergence of a new ideology of health and cleanliness, as well as changing perceptions of sexuality and bodily functions.

Our study is not so much concerned with the genesis of bourgeois or middle-class culture. The historical perspective is shorter. We are interested in the processes by which an expanding class comes to define its own way of life and thoughts as "Swedish culture" or simply as "human nature," along with its attempts to colonize and reform other groups in society who are seen as representing an inferior culture or lacking in culture. Our aim is not to present the cultural history of an epoch, but rather to discuss, using a historical perspective, the ways a cultural hegemony can be developed and challenged.

Much of the research on the making of middle-class culture has focused on ideas and ideologies. Our interest is directed at the problem of the way such ideas are anchored in the routines and trivialities of everyday life. How are the notions of the good and proper life related to cultural praxis? How are cultural messages embedded in the material world we create, and how is it that they are often communicated in a much more effective way through nonverbal rather than verbal forms of interaction? This type of silent socialization is found in the sharing of a meal, in the structure of work, in the physical arrangements of the home, and so on.

With this focus, the concept of *culture building* has become a central theme of our work. The term stresses the need to study culture in terms of process, focusing on the constant reworking of culture, on the handling of contradictions and inconsistencies, on the processes of learning and unlearning. The concept must not, however, lead to images of a conscious strategy in which blueprints are drawn up and construction platforms nailed together. People seldom view themselves as culture builders in their everyday task of integrating new experiences or giving new meanings to old knowledge. The structure and direction of this task are easier to see in perspective by the outsider, the researcher, than by the participants themselves.

We are not primarily interested in this process on the level of the individual; the focus is on the formation of shared systems of cultural meaning. Our perspective is materialist in the sense that we maintain that ideologies and cultural notions must be consistent with material experiences in order to be absorbed and to survive. The material basis of culture building is the simple fact that different groups of people live under different conditions, which produce different experiences. On the other hand, it is important to see that dreams, utopias, and new ideas about society contain a potential for change, a cultural force that may transcend existing material conditions and social frameworks. The new emerges out of the given.

So much for the theoretical considerations, which have been discussed in greater detail elsewhere.[1] Now for some of the limitations of the project. We stressed earlier that this is an attempt to describe some of the foundations of a dominant class's world view, using material from peasant and working-class settings for comparative purposes. In doing this, we simplify a much more complex social and cultural reality. We will start with the social world of the middle class, a notoriously vague term that is used interchangeably with "bourgeois" in the text. The problem is primarily one of translation. The Swedish word *borgare* comes closer to the German *Bürger* and lacks the rather strong ideological and sometimes derogatory connotations of *bourgeois*. This class defined itself mainly as bourgeois during the nineteenth century, while the term "middle class" became more popular

Introduction

during the twentieth century. As Peter Gay (1984) and others have pointed out, both terms cover a complex social reality and include rather different substrata and subcultures. For analytical reasons, we have chosen to put aside these internal divisions in our text, in order to concentrate on the shared cultural capital.

The developing bourgeois culture of the late eighteenth and the nineteenth centuries was formed in both dependence on and opposition to the old elite, the aristocracy. To understand the cultural profile of the bourgeoisie in this early era, we have to remember that its quest for power and standing in society was a battle waged on two fronts. The new class had to define itself not only vis-à-vis the old gentry but also vis-à-vis the common people, the peasants.

The bourgeois perception of the old aristocracy contained elements not only of distancing and polarization, but also of admiration and imitation. By the end of the nineteeth century, the bourgeoisie no longer represented an antagonistic subculture, having rather taken over the role of the dominant culture. In part this change was the result of a social and cultural merger with the thin social layer that the old elite represented, but it also came from shifts in the political and economic structure of society. The middle class in actual fact holds an upper-class position in Swedish society. It is scarcely possible to talk of remnants of a traditional upper class in Sweden, as it is, for example, in Britain.

We likewise give a simplified picture of nineteenth-century Swedish peasant culture, which was neither traditional nor without important regional and social divisions, differences we have discussed elsewhere (Löfgren 1980). Again, our purpose has been to generalize about some basic traits in peasant life and world view. Our discussion of the culture building of the working class contains similar simplifications. The research project of which this book is a part includes a number of studies of working-class life, as well as different subcultures within the middle class. References to them are made mainly in the notes.

Introduction

After these caveats, we would like to say something about our source materials. Our discussion of peasant culture relies mainly on the very rich collections of peasant traditions and folklore that are found in the ethnological archives, as well as on the extensive research literature on nineteenth-century peasant society. This is unusually well documented in contrast to countries such as England and France, where this type of extensive collecting did not occur. The material on peasant culture cannot be used without caution, as it often reflects the world view of the collectors and scholars. We often get a rather idealized and harmonious picture of rural conditions, which sometimes tells us more about bourgeois nostalgia and ideals than about actual peasant life (Frykman 1979).

For the reconstruction of middle-class life and thought, we have had to rely on a more mixed collection of sources. Although some earlier interviews and collections of traditions exist in the ethnological archives, the main part of our information comes from private sources —memoirs, biographies, letters, and diaries—as well as the flow of material from public discourse—newspaper articles, etiquette manuals, pamphlets on health and children's education, and so forth. Manifestations of the middle-class world view, cultural taxonomies, notions about the good and proper life can be found in everything from zoology readers to cookbooks.

The most problematic of these sources are the personal reminiscences, in which the past is suitably reorganized for the present, nostalgia dressed up as history. Just as early folklore collectors could lament the passing of a "golden era of peasant culture," we hear many sighs about "the good old days" in middle-class memoirs. In this genre, life was usually happier, healthier, or more natural before. Sometimes, however, the picture of the past is the reverse; the hard times of yesterday are described as a contrast to the rosier picture of the present. There is no room here for a more detailed discussion of the methodological problems of this kind of historical cultural analysis. We have

Introduction

tried to tackle these questions in other publications from the project (Wikdahl and Ekenbjörn 1980; Ehn and Löfgren 1982).

The Swedish version of this book was published in 1979. Since then much water has flowed under the bridge, both in our own work and in that of others. Although the text has been edited and partly rewritten to incorporate points and insights we have discovered later, references to the expanding international research in this field have mostly been made in the notes at the end of the book. A sequel to this book was published in 1985. It deals with the remaking of the middle-class and working-class cultures during the interwar years, the period of the making of the Swedish welfare state (see Frykman and Löfgren, eds., 1985).

Rational and Sensitive

•————————————————————————————•

CHANGING ATTITUDES TO TIME, NATURE,
AND THE HOME

Orvar Löfgren

The new dichotomy of work and leisure was above all a male concern. In the bosom of nature the stressed and harried businessman or civil servant could relax and cultivate his alter ego or find his true self, while his wife still had to look after her domestic duties. (Early twentieth-century photograph from the collections of the Nordiska Museet, Stockholm.)

· 1 ·

The Time Keepers

For most of us, time is an ambiguous concept. Time can be viewed as a natural biological rhythm, with the poles of birth and death, growing up and growing old. Time can be regarded as a framework that creates order in our everyday life, or it can be felt as a commodity always in short supply. Sometimes it can appear to be almost a mysterious current or a supernatural power governing our existence.

Time plays a key role in the social organization of all cultures, marking boundaries and transitions, phases and rhythms in the life of the individual and the collective, creating stability and structure. Yet time in itself is a continuum, and each culture breaks up the flow of time into sections, creating its own time with ordered periods and ages. People's conception and apprehension of time therefore vary from society to society, from age to age.[1]

How a culture conceives of time reveals a great deal about the way people live and think; it gives us a key to the understanding of a society's cultural foundation. In the same way, altered views of time can clearly reflect radical changes in society. If we wish to understand the extent of the transformation that Swedish society has undergone during the past hundred years, it may be well to begin the investigation with a study of the way culture shapes time.

The problem is, however, that there is not one time but many. The same culture can envisage, experience, and organize time in a number of different ways, with consequent problems of synchronization. But the variations within a single culture can appear small if it is com-

Rational and Sensitive

pared with other cultures; differences in concepts of time can then appear unimaginably large. Many Westerners visiting non-European cultures have experienced culture shock through confrontation with totally alien concepts of time. Yet we do not even have to leave Europe to experience this clash of cultures; it is enough to confront the view of time that existed in Swedish peasant society of bygone days. The parallels are striking. Nineteenth-century Swedes from the upper classes complained about the peasantry for exactly the same reasons that many Westerners complain about "primitive" societies: they have no grasp of time, they live a life of irresponsible and undisciplined laziness. Instead of husbanding the precious resource of time, the peasants squander it. We can follow this theme in countless reports and accounts left to us by clergy, doctors, officials, and early ethnographers.[2]

These people in authority felt that the peasants' difficulty was not just in husbanding time, but also in measuring it. In a mid-nineteenth-century description of peasant life, one clergyman left the following ironic report of the way the peasants of the plain measured time with reference to whether the fields were being cropped or lying fallow: "It was very usual that, if one asked a farmer the age of his little daughter, the answer might be something like: 'She must be four, because she's the same age as my brown horse, and it was born when the south field was in pasture'" (Nicolovius [1847] 1957:19). We hear the same complaint from a Danish clergyman who pointed out that the peasant rarely spoke of dates and months, instead fixing time by means of the various yearly tasks, "for the peasant does not care to concern himself with numbers, which are the yardstick of a nation's culture" (cited in Nilsson 1934:96).

Representatives of the upper classes were more shocked by the fact that many peasants could not even keep track of their own date of birth. In 1876 Nils Bruzelius wrote of the peasantry of Österlen: "Seventy or eighty years ago there were few people who could state their date of birth, usually answering that they were born 'at Easter' or 'when the rye was sown' or 'when the oats put forth the ear' " (1978: 106). We have similar examples from other parts of Sweden (Danver 1942; Hamenius 1972; Svensson 1967).

These lamentations reflect the meeting of cultures with different concepts of time: the new, standardized concept adopted during the eighteenth and nineteenth centuries by the aristocracy and the bourgeoisie, by clergy, officialdom, and industrialists, confronted the traditional peasant view and use of time.

"He Who Made Time Made Plenty of It"

Time for the peasant was neither homogeneous nor mechanical, but to a large extent anchored in the rhythm of nature. Yet it was not nature's rhythm alone that created time in peasant society; it was also the work of the peasant. Since production was so dependent on natural rhythm, on the alternation of light and darkness, cold and warmth, and on the periodic fluctuation of growth, the working year overlapped the natural year.

"Nature's calendar was almost sufficient for the peasant's year. The various tasks closely followed the changes in nature and could be dated with their help," notes Sigfrid Svensson (1967:16). Nature provided signs, which served as chronological reference points. People followed the melting of the snow, the movements of migratory birds, the burgeoning of the leaves, and the seasonal behavior of the animals.

For peasants in the southern Swedish province of Skåne (Scania), most of the weather signs concerned the agricultural work of the summer half. When the beech leaves began to sprout it was time to sow the oats, while barley could be sown only after the marsh marigold blossomed or when the oak leaves were as big as rat's ears. The best time to mow the hay was when the arnica was in bloom, and as summer pro-

*The rhythm of the working year, the changes in the seasons, and the
habits of the livestock organized time in peasant society. In northern
Sweden the summer removal to the mountain shielings and pastures
was one of the most important points in the yearly cycle. Here the
men are accompanying the cattle girls and their herds on their way
from the village of Myssjö in the province of Jämtland.
(Early twentieth-century photograph from the collections of the
Nordiska Museet, Stockholm.)*

The Time Keepers

gressed one could follow the changes in the fields and observe how the rye would "ear up, turn white, and then yellow" (Svensson 1967:16). As peasant children grew up they amassed a great store of knowledge about the natural calendar. They learned how to divide the natural year and the working year into seasons. Our fourfold division into spring, summer, autumn, and winter was too broad for the needs of the peasant farmer. Great regional variations in the rhythm of the natural and working years occasioned local differences in the way the year was divided. Spring in Skåne was known as *framtid* (fore-time), followed by *sommar* and then *skyr* (reaping), *efterhöst* (after-harvest), *vinter*, and finally *sivinter* (late winter). Other parts of the country could have even more seasons than this. The far north of Sweden, for instance, followed a completely different rhythm.

Chronology was thus far from homogeneous in peasant society. There were even differences within a particular area. The natural calendar and the working year for the farmer on the plains could be markedly different from that of the peasant who lived off forestry or fishing. There was a particularly striking difference in rhythm between peaks of intensive work and periods of rest (Nilsson 1934:102ff.; Svensson 1967:7; Löfgren 1973).

The association of the natural year and the working year meant that the peasant perceived time as a cycle, rhythmic and repetitive, but not at all mechanical. Time was short or long depending on the intensity and type of the work to be done.

This fluctuation is reflected not only in the way the year and the seasons were divided up, but also in the terms for the various parts of the working day, a subject studied by Bertil Ejder (1969). Local dialects once had a rich array of words that are now forgotten, replaced by hours and minutes. There were words that were based on the working rhythm, describing how long a team could plow without a pause, the time between meals, how long animals could graze the same patch of ground, or how long a horse needed to rest at the wayside. A now ob-

Rational and Sensitive

solete word like *reft* could mean a part of the working day in the form of a finished piece of work, a row of sheaves in the field, or a certain length woven on the loom. A *tåka* denoted a couple of hours working a threshing machine. *Ökt* and *orka* both meant a reasonable bout of work, while *pusthåll* was the distance that could be driven without a rest. A working day could be divided into a number of *bete* (bites), and here as in many other cases the division was based on mealtimes or pauses for draft animals to eat. The bouts of work were not of equal length, and they certainly were not perceived as such.

Time was therefore based on work. It was governed by the rhythm of work, by the need for food and rest for both men and beasts, by the time it took to become sweaty when flailing grain or tired when plowing. An hour in summer was therefore not the same as an hour in winter, an hour of watching grazing animals was not the same time as an hour's threshing. The length of the working day varied according to the work that needed to be done and the amount of daylight. People often worked until sundown.

In the same way that the many breaks for food gave the day its rhythm and variety, the working year received its structure from the periods of rest and the annual festivals. The ends of certain jobs, such as dung spreading, haymaking, and linen making, were marked by eagerly awaited feasts, which were landmarks in the annual rhythm (Löfgren 1973).

This heterogeneous chronology, based on the peasants' work, had then to be synchronized with the other cycles that governed their lives: the ecclesiastical year and the administrative calendar. In reality, however, these times were also linked to the working year. An important religious holiday could scarcely have developed at a time of year when the workload was heavy or the food supply meager. Again, there were regional rhythmic variations between holiday and everyday, between sacred and profane.

The Time Keepers

Since the church prescribed rest on holy days and the sabbath, people had to keep track of the days of the week. The church bells were a help here, not just ringing in holy days, but also marking the beginning and end of the weekday. Those who lived out of range of the bells had to devise other ways, such as homemade calendars, to keep sacred and profane days apart. They could otherwise lose track of time and become like the people in the cautionary tales, who forgot which day of the week it was, plowing on a Sunday or threshing on Christmas Day.

Time Becomes Money

It is obvious that our own sense of time has little in common with the way traditional peasant society viewed time. While the peasant's time can be likened to a wheel turning at the same gentle pace as the working year and nature's rhythm, our time is perceived more as a line projecting into the future. Broadly speaking, time for the peasant was cyclical, while for us it is linear.

The time according to which we advance is divided into compartments which must be kept distinct. People who are incapable of organizing or differentiating their time are considered impractical, perhaps even unreliable. Punctuality has become a virtue for us, and time a precious resource that can be saved or wasted. Our gaze is constantly directed forward. For modern man the ideal is to keep up with the times, preferably even to be ahead of one's time.

In addition, the contemporary system of time is highly rational and strictly formalized. Time is a unity that can be broken down mechanically into components: seconds, minutes, hours, days, weeks, months, years, decades, and centuries. These are measurable, standardized

Rational and Sensitive

units. Moreover, our use of time is highly specialized; for the peasant many activities could run parallel, but we have learned that there is a time and a place for everything.

These modern concepts of time have deep historical roots. The emergence of a new attitude toward both time keeping and time management has been traced to late medieval settings, where time gradually became a market commodity (Le Goff 1980). This process accelerated with the development of industrial production during the eighteenth and nineteenth centuries. New technology made new demands on time and time keeping. Industrial production expected more of both the worker and the organization of the work. Increased division of labor and production on an ever-greater scale required a disciplined sense of time that had been quite unnecessary in peasant society. Neither mass production nor mass administration is possible without the coordination and standardization of people's work and lives, and these were partially achieved by new norms of time.

The technological explanation is, however, scarcely sufficient. As E. P. Thompson has shown in a classic study of the transformation of the concept of time, it is more than a question of new technological systems demanding time discipline. Production technology is only one element in a larger economic system, industrial capitalism, which changes not only the methods of production but also the social and economic relationships and our way of thinking (Thompson 1967).

Working life is increasingly organized according to the principle that the worker sells his labor, his time, to the employer, who buys time. The success of the purchaser depends on how efficiently he can use the time he buys, not just by mechanizing the labor processes but primarily by intensifying and disciplining the efforts of the employees. The key words here are rational economic production and profitability. There develops a struggle for time between the seller and the buyer, a process that creates a clear polarity between production and nonproduction, between work and leisure.

The Time Keepers

This new development can be found in Sweden in the growth of a market-oriented form of agrarian capitalism in the eighteenth century. This transformation of agriculture turned some of the hitherto homogeneous peasant class into small businessmen, while at the same time it hastened the growth of a proletariat of landless peasants, the farm laborers and cotters.[3]

When the farmer is drawn into market production he finds himself in a totally new competitive situation. He is expected to produce in greater quantities at cheaper prices, whether he has a large estate or simply a peasant farm with a few maids and hired hands. He must view labor as a resource demanding proper management, and as a result the classic complaints about the laziness of the servants, their lack of discipline with regard to time, are now heard not only from the upper and middle classes but also from the farmer, the small businessman. The question of profitability becomes more and more prominent—is it better to pay laborers by the day, to hire them for a year at a time, or to operate a piecework system?

Here is a typical complaint, again from a clergyman, about the lack of industry shown by the craftsmen in one parish:

> The so-called tradesmen, in particular some carpenters and joiners, are careful to show that they can be industrious when they are working . . . for a certain fixed sum to be paid for piecework; but if they are paid by the day and also fed, without which it is scarcely possible to get them to come, it is galling to observe their pauses for rest, their five breaks for food, and in between these the few hours of work, when they scratch themselves behind the ears while they stand forever gazing at the log or the plank which they are about to work on, and their constant resting on the ax or the saw. Yet this is not considered theft, although they are stealing from their neighbor as much as any robber. Most casual workers and

Rational and Sensitive

lazy maids and hired hands could be included in the same class. . . . Nowadays one hardly ever encounters a modest profit for a faithful day's work; and if all this lack of discipline is to be counted depravity, then there are many depraved people here. (*Öller* 1800:200f.)

As the start of the nineteenth century, however, the boundaries between masters and men were not so clearly drawn in most Swedish peasant communities.

The divisions were sharper in large-scale agriculture, on the manorial estates, where it was more common to hear complaints about the slow working pace and poor time discipline shown by servants and casual laborers. From 1815 comes the following picture of work on an estate, on which it was considered

fortunate if the bailiff is ready at five o'clock in the morning to march out to the cornfield at the head of a troop of lazy farmhands, contumacious cotters, and tired peasants, the sort who, as soon as the bailiff is forced to turn his back to attend to other duties, lose their zeal for work, if they do not cease work completely. For these hired hands, who have no interest whatever in their master's welfare, there is no sound more dear than the bell that rings to indicate food and evening. (cited in Rehnberg 1967:54f.)

The bell that summoned workers to eat—known as the *vällingklocka* (gruel bell)—was one of the new methods of disciplining the efforts of agricultural workers. As Mats Rehnberg has shown (1967:27), the spread of the bell during the eighteenth and nineteenth centuries went hand in hand with increased production and new demands for efficiency and profitability in agriculture.

The management of the new concept of time became ever more im-

The "gruel bell" was a symbol of the new time discipline on large farms and manorial estates. It was rung to call the agricultural laborers to work and to signal breaks for meals. A rich folklore in the form of rhymes and ditties imitating the sound of the bell emerged during the nineteenth century; the message was often a social protest about hard working conditions and bad food, "blue gruel and sour herring." (Photograph by Gunnar Lundh. Nordiska Museet, Stockholm.)

Rational and Sensitive

portant for the farmer. As he developed into a small businessman and market producer, he learned how to calculate and budget not only his means of production but also time. During the course of the nineteenth century there came to be more and more farmers who kept diaries, bought calendars, acquired pocket watches and gruel bells, an indication of the new time discipline and the prestige associated with the mastery of time.[4]

Disciplining Time

The clearest example of the new discipline of time is found in the growing number of factories in the nineteenth century. A number of researchers have analyzed the growth of time as a discipline in European industry. Michel Foucault, in a study of French conditions, has shown that factory owners and businessmen made new demands on labor: "Time measured and paid must also be a time without impurities or defects; a time of good quality, throughout which the body is constantly applied to its exercise. Precision and application are, with regularity, the fundamental virtues of disciplinary time" (Foucault 1977:151).

The changeover was not easy. There are countless complaints about the poor punctuality and lack of serious concentration shown by the workers. People are said to waste precious time, they are indolent, lazy, without respect for the exigencies of time keeping, and so on. The workers have not yet learned that work and leisure are two completely different things.

Industrialization came to Sweden late, and the new industrial class was taken straight from the plow. The culture confrontation was therefore more marked here than in France or England. Textile workers were needed in the early wave of industrialization, in a sector that de-

The Time Keepers

manded a great deal of work discipline. Many of the workers came to
the factory irregularly, staying at home when urgent tasks on the farm
had to be finished. An English foreman in a spinning mill in Västergötland complained to an American visitor in 1857 about the bad habits of
the female staff:

> But the women, Sir, they cause problems. They're not used to
> such intensive work. At home they've always chatted and
> gabbled to each other while they work. I have a hard job
> keeping them attentive and careful. And they're full of
> mischief! Why can't two women meet without shaking a leg
> together? . . . It will take time before they are like the English
> and the Americans. . . . But they will learn.   (cited in Persson
> 1977:19)

How was such labor to be disciplined to carry out serious work and
taught to respect working hours? One aid in their training was provided by the factory regulations, which stated the workers' duties and
organized factory life into a precise schedule with fixed times and routines and with set fines to be paid by those who failed to keep their
times.

Another important tool for imprinting the new time norms was the
factory whistle. In the little weavers' village of Viskafors in Västergötland, the steam whistle blew three times every weekday morning; the
first blast was to wake the workers, the second was to remind them to
come to the factory, and the third to indicate the commencement of
work (Persson 1977:27). The steel industry in Eskilstuna began to acquire factory whistles in the 1870s when steam engines were introduced; they blew throughout the town to summon people to work at
six in the morning (Gårdlund 1942:307).

The steam whistle consequently became a symbol of the factory
owner's power over the workers' time. As clearly as the gruel bell, it

Rational and Sensitive

marked the change in life and imprinted in the consciousness of the local population the sharp new boundaries between work and leisure.

By the end of the nineteenth century piece wages began to supplant the older hourly wages in many industries, another stage in the development toward increased control of working time. This trend accelerated further in the twentieth century with the assistance of increased division of labor and time-and-motion studies. Jobs on the shop floor were subjected to ever more division, standardization, and routine. This stimulated extensive discussion about the struggle for time. It need hardly be said that there were huge differences between ideal and practice. Even within the working class there was an ambivalence about time discipline. Some groups of workers continued well into the twentieth century to assert their right to organize their work and even to take breaks and vacations when it suited them. The control of time became an important symbol of power in the workplace. The following picture of a Stockholm shipyard early this century shows a typical situation: "What speed people work at now compared to then! It used to be considered bootlicking to start work before the bosses came, and sometimes there was a delay of half an hour after starting time. . . . The problem of leisure probably wasn't given so much thought. People drank more alcohol at work then, and if you didn't feel like working, you could celebrate for a day or two" (Rehnberg 1953:71, 70).

The training of workers in a new attitude to time did not take place exclusively on the shop floor. During the nineteenth century compulsory schooling became an important means of disciplining time. The school, with its order in the classrooms, timetables, breaks, and ringing bells, prepared children for their future working life. It taught the children of the peasantry and the working class to live up to the demands made by industrial production on labor. The children of the bourgeoisie, by contrast, were brought up with a more complicated sense of time, loaded with a new symbolism and a new morality. These new disciplined and standardized time norms were internal-

The Time Keepers

ized through work and school and have become fundamental to the middle-class world view.

School created not only disciplinary time but also "evolutive" time, as pointed out by Michel Foucault, who notes that the new pedagogical doctrines of the nineteenth century stress education as a serial process consisting of a number of elements linked in chronological succession; this process echoes the "natural" progress of the human soul and provides guidelines for teaching methods. Organizing the activities in a straight line creates a linear time that is directed toward a fixed goal—time as career (Foucault 1977:160ff.).

Time in bourgeois culture thus becomes geared toward the future, obsessed with development, and the goal is to gain control over it. The important new message is that people create their own future. Time is in short supply and must be properly managed.

The values implicit here are directly linked with the ideology and view of mankind that take shape among the expanding bourgeoisie of the eighteenth and nineteenth centuries. Businessmen, merchants, government officials had to legitimize their new position as the leading social class. There had been no such problem in the the older society of the four estates, where the feudal nobility had an unquestioned position at the top of the social pyramid by reason of birth. The expanding, socially climbing bourgeoisie drew up a new charter of legitimacy, a mystifying ideology of personal qualities. It was by virtue of their competence and their high moral worth that the bourgeoisie felt entitled to assume a leading role in society.

In their development of a new moral system the bourgeoisie tried to distance themselves from the classes above and below them, from the old nobility with its prodigal life-style and from the gray mass of the people with their lack of discipline and culture. One of the cornerstones of the bourgeois world view is the importance of *control* and *economy*. It was essential to control oneself, with economy of emotion, money, and time. It was vital to learn to forsake present pleasure for

Rational and Sensitive

future security, to sublimate and repress uncivilized instincts and feelings.

Ronny Ambjörnsson has drawn attention to another important feature of the new system of values:

> The morality championed by the new man throughout Western Europe had developed in direct confrontation to the aristocratic life-style. For the landowning aristocracy the important thing was the *ownership* of the property, while for the upward-climbing bourgeoisie it was its *acquisition*, in other words the very motive force of the capitalist economy: work, constant investment, the inexorable logic of capital. (Ambjörnsson 1978:88)

The middle class saw itself as the representative of a new and better social system, where reason and morality would rule. This world view assigned a key role to the individual: "Make something of your own life!"

It might be objected here that virtues such as industry and thrift were also preached in peasant society, but in the more closed economy of self-sufficiency the concept of thrift had a different character. There it was a question of husbanding meager resources, building up a store for the winter, creating a buffer against crop failure and hard times. In short, it was the economy of caution. Bourgeois thrift and self-denial, on the other hand, were geared toward accumulation and future expansion: the world is wide open, the possibilities unlimited.

What then of the view of this earthly life as a scarce resource? To be sure, the church preached the importance of good husbandry of life, reminding of the hourglass which was slowly running out. Yet this caution was chiefly based on a view of the transitory nature of earthly life and the triviality of humankind in contrast to the eternal bliss awaiting the righteous in the heavenly kingdom. The bourgeois view of

The Time Keepers

life was totally different. The message here was: hurry up and make something of your life, seize the possibilities, calculate, invest, and expand.[5]

In peasant society the life cycle was collective; as people grew up and aged they moved up or down established and predictable steps. In bourgeois culture, however, life becomes a career ladder for the individual to climb.[6] The career mentality appears with great clarity in the pages of bourgeois memoir writers. It is a self-evident, fully internalized aspect of the view of mankind (which in bourgeois society was often synonymous with the view of men). The memoirs of Israel Holmgren, professor of medicine, are an excellent example of this career mentality. In a letter to his wife in 1910 he formulates his philosophy of life thus:

> My dear Ogge, if only I could manage to achieve something & make my name respected after my death. That is what I want. It is the best legacy I can leave my children and probably the only one.
>
> It means so much. I know myself what an incentive for assiduous work & integrity it has been for me to have inherited my father's name. I think I owe it to him to be a greater scientist than he, so that I need feel no shame over wasting what he has built up. And if I am allowed to live I shall certainly succeed. (Holmgren 1959:172)

The vision of life as a career was fundamental in the rearing of children, in particular, naturally, of boys. In his autobiography, the author Sven Lidman has described the incessant cultural bombardment to which children were exposed. He spent much of his youth at the home of his uncle, a grammar-school teacher and ex-officer, who wrote the following in a letter to his nephew in 1896: "You no doubt

Rational and Sensitive

understand that it ill becomes an old man to nag at young boys, who are mostly lazy, filthy, and deceitful. Use the hours well, otherwise you will lose years! . . . Compare blissful diligence with shameless indolence." In a later letter he says: "Prattle and carelessness lead to squalor and discomfort, misfortune and poverty—only well-planned work can bear fruit. . . . . I earnestly wish for you to have pleasure from your short life on earth, which can even be thoroughly enjoyable . . . if you use the hours properly instead of idling in bed" (Lidman 1952: 283f.). The message is clear: you are what you achieve. The language reveals to us this vision of life as a constant upward climb. Bourgeois culture often spoke of men with good prospects, or men in their best years, while today we talk of sacrificing something (or someone) for our careers, we describe a man as on the way up, at the turning point, at the height of his career, or at the end of his career.

This career mentality was firmly anchored in a definite social group —middle-class men. The working classes were not expected to have careers. Nor were women from the middle-class, although they had to show all the virtues of self-control and time management. The introduction to a popular good-housekeeping handbook that appeared in numerous editions at the turn of the century states:

> Time is money, as the proverb says. A good housewife must therefore, if only to save time, which in most cases can be said to be man's only capital, not only strive to be punctual and orderly herself, but must also demand this of the people whose duty it is to assist her. . . .
>
> A housewife who knows how to divide her time is always capable of keeping her house in perfect order, and will moreover have enough time over for some work that can bring her an income, or if this is not necessary, to regain her strength through some refreshing diversion or through the improvement of the mind. (Grubb 1889:3)

The Time Keepers

Even in the sphere of the home, the mentality that budgets and disciplines time is prevalent. A good housewife takes pains to create set routines for the servants' work, dividing the day and the week into duties and shifts (Nolan 1979; cf. Davidoff 1976).

Punctuality was a virtue preached not only in schoolbooks and etiquette manuals. Training in punctuality went on constantly in the bourgeois home, and from an early age. Memoir writers often record the iron rule that they had to be in time for meals.[7] Children were even given their own watches so that they could learn to assume responsibility for time, thus imprinting the norms even more effectively.

The goal was to create people with "built-in clocks," people for whom time was always clear and visible. The simplest way to make time visible was to furnish public places with clocks, which gaze down from church towers, school façades, waiting rooms. This development is especially clear in the furnishing of the bourgeois home. The silence of the drawing room was everywhere broken by the ticking clock on the table, the swinging pendulum of the grandfather clocks and wall clocks. Even in the silence children noticed the passing of time.

Birthdays and Anniversaries—Magical Numbers

"On this your special day we, your friends, would like to salute you. We see in you the ideal boss, the ideal family father. . . . You have built up your business into a model company, you have brought up your sons. . . . May you live to experience many more such days, and may we, your friends, have the benefit of assembling around you on the same rich scale. . . ." Here we have the classic introductory phrases of the Swedish speech held in honor of a fiftieth birthday, quoted from Elsa Nyblom's childhood memories of her middle-class home at the turn of the century (1946:115).

Rational and Sensitive

This ritual was as self-evident a part of bourgeois culture as it would have been unthinkable in peasant society. The new middle-class view of time and life emphasized the magic of numbers in a way unknown to peasant society. The celebration of birthdays, name days, and anniversaries became an important element in bourgeois social life. While peasant celebrations had concerned collective annual festivals and harvest feasts, the focus was now shifted to the life cycle of the individual, which was often based on mechanical time keeping and the new career mentality. Birthday celebrations are an example of such a ritual, which only began to be common among the peasantry and the working class around the turn of the century. Nineteenth-century peasants often found the bourgeois interest in birthday celebrations strange, to say the least. This clash of culture can be illustrated by a recollection from Skåne:

> I remember when I went to Hallaröd Elementary School, it
> was in 1895, and our teacher's birthday came around. All the
> children who wanted to and could afford it were supposed to
> contribute money for a present . . . many parents thought that
> they had "never heard anything so foolish or crazy as the kids
> going collecting money for the schoolteacher, we never heard
> tell of such nonsense before." In any case the teacher was
> given a lovely hanging lamp. . . . But our parents in the district
> thought they were "coming to the end of the world when they
> have to kick up such a fuss just because it's somebody's
> birthday." (cited in Danver 1942:17)

Such celebrations were a part of bourgeois culture and the bourgeois concept of time, in which an age that happened to be a round number of mechanical units was considered an occasion for festivity. The same applies to other anniversaries, such as silver weddings and club jubilees (Danver 1942; Swahn 1963; Rehnberg 1969).

The Time Keepers

It is in the archetypal Swedish fiftieth-birthday party that the magic of numbers is most clearly linked to the new concept of a man's career. On his fiftieth birthday the bourgeois man is at the height of his career, in his finest years. Since the career is anchored in his working life, it is primarily his colleagues at work and in business who congratulate him. During the decades around the turn of the century this rite of passage was extended to other anniversaries, such as the sixtieth birthday. Of all the festive accessories, such as flower arrangements, brass bands, and silver-handled walking sticks, the most blatantly obvious symbolic gesture is the presentation by the colleagues of an inscribed gold watch.

Nostalgia and the Cult of Progress

The career mentality is intimately connected to the faith in the future nourished by the bourgeoisie, a belief in evolutionary progress; but parallel to this creed we also find a nostalgic longing for the past. As Richard Sennett observes, a wave of nostalgia swept through bourgeois consciousness during the nineteenth century (Sennett 1977:168ff.), and this nostalgia is most clearly marked in the memoirs.

The bourgeois looked to the past for different reasons than the tradition-bound peasant. Of course, both used history to legitimize present actions, but when the peasant clung to tradition it was because of a pragmatic attitude toward sure and well-tried knowledge. The backward gaze of the bourgeois had an almost mystical, romantic character. The peasantry, for example, had none of the ancestor cult prevalent among the nineteenth-century bourgeoisie. Insofar as the peasants kept track of their ancestors, it was generally for concrete economic reasons: traditions of farm ownership, land rights, and the like.

Rational and Sensitive

It was among the bourgeoisie that the tradition arose of setting up family altars in the form of portrait collections on the grand piano, and the later custom of lighting candles on relatives' graves. These were ways to create a symbolic estate, giving sanctity and mystique to blood ties.

Nostalgia takes a number of forms in bourgeois memoirs. They may idealize childhood as a time when all was simpler and more natural, safer and more genuine; or they may show a fascination with family ancestry and genealogy; or perhaps most interestingly, they may take an almost fanatical interest in history and historical personages. The latter appears clearly in many childhood memories. History was a living reality in the nursery, in children's games and in teenage dreams.

There is an example of this combination of nostalgic longing for the past and belief in evolutionary progress in Alice Quensel's description of her early years in a bourgeois home in Stockholm at the turn of the century. Her childhood was a time when "development was still leading to better conditions in every respect," yet she was even then engrossed in history, constantly identifying herself with heroes and kings, and the scenes and anecdotes that were so important for the bourgeois view of history:

> History was there from the beginning—I do not know how early it came into our existence, which I cannot remember ever lacking a historical background. Mother read historical novels to us, and well before we started school we knew all the kings of Sweden and their queens and much besides. . . . But we also played living history. My two elder brothers and I were Gustav Vasa, Gustav II Adolf, and Carl XII—how these kings could have lived at the same time was a ticklish problem which, like many others, was best solved by being ignored. We would meet to discuss our generals and our councillors, all of whom we naturally knew by name. (Quensel 1958:42f.)

The Time Keepers

In the Quensel home, where the father was a government official, the children's games and fantasies were thus dominated by history, which was of course synonymous with the history of heroic kings. The same obsessions are encountered in other memoirs, where history is acted out and children live the roles of crusaders, generals, and explorers.

This form of history was an important element in bourgeois life, a dominant feature of the child's world of ideas. In the myths that were woven with the aid of history books and pictorial representations of historical scenes, the child was provided with role models. Like the bourgeois world view on which it was based, the idea of history was synonymous with the history of individual personages: men or women who raised themselves above the multitudes, taking their own destiny and that of their nation into their hands.

It is obvious that the historical fantasies that were created in nursery games and tin soldier battles, in the declamation of heroic poems, in the historical tableaux enacted at family parties, in school education, and in torchlit parades to commemorate great kings were all myths that were firmly anchored in the present, in the contemporary bourgeois views of man, society, and the nation.

The Tyranny of Time

By the time the present day approaches, the new concept of time is firmly rooted in our consciousness. It has become natural and self-evident. Today there is a tendency to make time into an object, a power with a mystical life of its own. We are no longer masters of time. This objectification is reflected in language: time is slipping away from us, time is passing, time is running short, and sometimes time stands still and we have to kill time with various pastimes. In the past century we have become more and more obsessed with the importance of speed as a temporal criterion.

Rational and Sensitive

Many people feel that they are under a tyranny of time. If only there were more time to allow us to do all we want to do. We have more and more times that have to be synchronized, deadlines to be met, times that cannot be allowed to overlap. Time must always be linked either to work or to that period of fervent activity which we choose to call leisure. The art of waiting, which the peasant knew so well, has died out. Waiting can now be unbearable, and many people feel stress if they have to spend any time in unproductivity. Running after the bus is preferable to waiting five interminable minutes at the bus stop. The old bourgeois virtue of economy may have given way to an ideology of consumption, but it is still a virtue and a frenetic sport to try to save minutes or seconds: finding a shortcut through town or a supermarket checkout where the waiting time is half a minute shorter.

Yet our culture does not have a homogeneous representation of time—there are variations in both time keeping and attitudes toward time among different social groups. Rita Liljeström has pointed out the differences between men's and women's concepts of time (1979:144). In the same way, the tyranny of time has different effects for the manager and the worker on the shop floor. The poet Göran Palm, who spent a year as a factory worker with LM Ericsson, captured the following typical features of the workers' apprehension of time:

> But for the great majority of shop-floor and office workers . . .
> the eternal problem seems to be to make time on the job
> pass. Of course, it happened occasionally that even I forgot
> the time at LM, for example when a discussion arose, when a
> difficult order had to be completed, or when something un-
> usual happened, an accident, someone treating us to a cake
> before leaving the company, and so on. But I often looked at
> my watch. And when I looked at the time it was in the hope
> that it would be more than it was. Almost always! As a rule it
> was not as late as I had hoped. Time often crawled. Some
> days it appeared almost to stand still.

The Time Keepers

This was not a peculiarity of my watch. People who worked in places where they could see a clock on the wall claimed that it was a mild form of torture. The second hand terrorized them. During the minutes before every break it would drag round in slow motion, but as soon as the bell rang it would chase furiously round the clock. . . .

When the present is not good enough, people put their hope in the future. Then it is a question of finding as much as possible to look forward to and long for, to escape the power of the present. At eight in the morning, for example, I began to look forward to the nine o'clock break. At ten o'clock I began to look forward to the coffee break. When the coffee was finished I looked forward to the bell that signaled going-home time.

This sort of petty longing soon becomes a habit.

Since most people at LM work a five-day week, Friday is by far the most eagerly awaited working day. . . .

Yet these beacons of the future which go out once a week are not enough. Already in November comes the vision of Christmas, and by February, Easter is on the horizon. Scarcely has Ascension Day passed before Whitsun rises over the roof of LM like a morning star.   (Palm 1974:148ff.)

While the blue-collar workers may feel that the bosses are "hanging from the hands of the clock," the white-collar workers feel that they have time under control. They can plan and divide time with the aid of the planning calendar—a cultural feature that is an important part of today's representation of time. It might be said that there is an important cultural barrier in modern society between those with and those without a planning calendar. The calendar has become a status symbol, a symbol of the freedom to control one's own working time. But this freedom is mostly only symbolic. We can observe how the planning calendar and weekend courses in time management create a new

Rational and Sensitive

tyranny of time, which slowly and imperceptibly shapes the way the calendar user conceives of time. This subtle control is reflected in language. When the civil servant, the department head, or the university professor takes his diary out of his pocket, his way of thinking is governed by it. He leafs thoughtfully through it and notes where there are gaps, breathing spaces, an empty day or an empty week that can be filled with the ballpoint pen. With the aid of the calendar, time can be covered with a grid of hours, days, and weeks, units to be filled with notes and appointments.

The material structures with which we equip ourselves have a greater power over us than we realize. Increased demands for exact time management and measurement are reflected in our equipment. Today's digital watches freeze time into not only hours and minutes but also seconds; today's calendars divide time more finely, with spaces for every hour of the working day. We are thus constantly reminded that time is precious, that every hour must be consumed in a rational and efficient way, whether at work or at leisure.

The Social Construction of Time

Time is difficult to grasp. When a conception of time is internalized it becomes a matter of course; it exists as an undercurrent, a more or less unconscious structure of our daily lives.

When comparing our contemporary images of time with those of an older peasant society, we must be careful not to romanticize traditional time keeping in terms of a "natural time." In the same way we cannot talk of a clear-cut division between a traditional cyclical temporalization and a modern linear one. I started by stressing that every culture or era organizes and experiences time in many ways. The cyclical rhythm of nature's calendar did of course play an important role

The Time Keepers

in the peasant representation of time as well as in the structuring of the ritual life, but this did not mean that time was perceived as cyclical, static, or oriented toward the past. There existed a linear time in peasant life as well, related both to the constant need for planning for the future and to religious time, with its focus on the stations of this life and the next, Both time keeping and attitudes toward time tend to change contextually in any given culture.

In the same way it is clear that modern concepts of time not only differ between social groups but also situationally. In the routinization of everyday life, in the repetitions of the working week, we live in a cyclical time parallel to our linear temporalization. We may experience moments of "being," of timelessness, as well as moments of stress when time flies too fast.

The complex relationships between different representations and perceptions of time may also create apparent cultural paradoxes. Some of the contradictions in the new middle-class attitudes to time have already been pointed out: orientation toward the future, the cults of speed and career on the one hand, and of nostalgia on the other, a yearning for the good old days when time was abundant and natural, or utopian dreams of living in a harmonious state of timelessness.[8]

The gradual emergence of an abstract, standardized, and quantified time keeping has also had a varying impact on different sectors of society. The traditional time that revolved around the yearly tasks survived in some spheres of production, while others rapidly came to be based on timed labor (Thompson 1967:70ff.). Anthony Giddens has pointed out that this view of time as a market commodity tended to create a division between public and private time in nineteenth-century society. In the public sphere of production, time was under the supervision of clocks, regulations, timetables, and calculations, while time in the private sphere continued to be experienced in more traditional and qualitative forms (Giddens 1981:130ff.).

It is also important not to reduce the introduction of disciplinary

Rational and Sensitive

time keeping to a tool for industrialists and buyers of time. When the agricultural laborers on the manor farm bought their own watches, they could start to check the chimes of the gruel bell, and in the same way the standardization and control of time could become a weapon in the hands of the unions in their fight for a fair day's pay for a fair day's work.[9]

The disciplining of time is more than a matter of minute hands, diaries, and budgets; it also has to do with a moral judgment of the quality of how time is used. In the polarization of work and leisure, nonproductive time came to mean "free time," but with the successful working-class struggle for more of this commodity, the elite started to entertain apprehensions about this new freedom. Were common people really ready for so much free time? Did they have the cultural competence and the sense of responsibility necessary to manage their own time in the proper manner? Such questions were debated with a growing intensity. An example of this concern may be quoted from 1936, when a heated debate on workers' rights to one week's holiday was raging; the text comes from the English edition of the catalog of the first big Swedish exhibition of leisure life:

Leisure time should certainly be *free* time without any burdensome obligations and wearisome restrictions on the individual, yet on the other hand it should not be a *dead* time frittered away on idle amusement which can only lead to dissipation, or on listless loafing which breeds boredom and dissatisfaction. If the people are unable to fill up their leisure hours in such a way that they derive health and pleasure from it, then it is for the community to help them by advice and action, give them the possibility of spending their leisure time in a richer, finer and more profitable manner. The leisure time in this way becomes a concern of the community with an importance as great as that of working time.

The Time Keepers

Ideas of rationality and effectiveness may penetrate the private sphere of life, but the cultural polarization between work and leisure, between public and private, is a basic theme in our contemporary lives. The following two chapters will examine some of the ways in which these polarities have been organized and perceived.

· 2 ·

The Nature Lovers

"The most deeply ingrained trait in the Swedish temperament . . . is a strong love of nature," wrote Gustav Sundbärg in his book on the Swedish national character in 1910. It was this devotion, he argued, that had created the country's great natural scientists, explorers, and poets, as well as giving Swedish music and imagination their special flavor. "This feeling is equally warm among both high and low—albeit not equally conscious—and this strong attachment to nature, which in some cases may produce wild and unruly emotions, is on the other hand the most profound explanation of the indestructible power and health of the Swedish nation" (Sundbärg 1910:4f.).

His reflections have been echoed, though in less bombastic terms, by later observers, both natives and nonnatives: Swedes are above all nature lovers.[1]

These stereotypes are confirmed in contemporary images of Swedish life: the weekend excursions out into the countryside with coffee and sandwiches, the bands of joggers, skiers, and hunters roaming the forest. One need only look at the extensive hunting-and-gathering economy of berry picking and mushroom collecting out in the woods, or the enthusiastic toil in suburban gardens, or holiday images such as the Friday evening ritual of mass escape to the country cottages or trailer camps, the frantic hunt for sunny hours on the beach, or the incessant rain and the complaining children in the rented summer house.

The statistics may provide such fleeting images with a more stable foundation. The 8.5 million Swedes together own more than 600,000 country cottages, even more leisure boats, and close to a million of them also engage in sport fishing.[2] Ratings show that few television programs can compete with those on nature and wildlife.

This love of nature seems so stably anchored in today's Swedish life-styles that many argue that it must always have been the case. This attachment is seen as one of the traditional elements in contemporary life, something that creates a continuity between a peasant culture of the past and modern society. Such a view begs the question: how did nineteenth-century peasants experience the landscape; in what ways did their attitudes toward nature and wildlife differ from or resemble ours? The following discussion will center not so much on man in the landscape as on the landscape in man: the ways in which our images of nature are organized by culture.

The Peasant Landscape

In peasant society the landscape was seen as a sphere of production. An economy dominated by an intensive use of many resources demanded an extensive knowledge of the natural surroundings. Peasants, craftsmen, hunters, and fisherfolk had to learn how to read, classify, and manipulate the ecosystems of which their local settings were constituted.

The landscape was not a single workplace but many. Each economic activity had its own cognitive map or frame of reference, and these could overlap. The mountain man did not walk in the forest, he walked in the timber forest, the birchbark forest, the wildfowl forest, or the elk forest. All these hunting-and-gathering activities had their own cultural filters, different ways of perceiving and reading the landscape (Campbell 1936).

Nature was an unruly force which the peasant had to fight or find ways to coexist with. Here a chain has been formed to keep the swidden fire at bay, by men from the village of Mangskog in the northern province of Värmland. (Photograph from 1911 in the collections of the Nordiska Museet, Stockholm.)

The Nature Lovers

The language tells us how rich and differentiated this knowledge was in a subsistence economy. It is no coincidence that a peasant of the plains could name seventy-five different types of soil back in the 1880s, that some fishermen had twenty-five different terms for herring, or that the northern Lapps needed to differentiate between forty types of snow. Such examples show us where the focus in landscape use was located (Löfgren 1976 and 1981c).

This peasant world may seem a very distant land in today's highly urbanized settings, and it can be difficult to imagine how close to nature people lived in an economy in which the slightest shift in weather, vegetation, or animal behavior was noted and assessed. The knowledge of this landscape of production was based on a long-accumulated tradition, which gave the elders a key role in socialization. Their knowledge was relevant and sought after by the young generations, who had to learn to master nature with limited technical means. The process of learning became a long-term one, the occupational training of a farmer, a hunter, or a craftsman continued more or less during his whole life. The ability to read, interpret, and transform the landscape grew step by step, and it is important to remember that this process of learning was based more on participation and imitation than on formal education. People were not taught, they learned.

The actual knowledge was, of course, dependent on the economic pattern and on the resources exploited in the local ecosystem. In an earlier study, I have discussed how farmboys and fisherboys who grew up in the same coastal village came to experience the landscape in very different ways. Fishermen's sons were socialized into a maritime landscape. They learned to see the underwater landscape with its sandy plains, seaweed forests, mountains, rocks, and wrecks; they learned to identify and judge the slightest change in weather and wind, wave movements and currents. Their meteorological knowledge was more complex than that of the farmboys, who on the other hand became experts on fields and pastures. For them the sea remained

Rational and Sensitive

mainly a background set piece to the activities on land (see Löfgren 1977:143ff.).

In the same manner, woodland children were trained to observe the details of the landscape, a prerequisite for becoming skilled wood craftsmen. This learning process has been discussed by Agneta Boqvist in her study of the Bollebygd region of Västergötland, where people lived by forestry and woodcrafts:

> Every craftsman has a fantastic store of knowledge, which includes all kinds of knowledge about the characteristics of different types of wood: that birch absorbs water, that pine leaves a taste, and that alder and aspen are light woods best suited for clogs, but that the latter splinters easily; that free-growing spruce close to bogs is well suited for plaiting mats and herring baskets, and that fallen fir is lighter and tougher than birch; that staves for casks are usually made from pine, but that the hoops are made of pine withies. Just by looking at a growing tree, a basket maker can judge if it is fit material for baskets.
>
> This knowledge was based on lifelong experience acquired by growing up in the woodlands and surrounded by crafts. . . . People spent a great deal of time in the woods, berry picking, assisting in the logging, in search of grazing cattle, and on the road to school or to friends and kin in other villages. There were usually shortcuts through the forest and numerous beaten tracks. (Boqvist 1978:105ff.)

In order to facilitate the assimilation of this broad knowledge of nature, peasants often made use of folklore. Children learned rhymes, ditties, and mnemonic rules about the habits of animals or the uses of plants. This colorful folk literature included sayings "from the time when animals and plants could speak" and advised people, for ex-

The Nature Lovers

ample, about which kinds of leaves could be used as animal fodder. In one example, a sheep warns: "Break birch leaves, break rowan leaves, but never maple leaves: they are broad to the eye but thin to the tooth." In another rhyme a cow advises: "Sallow leaves fatten me, aspen leaves feed me, rowan leaves starve me, alder leaves flatten me" (af Klintberg 1975:284ff.).

For the first generations of folklorists, this kind of lore was seen as a survival of an animistic peasant religion, but it should rather be seen as a simple aid for the memory. In other cases, the pedagogical message may not be as direct; the rhymes and rules have more of a classificatory function. Through them children learned to distinguish different types of trees, to register the shifts of the seasons, and to observe the behavior of animals.

The Magical Landscape

The peasant was never alone in the landscape. Farmers, fishermen, and hunters moved in magical surroundings, populated by supernatural beings like trolls, gnomes, wights, and night-mares. Some of these beings were defined as *rådare*, meaning the magical rulers of nature. They guarded natural resources and could influence weather, wind, and growth. These rulers were seldom defined in terms of good or bad. Their behavior was ambivalent: on the one hand, they could punish breaches of norms and taboos or seek revenge; on the other hand, they could assure people of good crops or warn them of approaching storms.

The *skogsrå*, the siren of the woods, demonstrates this ambivalence. For many charcoal burners she was a living reality. She watched over the charcoal stacks, and many a man could tell stories about being awakened in the middle of the night by a strange sound, a shrill laugh,

Rational and Sensitive

a bellowing animal, only to find out that the stack just had caught fire. In return the *skogsrå* could demand that the charcoal burner keep his workplace neat and not disturb the wild animals in the surroundings. If he broke any of these unwritten rules, the disposition of the *skogsrå* could change swiftly, and he could suddenly find himself dogged by misfortune.

In the same way, the rulers of the sea played several roles. Fishermen could make small offerings to them, such as a silver coin or a drop of aquavit to bring them luck in their fishing. Such allies could warn of bad weather, but those who offended them risked having their nets damaged or their luck destroyed (Löfgren 1981b).

Supernatural beings policed the landscape, guarding boundaries between different spheres of activities and territories. Jochum Stattin has described in a recent study (1984) how the water spirit *Näcken* could appear in situations of transition, scaring away people who stepped into forbidden territories or found themselves in the wrong place at the wrong time.

Examples like these illustrate how beliefs in the supernatural inhabitants of the landscape structured the peasant perception of nature; they also mirror important elements in their world view, ideas about the proper and improper use of natural resources, definitions of right and wrong.

The rich folklore material also mirrors the shifting focus of the peasant economies. In northern Sweden, where the economy was dominated by extensive stockraising and dairy farming, the little people of the underworld, called *vitterfolk*, were cattle breeders. Supernatural tales tell of cowbells sounding mysteriously in the midle of the forests, of sudden meetings with the cattle herds of the little people, and of attempts by peasant girls to steal one of their small cows with the help of magic. As the economy largely centered around milk production, it is not surprising that the special characteristic of the *vitterfolk* cows was their amazing milking capacity.

The Nature Lovers

In this part of the country, the cattle were driven to summer pastures in the mountains, where they were milked and tended by the farm women who lived in outlying shielings (chalets). Life in these shielings was marked by the knowledge that humans shared the setting with the little people of the underworld, as the folklorist Åsa Nyman has pointed out:

> People's relations to the underworld folk were rather difficult.
> You had to be on good terms with them, or else they could
> punish you or seek revenge. On the first arrival at the chalet a
> polite "Good day" and a request to borrow lodgings for the
> summer were called for. It could well be that the rightful in-
> habitants of the forest had not had time to move away. As
> they were invisible, there was always the risk that they could
> be accidentally hurt, which could bring about severe
> repercussions. The belief in these beings colored to a great
> extent the everyday life of people and the ways they related to
> nature. They had to be careful and wary in all kinds of tasks
> and activities. When emptying out a pail of hot water, they
> usually called out loud to give the underworld folk a chance
> to move away. And they refrained from noisy behavior after
> sunset, the time which above all was regarded as belonging to
> the supernatural.   (Nyman 1972:61f.)

Even out in the wilderness, the peasant was never quite alone. The rural physician Fredrik Borelius remembers this feeling from his childhood in the far north of Sweden:

> The invisible people travel the same roads as ordinary
> people. On a path to the mountain shieling in Ångermanland,
> which I have walked many times, people used to meet them.
> They never saw them, but became aware of the meeting when

Rational and Sensitive

the cows moved out of the way. Then a person had to do the same and also give a polite greeting; the *vitterfolk* had older rights to the roads than people. In my childhood I heard of a man . . . who moved a fallen tree from a track in the forest. An old mountain troll came and thanked him for clearing her path, and in return she cured him of the falling sickness. (Borelius 1936:98)

The Industrial Landscape and the Cult of the Exotic

During the nineteenth century this magical landscape withered away, as nature was conquered by science and technology. Surveyors, engineers, industrialists, and scientists colonized this new industrial landscape and discovered new economic possibilities. The agricultural landscape was rearranged in geometrical patterns for rational exploitation. The hunt for raw materials for the expanding industries made new, attractive resources out of land that had previously had only marginal value, if any. Nature was seen as a kingdom of slumbering riches, waiting to be exploited.

The new systems of communication changed the map. The railways ran straight as arrows through forests and marshlands. The steamboats found their way through lakes and new canal systems. The traditional winter roads, created for horse and sledge, lost their importance. Old centers of communication and commerce were abandoned for new railway towns and ports.

Through industrialization and urbanization, many local settings ceased to be landscapes of production for the majority of the population. Industrial technology made the steps between the raw materials of nature and the finished product many and complicated. A new distance from nature was created and there was far less need for direct

The Nature Lovers

and practical training in the use of natural resources. Children no longer learned about nature by following the adults in their landscape activities; training was moved indoors into the schoolroom, and nature increasingly came to be experienced with the help of media like the textbook and the wall chart. A screen was erected between learning and firsthand experience.

This technological and scientific colonization of nature also helped to shape an ideology that saw man as the master of nature. The possibilities of controlling and manipulating nature seemed much greater than they had been for the peasants. These new ways of using and experiencing nature contain some striking paradoxes. Science and technology clear the landscape of all peasant mystique and superstitions, but in its place a new mysticism colonizes the landscape. A new division of labor creates two types of landscape, which rarely overlap. The landscape of industrial production is ruled by rationality, calculation, profit, and effectiveness, while another new landscape of recreation, contemplation, and romance emerges—a landscape of consumption.

This complex cultural change cannot be explained solely as a product of industrialization or technological development, for its genesis also lies in the birth of the Romantic eye among European intellectuals and artists toward the end of the eighteenth century and the beginning of the nineteenth. The Romantic attitude toward nature mirrors important elements in the new world view of the bourgeoisie, the novel ideas about individuality, the nostalgic search for a utopian past and an unspoiled natural state. This was the period of the lonely wanderer, exploring both himself and the wilderness in search of true nature. Artists and authors became the vanguard of the new tourism.[3]

It is not, however, the whole of nature that becomes part of this new cult. Logically enough, it is nonproductive nature that attracts the attention. The first tourist pilgrimages were not to agricultural scenery but to the wilderness. It was the rugged and exotic landscapes that attracted these pioneers: the Alps and the mountain world. An anony-

Rational and Sensitive

mous writer in the 1895 yearbook of the Swedish Touring Club asserts that: "A touring club is usually born in the mountains. It is the grandiose, powerful alpine world that first and foremost awakens this love of nature" (STF:s årsskrift 1895:vii). This love of the mountains fits nicely with the bourgeois world view, as Roland Barthes has pointed out (1972:74). It is the majestic mountain, the naked gorge, and the untamed rapids that dominate the early guidebooks. This landscape not only represents the wild and exotic, but also the solitary and aloof, the fresh and pure. The new interest in mountaineering and wilderness treks mirrors a masculine cult of asceticism, achievement, and individuality. The man who endures hardship and deprivations to conquer a mountain single-handed is performing a ritual that expresses a basic theme in the new world view. He masters both an inner and an outer nature. This moral theme was expressed thus by an alpine enthusiast: "The possibilities afforded by the passion for mountaineering can only be understood by those who realize that it is the step-by-step achievement of a goal which is the real pleasure of the world, that the accomplishment of an undertaking can bring a person infinitely more enjoyment than, for example, the contemplation of beautiful scenery" (Améen 1889:54).

Alpine travel was a way of buying hardships, so it is not surprising that the mountain peasants viewed this way of spending time and money with some dubiety: it seemed like work without a purpose, and they even called it recreation!

The wild, exotic, and majestic were found not only in the mountains but also on the coast. The rugged west coast of Sweden, dominated by rocks, heather, and sand, had been considered the height of ugliness by earlier generations of upper-class travelers; the Romantic eye transformed it into something beautiful and fascinating. Again, the strong moral flavor in the judgment of the landscape is notable: the seacoast represented untamed simplicity and solitude. Like the mountains, the coastal landscape was not only morally superior, but also healthier, far removed from smoking factories and noisy cities.[4]

The bourgeoisie, bearing walking staffs and picnic baskets, colonized the wilderness. Here the party has discovered a spectacular waterfall as a suitable backdrop and panorama. The raging torrent was a favorite element in the cult of wild and exotic scenery. It represented some bourgeois virtues in its demonstration of ungoverned strength and individual freedom. (Photograph from the turn of the century in the collections of the Nordiska Museet, Stockholm.)

Rational and Sensitive

In the new tourist pilgrimage to the coast and the mountains it is also possible to detect a curiosity about the primitive and picturesque life led by the natives of these regions, "these simple but sound and capable people of the lower classes," as they were described in the yearbook of the Swedish Touring Club (Lindroth 1903:135). It is hardly a coincidence that the fisherman, that born individualist and gambler, was a much-loved stereotype in the social landscape of the urban middle class. This confrontation between two worlds has been described (in a somewhat self-congratulatory manner) by the author Ludvig "Lubbe" Nordström, who worked for a year as a hired fisherman in a small coastal community, where visitors from the newly built hotel came down to the harbor to observe the life of the locals:

> And the lazy city females came down to look at us. They asked about everything, standing in a line on the jetty in the blazing sun. "And isn't it dangerous out at sea, when a storm blows up? And isn't it cold to lie out in the boat?" And they looked at the local girls and at me. At my naked, tanned, and hairy breast, which glittered like an African's under my open shirt. And the eyes of the pale city females shone; the glistening water, the boat, and we fisherfolk were mirrored in their moist eyes, and the corners of their mouths watered, the saliva coated their teeth as in anticipation of a good meal. Those city females, those city females! (Nordström 1907:61)

The coast and the mountains, the fisherman and the lonely herdsman in the wilderness thus came to be important elements in the new, exotic landscapes, but the interest in these kinds of settings was also linked to a new way of looking at nature in terms of views and sceneries. The Romantic eye sought the panorama, a vantage point from which to take in a mountain view or a seascape. An arduous climb was rewarded by a breathtaking view of wide horizons, along with a feeling of control, of having the world at one's feet.

The Nature Lovers

The new landscape aesthetics contained ideas about what kind of scenery was exotic, interesting, beautiful, genuine, and natural. At the very top of this ranking list one could often find the sunset, viewed from a mountaintop or a seaside cliff. This scenery satisfied many of the new emotional longings. Observing this view alone or with silent companions was a form of aesthetic worship, an experience of serenity, sanctity, and wholeness. The absolute stillness, the dying of the day, the open landscape, all gave a feeling of total belonging, of a quiet ecstasy. The beholder felt that time stood still, or experienced a "natural" time, being totally immersed in the landscape. It was like a ritual return to a mythical past and a real life (Löfgren 1985a:92ff.; cf. Grossklaus and Oldemeyer 1983:169ff.). The paradox is that these feelings can in some ways be seen both as a result of a new alienation from nature and as a domestication of nature.

During the nineteenth century, the wilderness was organized and tamed. Expeditions into the countryside, by train, by steamboat, or on foot, were based on an idea of collecting beautiful landscapes. Planned footpaths, guidebook listings, and newly erected sightseeing platforms structured the enjoyment of the scenery: "Look, here is another beautiful view!" People learned unconsciously to frame the landscape, to create closed spaces.

This process of cultural framing was also shaped by other factors. One important condition was the changed modes of transport. As horse-drawn coaches and carriages were replaced by railway compartments and steamboat lounges, the perception of the landscape became different. Nature was now experienced as a scenic view gliding past the window of the train or the porthole of the steamer. Travelers learned to focus their eyes on the distant fields, not on the rapidly passing foreground. From these observation posts the landscape looked rather like a framed painting or a photograph (Schivelbusch 1977:51ff.).

There exists an interesting interplay among different genres developed in the nineteenth century, between the grand landscapes in oil,

Rational and Sensitive

the watercolor sketches of both artists and tourists, Victorian amateur photography, and the popular exhibitions of panoramas and dioramas. The Sunday family outings could be directed to scenic views outdoors but also to art galleries, where the same majestic views were presented in oil, almost as real as life. In these genres, ideas about how to look at nature and what to look for were institutionalized and notions about the picturesque, idyllic, exotic, and grandiose were expressed.

For the urban tourists, nature could become a collection of frozen images, a string of pictures. Toward the end of the century, the new techniques of cheap mass reproduction made it possible to bring these views back from one's travels and share them with friends. The scenic postcard was born out of a new mode of seeing and in turn came to structure this new perception of the outside world. The selection of suitable motifs for postcards helped to define and reinforce the idea of a beautiful, interesting, or exclusive view. The five-star views were not only listed in the local guidebook, they could also be bought in the souvenir shops. The postcard thus helped to organize the landscape, but it also captured the viewers' moods. It mass-produced the feeling of a sunset, the sacredness of a mountain panorama. In some ways the postcard made it easier to share these very private emotions, which were so difficult to verbalize (Löfgren 1985a).

The paradox of the domesticated wilderness is also evident in the interior decoration of the late nineteenth century. During the 1850s and 1860s, the parlors and drawing rooms of the bourgeoisie were colonized by exotic and emotionally loaded natural motifs. Winding lianas and wild plants patterned the carpets, indoor palms and other exotic plants swayed in the windows. Even more exotic landscapes could be found on the fire screen or on the embroidered cushions nearby. The visitor could relax on the rose-decorated sofa, leafing through albums depicting scenes of untamed nature or just letting the eyes wander toward the impressive landscape in oil on the opposite

The Nature Lovers

wall, where agitated waves battered the rugged coast or the blue mountains melted into the horizon; a landscape big enough to give the observer the feeling of walking right into it. In less affluent homes one would have to be content with the majestic stag at sunset in the form of an oleograph or a cross-stitch embroidery (Paulsson 1950:2.362ff.). The cozy home and wild nature were united in a contrast to the hectic life out in the sphere of business and production.

How Nature Became Natural

In these ways, nature came to stand for the exotic, and the exotic became domesticated. In the next step of this new development, nature became natural. During the nineteenth century the polarization between nature and nonnature became sharper. Nature, the recreational landscape, was given qualities that made it the very antithesis of all that was defined as unnatural in middle-class life. Nature came to stand for the authentic and unaffected in contrast to the artificial, manmade, and commercialized milieus of the urban world.

It was toward the end of the nineteenth century that this view of nature came into focus in Sweden. This was the period of a new Romantic attitude to nationalism. Writers, artists, and scholars searched for a new national identity in the landscape and in history, an identity that stood in contrast to the conservative patriotism of earlier generations who dreamed about a heroic and martial past. This was the new nationalism of progressive liberals, who embraced a cult of the simple, the genuine, and the natural.[5] The artists painted scenes of rural landscapes and everyday life under the slogan "Paint Swedish!" or, as one of the chief ideologues put it:

> Our art should . . . be just like our nature! It should express
> our special character and the feelings of our hearts, using for

Rational and Sensitive

this purpose the colors and forms of our country and our people. We must take to art for the sake of nature and not for the sake of art.

Art shall grow in the country, because nature sings in the breast of the entire nation and demands an expression—an art. And the artist must be one with the whole people. It is only thus that a genuine and deep-rooted art can be created, one that will live in history as Swedish art. (Bergh 1900:135f.)

Nature was animated into a symbol for Swedishness and a national fellowship above class boundaries. Now it was no longer the wild mountains or the stormy coast that were the favorite landscapes, but rather the nostalgic and melancholic settings: the whispering pine forest, the silent, starry winter night, the grove of young birch trees, the wood anemones in the forest clearing. The dramatic and exotic landscapes gave way to the intimate and melancholy, but still it was the solitary landscape, uncontaminated by human presence, that was preferred.

During this period, nature and nation were united in a patriotism that defined itself as progressive and forward-looking, in contrast to conservative jingoism. The combination of patriotism and tourism was emphasized in the program of the Swedish Touring Club. One of its founders, a geologist, states this ambition with the help of a poetic quotation:

And if we can at all succeed in awakening in our Swedish youth, who carry the future of their fatherland on their shoulders, this fiery enthusiasm for our *whole* country, this unwavering conviction that every part of it is indispensable, then the Touring Club will have fulfilled its most finest task, and *then, O, Mother Sweden!*——

The Nature Lovers

Then shall the Muscovite in vain
with his race thy courtyard threaten.
(Svenonius 1892:41)

To these two foundations, nature and nation, were added history
and the home district. As peasant culture was threatened by industrial
development, the interest in the natural, indigenous people increased.
Scholars and folklore collectors saw themselves as a rescue team picking their way through a landscape of cultural ruins, where scraps and
survivals of traditional life-styles could still be found. Through their
enthusiastic work they helped to construct the myth of a traditional
and national peasant culture. In this new mythology the province of
Dalarna (Dalecarlia) in northern Sweden came to represent the typical
traditional peasant culture, the good and natural life of the old Swedish peasant population. For the urban middle class, Dalarna became a
place of pilgrimage, a search for what was genuinely Swedish. A tourist
in the 1890s describes his impressions thus:

Here you still get a breath of old times and see a last glimpse
of the disappearing Dalarna. For people in delicate health
who do not want to undergo hardship, the village of Leksand
offers the opportunity to see an image of the Sweden of our
ancestors in fully civilized surroundings. These blue mountains, the high, forested ridges become doubly beautiful
when one sees people in folk costume moving around among
them, a naïve race, still with a zest for life, dancing to the
sound of fiddles on Saturday evenings, down on the shore of
Lake Siljan; or when one glimpses the bands of churchgoers
in national dress among the rows of airy birches leading up
to Leksand Church. In this wonderful Dalarna with its sound
people, its cottages, its old customs still preserved up here,

Rational and Sensitive

everything is genuinely Swedish as in no other province, and nowhere else does one feel so happy and proud of being Swedish. It may be Sunday, with its gathering of people in national dress in the temple, that gives the most powerful impression of the treasury of old-fashioned sentiment and poetry we Swedes still have up here in this province, which is the heart of Sweden and the jewel in the crown of our king. (cited in Näsström 1937:80f.)

Here the middle class could play peasants, get back to nature, and dress up in the local costumes, which were called "national." A sketch from a tourist hotel in Dalarna in 1915 describes this feeling: "You wake up rejuvenated. The old man becomes a youngster again, and the ladies, who never get older than middle age, feel like teenage girls and playfully dress up as local lasses in order to charm their blasé admirers with a rural naïveté" (cited in Rosander 1976:222).

Why was Dalarna chosen as the original home and model of Sweden? In many ways the peasant life of this province was atypical. One reason was, of course, the fact that it was still possible to find a picturesque peasant life there at the beginning of the twentieth century, with traditional costumes and customs. But the atypical life of the Dalecarlians also fitted the middle-class mythology of "the old peasant society." The social differences were smaller here than in many other parts of the country. There was no large rural proletariat to disturb the image of a happy village *Gemeinschaft*. Here one found the stereotypes of a freedom-loving, individualistic, and principled peasantry, embodying honesty, honor, and love of traditions. They represented the kind of ancestors the middle class wanted to have in their cultural charter.

This mythology was furthered by the efforts of the first generations of ethnologists and folklorists, who directed much of their collecting

The Nature Lovers

efforts to the villages of Dalarna, thus helping to give this idiosyncratic region a central position in the construction of "traditional peasant life."

This new cult of nature and the peasant heritage was the foundation of Swedish ethnology, one of the fashionable disciplines of the 1890s, which provided ideological ammunition not only to the public debates on culture but also to architects and community planners. The traditional village became a utopian model for community life.

The first open-air museum in the world, Skansen, founded in Stockholm in 1891, was an important manifestation of this new interest and also an instrument of socialization for the urban middle class. The whole family could go there to wander around the reconstructed cottages and farmsteads and find confirmation of the mythology of the old peasant society. In an article from 1892, the author Gustaf af Geijerstam describes a visit to Skansen: "This exhibition of old Swedish life affected me like a dream, a great folk poem turned into a reality, which activates all the powers of the imagination." He further stresses that it is not only the need for recreation for the nerves after an intensive city winter that creates a longing for rural pleasures, but also that this need "is related to the inner feeling for the primitive that any human harbors, even when he leads a life that is outwardly as different as it could possibly be. It is the primitive that we city dwellers seek during summers in the countryside, the primitive and its tranquility" (cited in Näsström 1937:76).

The cult of the peaceful countryside and the old peasant life can be seen as an attempt to create a common national identity in a period of sharpened class conflicts in Sweden. The old national symbols, like the royal family, were no longer the rallying points they used to be. The traditional harmony of village life, where everybody knew his or her station in life, seemed very attractive in these times of rapid change and unrest. On the other hand, this cult of nature and folk life

Rational and Sensitive

was part of a progressive ideology. This paradoxical combination of a firm belief in progress and a nostalgia for the old days can be found among many of the radicals at the turn of the century (Sundin 1984). Both liberals and socialists used the image of an egalitarian peasant society as a model for the future, which also expressed a longing for a natural and simple life in a society that was sometimes felt to be overcivilized.

Karl-Erik Forsslund was one of the main ideologues of this new movement, which preached the virtues of simplicity, the athletic life, a belief in progress, and love of one's native district. This was the birth of today's Swedish cult of the sun and the body. Forsslund's teaching was a curious blend of regional Romanticism, Nietzscheanism, and socialism. Ture Nerman has attempted to characterize the movement:

> What did all the young people who fervently adopted the doctrine mean by beauty? A little of everything, really. . . . It included the temperance movement's nature worship, the progressive spirit of the theory of evolution; it was sun worship and folk dances and looms and handwoven cloth, and it was total scorn for antimacassars and Athenian shelves with plaster cats and porcelain idylls; we battled against the pathetic mahogany furniture of the eighties and painted over the large-flowered wallpaper with plain red or other colors, but always monochrome.   (cited in Stavenow-Hidemark 1971:88)

This gospel stressed the distinction between natural and unnatural, between country and town:

> We were the youth of the time who hated the city culture of chimneys and chimney-shaped clothes—trousers, top hats,

The Nature Lovers

and the like—and we ourselves went around with long hair
like artists, with full beards if possible, wearing short trousers,
preferably of homespun, and large flapping scarves. We felt
such a *joie de vivre* and delighted so in our youthful strength,
full of idealistic missionary pathos and a burning faith in life,
that we went everywhere, even along the city streets, singing loudly of walking "over dew-soaked mountains." And the
girls had the open-air grace of Skansen and liked to be called
"lasses" and had long hair in braids hanging down their backs
or demurely pinned up in rings around the ears. And perhaps a large bronze clasp on their blouses. That is what we
were like. That was the fresh-air manner in which our
chieftains were dressed.   (Nerman, cited in Näsström
1937:161)

This milieu at the turn of the century saw the development and ideological charging of concepts associated with the word *hem* (home):
hemkänsla (feeling for home), *hemlängtan* (homesickness), *hembygd*
(home district). The first phases of the *hembygd* movement had a utopian touch, a revolt against the artificial life-style of the bourgeoisie,
but it was soon dominated by nostalgia. As Hermann Bausinger has
pointed out, the corresponding German *Heimat* ideology originated
from a new need for security in a world with ever-widening horizons
and increasing rootlessness. The nostalgia for the home district was a
defense against all that was foreign and changing (Bausinger 1961:
85ff.). The paradox is obvious. The new Romantic view of the home district was an attempt to turn back the clock, to anchor the rootlessness
in the traditions of peasant society. Yet what was recreated was not so
much the landscape of peasant culture as the myth of the way it was
and the dream of the way it ought to be. There was a longing for a secure society with no class conflicts and no outsiders.[6]

Rational and Sensitive

Summer in the Country

"I have deliberately delayed mentioning the best of all: our summers," writes the industrialist Herman Lagercrantz in his memoirs (1944:32). His description follows the pattern of many other bourgeois memoir writers. In the normally sober and rather dry accounts of climbing the career ladder, the style suddenly changes. The figure-conscious businessman and the graying official are seized by a surge of emotion and sentimentality when they think of the summer vacations of their childhood:

> For many Stockholm children, the years of growth are divided into two halves, which are so dissimilar that there can hardly be a single point of contact between them. On the one hand there is a dark winter filled with compulsory school and homework, broken only occasionally by Christmas and winter sports—in my time more skating and tobogganing than the skiing of later years. On the other hand there are the long, bright, free days of summer, when life was a game played in birch groves or on glittering waves. (Lagercrantz 1944:32)

Bourgeois culture often equates nature with the summer; love and nostalgia for nature are anchored in memories of the delights of summer vacations. This is another example of the compartmentalization of life: summertime in the country had very different qualities from everyday winter existence in town. Vacationland ritualized further the boundaries between work and leisure, between efficiency and emotion.

Nature is not just a compensation, it is a place of refuge in direct contrast to "the other life." Here, for example, is a description of Wilhelmsberg, a country house outside Gothenburg toward the end of the nineteenth century:

The Nature Lovers

Wilhelmsberg is no large estate with fields and forests. It is a
little country house out in the country, a little haven in the
bosom of nature, far from the restless world of business in the
nearby city. The adjoining land consists of no more than a
few acres situated between the mountain slopes. The garden,
cultivated in the favorable soil between the mountains, provides crops of delicious fruit every year, and shady bowers for
repose on close summer evenings.   (cited in Paulsson
1950:1.337)

There were many ritual devices to mark the transition from town to
country, from the world of work to carefree leisure. We can observe
just how quickly children learned this magical transformation. The experience of the great ceremonious removal by steamboat or overland
was etched in the memory.

Once out in the summer idyll, the naturalness of summer life was
emphasized by the simplicity of the physical environment. White is
the color of summer. The white house had bright rooms with light,
simple furniture. There is often a marked contrast with the dark, heavy
city apartment. Out in the garden, summer people stroll in white linen
suits and straw hats, while newly painted canvas shoes tread on the
soft, well-groomed grass of the croquet lawn.

The childhood memories give an almost sacral character to summer
vacations. Life in the country symbolizes all that is genuine, warm,
emotional, and magical. A clear example of these attitudes and this
language is a description of summer vacations around the turn of the
century by Alice Quensel, daughter of a state official:

Our home on Luntmakaregatan was squeezed between rows
of houses in a narrow street. In a purely physical sense the
horizon was limited, and although the inner dimensions
must be considered large by today's standards, it was natural

Rational and Sensitive

that freedom was a seductive, enticing concept. No day of the year, scarcely even Christmas, was as longed for as the day of the spring removal. The *countryside* was for us city children not merely a romantic idea, it was a need we felt and a boundless happiness. . . .

Nothing on earth could appear more dear than to be welcomed out there one day at the beginning of June, when the lilac in the fragrant hedges blossomed, and we, free as birds, could run around and once again find our way about the bowers and the hills. . . .

Children those days had long weeks of summer vacation. There was no thought for work other than running errands for Mother or, for the bigger children, looking after the little ones. (Quensel 1958:121–126)

Strindberg has given us a literary picture of a bourgeois summer paradise in a tale that describes life in the fashionable bathing resort of Furusund in the last decades of the nineteenth century. It is a picture of idyllic sensualism, where everything appears "arranged for the three-month-long festivity known as summer" (Strindberg [1902]1962:7):

He wandered along a level path, soft as a carpet. There were sofas and tables placed out as if it was one great hall, where everyone belonged to the aristocracy and all were visiting one another. . . . When he had walked for a while, he saw a party parading toward him with singing and music. It was an ordinary weekday, but they were all dressed in light Sunday colors. . . .

He could see through the windows of the huts, and there were people in their best Sunday clothes resting; even the maids were sitting on the kitchen steps, their arms crossed, doing nothing. (Strindberg [1902]1962:27f.)

The Nature Lovers

Summer vacations meant something else to many people: a time for them to discover themselves, become complete; an existence in contrast to a fragmented and discordant city life. Town dwellers should ideally enjoy at least two or three months of this bright, simple life every year. Although the father may not have been able to be there all the time, he arrived every Friday evening on the boat or the train and changed from his city suit to a straw hat and white clothes, changing at the same time into a new person.

Town and country, work and leisure have thus come to mean separate lives in the twentieth century. The flight from the town is felt by many Swedes today to be a return to nature. Weekends in the summer cottage or the trailer park allow them to live a genuine life close to nature. This pattern was already developed in bourgeois culture at the turn of the century. An early example of summer cottagers is the Tegnér family:

At the age of seven I came to Småland. My parents knew that the fresh highland air would be good for their asthmatic, highly strung boy with his weak heart and muscles.

Now I sometimes wonder whether [the poet] Verner von Heidenstam could really have loved the stones and the soil of Östergötland as much as we cottagers loved our hill in Småland and all that was to be found there—the deep, thick spruce forests, the dry, sun-drenched pine plateaus, the balmy groves of hazel, linden, birch, and alder, the rich soil we dug, the gravelly reddish-brown subsoil, the confoundedly stubborn little juniper bushes that we had such trouble uprooting. . . .

Yes. For we became cotter children. Our father (and indeed our whole quartet) was so delighted with the Södra Äng farm . . . where we spent that warm, pleasant, wild-strawberry summer of 1896, playing croquet on the lawn between the li-

Rational and Sensitive

lac bushes and the grain shed and climbing our own stout side bough of the largest cherry tree, that he leased the very best forest slope to the northeast and built for us there the most marvelous cottage. . . .

In long, sweaty summer weeks year after year we cultivated Swedish soil, the heart of Småland; farthest up in the parish of Norra Solberga, in Sola, which is not like other places in this difficult world, but rather the very Center of the Earth . . . and the abode of Peace and Bliss. (Tegnér 1963:77ff.)

This was how the alternative world was constructed, the place of summer refuge where people were ritually transformed.

Let us summarize the main features of this transformation. Industrial society splits human life into opposing worlds such as home and the outside world, work and leisure, production and reproduction. At the same time it creates a new ideology of the possibility of becoming a whole person in a partial world. At leisure in the home or in the country, we can become complete and genuine people, living a full life. We find a compensatory sphere governed by quite other laws than in the sphere of production. It is important to see the connection here: love of nature is one of the foundation stones in the new, emotionally charged intimate sphere, so nature is quite logically assigned the same qualities as the other building blocks of this new world.

It is striking how many features are shared in common by the pictures of nature, the home, and femininity: naturalness and genuineness, peace and tranquility, comfort and warmth. These are the reverse of the production sphere, with its efficiency and cold rationality. The bourgeois man learns not just to rest in the warmth of femininity, but also in the bosom of nature and the home.

This new vision of nature has a striking degree of home comfort. A description of a stay in a boarding house at Kinnekulle sets the tone:

The Nature Lovers

When one sits on the verandah and looks out over the garden
before one, with its beds of dahlias, and further away the
cornfields, the forest, and the sea, the thought never occurs
that one is not at home. One feels that one is in a calm and
peaceful place in the world. A certain peace of mind steals
over one. The sea of thoughts is becalmed. One sinks into
daydreams. And one finds that few things are as delightful as
dolce far niente at Kinnekulle.   (Améen 1890:68)

No emotion in nature need be bridled, but all can be given free rein.
The most single-minded businessman or the most dutiful bureaucrat
is moved to tears by the sight of a slope covered with wood anemones
or the memory of childhood summers. Emotions that are otherwise
correctly channeled and disciplined can be given free play in well-
defined situations.

Gustaf Näsström gives the following description of a young friend
who as a student was intoxicated by Forsslund's teachings:

He became at length an exemplary official, who for the six
days of the working week looked forward to the seventh, and
yearned even more for the vacation, when he could tie up his
knapsack and set out on adventurous rambles in the wilderness. His life was richest then; perhaps he lived to the full
only then. Longing away from the city and ordered work, a
dreamer in green forests and hazy blue mountain moors. Is
this fate not typically Swedish?   (Näsström 1937:160)

This passage highlights yet another important ingredient in the bourgeois view of nature. The surge of emotion occasioned by the landscape, an emotion so profound that it is felt to be something character-
istically human; the bourgeois feeling for nature is the only natural

Rational and Sensitive

feeling. Let us return to Senior Juror Tegnér's family in their summer
cottage:

> Can any children have *felt* as we cotter children did for the
> tiniest little rocky ridge, only a few yards high, thinly over-
> grown with catchfly, an odd tree stump red with wild straw-
> berries, surrounded by ferns? Because Our Mother's Cottage
> could be glimpsed red through the rowan trees by the fence,
> and the voices of the people of the house could be heard oc-
> casionally beyond the buzzing of the bees, below the chirping
> of the birds.   (Tegnér 1963:79)

No, real cotter children would no doubt have had difficulty in feeling
the same surge of emotion for the land around the cottage. The internalization of this new view of the landscape was so thorough that
most of the memoir writers, like Torsten Tegnér, take their own view of
nature as something self-evidently Swedish. It is seldom that any other
reality is allowed to intrude in this summer paradise, the reality that
this life of summer pleasures was granted to a sheltered minority of
families at the turn of the century.

   Real cotter children found the life of the summer visitors fantastic,
almost unreal. A native of Bohuslän left the following recollection from
the beginning of this century:

> We called them the visitors or the gentlefolk. There was a
> wide gulf between them and us. Most of them owned one of
> the big summer villas that faced the sea, others rented rooms
> from the local people. They usually arrived a bit into June,
> when the schools had closed. . . .
>
>   The visitors were a part of society, only they were admitted
> to the society drawing rooms. They arranged bazaars and
> charitable works. Along came the older ones with their fine

The Nature Lovers

titles, the high-school graduates with their white caps, and the young unmarried daughters, society girls, wearing white lace dresses with pastel-colored silk ribbons around the waist. . . .

My grandparents' house had been sold to a factory owner from Gothenburg. They had three children of about the same age as us. We were playmates for a number of summers. Our mother was careful to see that we were clean and tidy, and anxious for us to behave properly. They had a playhouse in the garden, a swing for several people at a time, croquet, and many, many other things. We knew when they were coming, and we sat expectantly on the sofa, looking down the road; we saw the carriage pull up, and they came up to fetch us straight away. This was in our early childhood, but the picture changed; there came years when we waited in vain. Whether it was their parents or they themselves who had grown older and realized that we were no longer suitable company, I don't know. But it broke us to the heart, the disappointment was so great.

But the summer visitors tickled my curiosity. We used to sneak up to the window and peep in when they were dancing in the society drawing rooms. We knew them all by name, knew where they lived, and sometimes pretended that we were them. (Jirvén 1971:86f.)

This sort of recreational landscape was a meeting place for different classes, a confrontation between different worlds. Concepts like leisure and vacation had very little relevance in working-class life at the turn of this century; spare time after school was to a great extent occupied by errands and extra work. As working-class people gradually got the chance to develop a life of leisure and started to visit the countryside and the seaside on day excursions, weekends, and holi-

Rational and Sensitive

days, many middle-class observers began to complain about the lack of manners shown by the new intruders. Journalists and cartoonists caricatured the holiday mores of these common people with varying degrees of contempt and irony.

One of the problems with working-class vacationers was that they did not know how to behave. W. W. Thomas, Jr., envoy extraordinary and minister plenipotentiary of the United States to Sweden, once found himself crowded out by a large party of miners and their families during a summer steamboat journey out of Stockholm and complained bitterly about the consequences of democratized travel:

> For the moment any number of individuals become demoralized into an excursion, they develop a fatal facility of appropriating all the accommodations, eating all the food, filling all the cars and boats, and crowding and hustling the politeness and patience out of everybody else. . . . There was no place to sit down, and scarcely any room to stand up, and how these miners and their prolific families could enjoy this sort of thing I can not conceive, unless they were sustained by the happy consciousness of traveling at reduced rates. (Thomas 1892:505).

Another complaint had to do with the idea that working-class people often profaned nature. There were too many noisy voices and boisterous picnics with accordions, beer, and card playing, and far too little of that aesthetic asceticism which middle-class nature lovers regarded as the proper mode of conduct in the sacred halls of nature. There was simply too much of the herd mentality in the ways working-class people used the landscape and not enough contemplation. It was questioned whether common people really loved nature the way it deserved to be loved, or, as the art critic C. G. Laurin put it in 1909: "A shepherd boy usually has no eye for the sunset over the sea or

This picture of an excursion train from 1907 contains several of the classic, middle-class stereotypes of working-class holiday making: noisy music, unrestrained drinking, and uncontrolled collective enjoyment. (Watercolor by Erik Tryggelin, Nordiska Museet, Stockholm.)

Rational and Sensitive

the beauty of the white swans flying over dark blue waters."[7] One of August Strindberg's characters describes this class difference in a similar way: he describes his bourgeois friends as being able to "watch nature as you might some noble and uplifting play! Laborers don't see nature like that: the fields are bread, the woods are timber, the lake is a wash-tub, the meadow cheese and milk—the whole thing earth —without a soul" (Strindberg 1967a:261).

For the urban working class, the recreational landscape had other qualities. In a world of overcrowded lodgings and few public meeting places or institutions, the nearby countryside represented an open social space, a territory for meeting and socializing. Groups ranging from family parties to workers' associations made Sunday excursions into the countryside. A description of such an outing from Gothenburg to the nearby coastal community of Lysekil in 1899 illustrates this new tradition:

> Now came the time when all were to share a meal together. The whole plain, which unfortunately could not muster a single tree to provide shade, and which therefore was burning hot, was all at once filled with happy people. Boat after boat arrived with local stone workers, bearing their red flags. When all had arrived, the music rallied the participants, and Mr. Clausen held a forceful welcoming speech, in which he regretted that it had not been possible to find a more shaded meeting place, because the upper class, which monopolizes everything else, also controls these. (cited in Holmgren 1983:95)

The summer landscape could thus become a scene of confrontation, a fight for territory and access to nature. For many urban working-class families the countryside also represented an economic resource, a way of eking out meager wages by gathering anything from

The Nature Lovers

firewood to berries. Most of them still had relatives or friends out in the villages, as the making of a Swedish urban working class was a relatively late phenomenon.

Our Animal Friends

Another middle-class worry had to do with the relations peasants and workers had with the wild inhabitants of the landscape, the animal world. In the 1911 definition of culture quoted in the Introduction, one of the important signs of civilization was "kind treatment of domestic animals and other living creatures." For an understanding of the complex attitude toward nature and the natural that developed in nineteenth-century middle-class culture, it is also necessary to look at the relations to those living creatures of the natural world. In the images of animal life, new polarities between the wild and the civilized, the natural and the unnatural were constructed.[8]

A common complaint of urban visitors to the countryside in the nineteenth century was the proximity of peasants and domestic animals. The physical propinquity to farm animals was often seen as revolting, even dangerous; living so close to animals was bound to make men more bestial. Another repugnant trait was the brutality and callousness witnessed in the peasant treatment of animals and in their hunting and trapping methods. These accusations became much more common toward the end of the nineteenth century: the whole peasant attitude to animals was one of cruelty mixed with old superstitions. The growing intensity of such complaints, however, tells us more about the world view of the new urban middle class than about peasant attitudes to animals.

Peasant relations with the animal world were certainly of a different kind. The habit of keeping small animals in the living quarters of the farm, which was still common in many parts of Sweden at the end of

Rational and Sensitive

the nineteenth century, was an example of the very pragmatic attitude to animal husbandry. They were kept indoors not only for the warmth they gave but also because it was better for them. Hens laid more eggs, young calves grew stronger faster. In the same way, there was never much fuss about the nonproductive aspects of animal care. Cows were usually starved during their winter stay in the stables when they were not producing milk, and they were seldom groomed. Animals, both wild and tame, were primarily an economic resource for the benefit of man, and as. it said in the Bible, they were soulless creatures and should be treated accordingly.

Growing up in peasant society provided as extensive knowledge about animals as it did about the landscape. People learned how to get the most out of the livestock and how to protect it from sickness and other dangers. Knowledge of the habits of wild animals was not only part of hunting-and-trapping expertise, but could also be used to mark the changing seasons and to warn of shifts in the weather. The future could be foretold by interpreting the behavior of some species; others warned of accidents and death. Some of them could change a person's luck; others were the helpers of supernatural powers.

One basic theme in the folklore surrounding animals was the peasant idea of limited good and the notions of luck and envy. Luck in cattle raising, fishing, hunting, and other economic activities was an individual asset under constant threat from others in the community. One person's luck could be another's misfortune. A successful peasant had to watch out for the evil eye and the envy of others, while misfortunes could lead him to start thinking about who was out to steal his luck and by what means (Löfgren 1981b:75).

The idea of the magical destruction of luck was especially strong in animal husbandry. A sick animal, a lame horse, or a cow running dry could threaten the precarious balance of the household economy, and therefore it is not surprising to find a large body of folk medicine in

The Nature Lovers

this field, consisting of both cures and preventive treatments or rituals. Sudden illness or damage was often interpreted in terms of magical destruction, which could be caused by certain wild species being out of place, like the weasel or the hedgehog appearing in the stables, or by supernatural spirits. Destruction could also be the work of evil neighbors: "Who has been riding my horse sick and sweaty in the stable at night?" "Who is stealing milk from my cow by sending a magic hare to suck the udder?" There was a large body of magical techniques by which one could steal the courage of the cow or "shame a horse," as the saying went.

This whole body of magic and witchcraft was very much a reality in the peasant world view until the end of the nineteenth century. It possessed its own logic and rationality and reflected fundamental tensions in the peasant economy and ideology. As middle-class science and rationality colonized nature, however, these kinds of beliefs came under increasingly heavy attack. There is a parallel here to the development in attitudes to the landscape. Peasant magic was scorned by science, and the folk medicine of local cow doctors was ignored by the new nineteenth-century professionals, veterinarians and zoologists.

Zoologists and botanists created a new scientific order in the natural kingdom, following in the footsteps of Linnaeus and other scientists of the Enlightenment. By the end of the nineteenth century, the new scientific taxonomies had permeated all kinds of discourse on the animal world. One could be quite sure that upon entering the main gallery of the new Museum of Natural History in Stockholm in 1896, the first item one saw would be a showcase with a splendid group of stuffed gorillas. One could just as easily guess the name of the first species presented in volume one, chapter one of A. E. Brehm's *Life of Animals*, the standard animal encyclopedia, in both the 1898 and the 1956 editions. The first illustration was of a rather proletarian-looking skeleton of a gorilla, flanked by a rather more gentlemanly

Rational and Sensitive

Homo sapiens (Löfgren 1985b:196). All animals had found their proper place and station in the orderly system of the natural world.

As old peasant magic was replaced by a new middle-class mystique in perceptions of the landscape, attitudes toward the animal world were being charged with new cultural values and emotional content. There is an interesting paradox in this development, because at the same time that people felt a growing intimacy with animals and developed anthropomorphic dialogues with them in theory, they distanced themselves from them in reality. People became increasingly disgusted by the bestial behavior of animals. Their lack of shame and propriety was only a reminder of all the things the bourgeoisie were trying to repress in themselves. One of the mainstays of their idea of self-discipline and civilized behavior was, of course, the denial of the animal in man. Only people belonging to the lower stages of cultural development could live like animals.

There is a striking parallel here to the changes in attitudes toward nature. One of the preconditions for a more Romantic and sentimental view was, as we have seen, the gradual withdrawal from an active or productive use of nature.

One important thing to remember about eighteenth-century urban settings in Sweden is that they were in fact very rural. The burghers still lived in close contact with both farming and animals. Artisans, merchants, scholars, clergymen, and civil servants often combined their occupations with subsistence farming. During the nineteenth century, however, the urban and rural worlds were increasingly segregated and bourgeois children grew up having far less contact with the realities of the pigsty, the stables, and the fields. Animals were something to be read about or looked at, rather than things to be handled in everyday life. It was love at a distance.

There were, however, some animals with which people maintained contact even in city life, perhaps even more so than in previous generations. At the same time that the urban bourgeoisie was complaining

The Nature Lovers

about the cohabitation of men and animals in the peasant villages, distinctions were being created between animals. Pets became very important in nineteenth-century bourgeois society. The history of pets goes much farther back, of course, especially in aristocratic settings, but among the bourgeoisie, a new intimacy developed in relation to dogs, cats, canaries, and goldfish. While it was considered highly improper to have piglets or hens running around in the living room, a lapdog in bed or a kitten on one's knee was something quite different. The boundaries between pets and other animals are elaborated in many ways: not only are pets allowed indoors, they are also given names and even a decent funeral, they are taboo as food, and so on.

Pet keeping in Western society is a complex phenomenon. It contains a narcissistic element that has increased over the last century. Animals make good companions because they can be shaped after one's own wishes. In some ways they are better than humans; their love may be more genuine and less demanding. One can mirror oneself in the imploring eyes of a pet, and one can choose a companion to reflect one's personality.

Out of the idea that some animals bring out the best in man grew new moral hierarchies in the nineteenth century. Some animals became nobler and better than others, mainly those with which people could identify and sympathize.

Identification was not limited to pets, however; there were other species that ranked highly and were felt to deserve human friendship and protection. Societies for the prevention of cruelty to animals developed in Sweden during the latter part of the nineteenth century. They sought to protect animals not only because of their use to humankind, but also for moral and religious reasons. Caring for animals was thought to make people into better human beings (Sundin 1981).

It is not surprising that the first of these associations was the Society for the Friends of Small Birds, founded in 1869. In the bourgeois world view, bird life provided both moral lessons and a utopian ideal. This

Rational and Sensitive

special interest in feathered friends can be explained in several ways. One important fact was that birds did not seem so bestial. They were reasonably clean in both thought and habit; their life seemed sweet and ethereal. They did not wallow in the dirt but moved in the clear skies, they did not grunt or grub but sang their exquisite song from trees and bushes. Even their sexual life had a certain refinement, hardly found among dogs and pigs, not to mention rabbits.

In many ways, birds were paragons of bourgeois virtues compared to other animals. Most of the small birds lived in stable nuclear families and took care of their offspring in the secure nest. They also represented the soul of liberalism and individualism, as free, democratic, but industrious citizens of the heavens.

However, even bird lovers and ornithologists did not embrace all birds with the same enthusiasm. There were good birds and bad birds. Most of the little singing birds were considered nice. They built fine nests, were vegetarians or insect eaters, mated only once a year, and never troubled other nesting birds. Many of them returned faithfully year after year, it was hoped with the same mate. Their life was characterized by values like domesticity, matrimonial fidelity, and thrift.

Bad birds, on the other hand, had to be kept in check. They led wicked lives, attacking the nice birds. They lived on prey or carrion. There were even those who laid their eggs in other birds' nests, without a glimmer of parental love. For many bird lovers, the really bad bird was the sparrow. Its voice was shrill, its plumage a dirty gray, it moved around in noisy mobs, behaved aggressively, and lived on grain and horse manure. It also mated incessantly and built untidy nests. Sparrows were often described in rather proletarian terms. They came to symbolize city life, the urban sprawl that threatened the rural idyll. These sons of the gutter certainly were not worthy of bird lovers' attention and protection.

The membership roll of the Society for the Friends of Small Birds makes impressive reading, dominated as it was by senior civil servants

The Nature Lovers

and businessmen.[9] The activities of the society were, however, mainly directed toward children and schoolteachers. A basic idea was the educational purpose of bird protection: "Love of nature is a strong force in shaping young minds to contentment and happiness, and in moral and religious terms it is always beneficial; the heart becomes susceptible to the good, the right, and the beautiful" (*Sällskapet småfoglarnes vänner* 1869:37). Birds can also set good examples for family life and relations between parents and their offspring. In a talk on "the gifts of small birds to their young friends," one of the members lectured on the family life of the chick, who "passes through the tenderest of all schools" before Mother Hen lets it out into "the struggle for life that exists even in the chicken run."

Young members were not only subjected to lectures; they also made excursions into the countryside with banners and music, to plant trees for future bird life. They were taught to fight the shooting of small birds and the plundering of their nests.

Birds were not the only animals used in the education of children. Other species were of great help as moral examples, for instance in the problematic task of sexual instruction. The mating of farm animals, which was a fund of sexual knowledge for peasant children, was an experience from which bourgeois children needed to be sheltered, or exposed to only in the form of theoretical and anemic presentations in the biology readers. In this field of education, a balance had to be struck between using animals as good pedagogical examples on the one hand, and making sure on the other that the boundary between human and animal sexuality was very clearly stated.

During the nineteenth century, a zoological world for children was created, in which animal life was reorganized for suitable educational ends. Polygamous tendencies were repressed. In schoolbook illustrations the harem cock was transformed into a proud family father, posing together with Mother Hen and their two chicks. Other farm animals posed in the same nuclear family pattern. In the entrance to the

Rational and Sensitive

Biological Museum in Stockholm, built in 1893, the visitor is still confronted with a stuffed mother bear on two legs, holding her cub in a tender embrace, a reminder of the natural instinct of motherhood.

Since direct talk of human sexuality was taboo in Oscarian education, flowers and bees had to come to the rescue. In manuals of reproductive functions, children had to work their way through the sexual life of the poppy, the starfish, the hen, and the dog. As one climbed up the biological ladder toward *Homo sapiens*, the problems began. Was human sexual life guided by nature or culture? One textbook author argued against those who maintained that it was unnatural to repress the sexual urge:

> Even the most superficial study of nature would show them that the union of the sexes among other living creatures only has the goal of securing the survival of the species, and that animals are often forced to repress their sexual urge and to forsake the feelings of lust related thereto, as well as to other functions of life, without it doing them any harm at all.
> Why should Man alone have the right to aim lower in life?
> (Cederblom 1909:2.41)

Another author chose the opposite line of argument. The difference is that animals cannot feel love in the same way as humans can. Although we may admire the instinct of love we see in feline and canine parents, we must remember that human love is something higher and more refined. This is the kind of love which purifies our sexual life. Men have a procreative instinct, just like animals, but for the animals this is a blind instinct. We, on the other hand, control this instinct through our willpower (Panduro 1922:35). Thus the animal world can be used both to legitimize human morality with the help of arguments from the naturalness of natural life, and to draw a distinction between *Homo sapiens* and animals.

The Nature Lovers

Another rewarding field of analysis is the transformation that animal stories and fables undergo as they pass from peasant tradition into children's literature. We may find the same fables in both settings, but in peasant tradition they tend to lack the strong moralizing element that is so marked in Oscarian literature. The rich fauna of animal stories in Swedish folklore had a burlesque flavor and were intended primarily for entertainment, not moral instruction. The transformed animal stories that found their way into children's books preached bourgeois virtues such as parental love, patriotism, self-discipline, long-term planning, and thrift.

Being Close to Nature

All cultures carry on dialogues with animals. Values, personality traits, hierarchical notions, and moral principles are projected onto the animal world. This anthropomorphization may then be used in arguments about what constitutes "natural behavior" or a "natural order" in discussions about human behavior and society. The animals talk back to us.

In this comparison of peasant and bourgeois attitudes toward the animal kingdom, I have tried to show the parallels between the perceptions of the landscape and the perceptions of its wild inhabitants. It is the alienation from the natural world that is a prerequisite for the new sentimental attachment to it. Nature must first become exotic in order to become natural.

The comparison with peasant life has been used to illustrate how fundamentally different these new images of nature were. The alleged indifference to the beauty of the landscape and the callous treatment of animals of which peasants increasingly came to be accused reflects this change. Peasant thinking and behavior became a totally different world.

Rational and Sensitive

Although peasants had a very pragmatic view of animals as productive resources, there for the good of humanity, the whole idea of conscious cruelty toward animals was probably most alien to peasant thought. The accusations of neglect and indifference also miss the point that relations between humans and animals could be very close in peasant life. A strong attachment could be formed between the stableboy and the favorite horse, between the farmer's wife and her best milking cow. One could confide in these animals and get warmth and affection from them.

The changing middle-class perceptions of animals and nature cannot, of course, be reduced to simply a question of class; they also had to do with the more general process of urbanization. It is especially among the sections of the nineteenth-century bourgeoisie which became increasingly alienated in their everyday life from animals and a productive use of nature that this new sentimentality emerged. However, the new ideologies of nature had a more complex background than that.

First of all, they were shaped by the increasingly scientific approach to nature and the animal world, which produced a hierarchical relationship between scientific knowledge and popular knowledge and a way of structuring the natural world based on symmetry, rationality, and order. It also created a notion of human objectivity and analytical distance from other living creatures.

Second, there was the new empathy, the heightened sensitivity and sentimentality toward nature and parts of the animal kingdom, and the construction of new hierarchies of closeness and identification. This process was also clearly related to the increased educational importance of animals in the nineteenth century, especially in the development of a much more intensive and complex schooling for children. The ways in which the animal world was organized and presented in this context did not necessarily have to correspond to the ways in which adults thought about animals.

The Nature Lovers

Third, there were the ways in which the view of animals was used in the cultural warfare of class conflict. The moral and cultural supremacy of the rising bourgeoisie was legitimized by the fact that they saw themselves as treating animals in a much more civilized and sensitive way than the callous proletarians who flogged their horses or the ignorant peasants who maltreated their dogs. In this process of legitimation, the notions of bourgeois superiority to the superstitious common people also played a role.

Animals were not thought of or used in the same ways in these different domains, but such contradictions need not have constituted a problem; they could be successfully compartmentalized or mediated. It may, for example, seem paradoxical that the industrialist who was a member of the Society for the Friends of Small Birds could be moved to tears about the problems of the little thrush, while showing a marked indifference to the sufferings of his own workers. That paradox can in part be explained by the fact that bourgeois culture was organized around a polarity between the spheres of production and nonproduction. In the productive sphere, the laws of rationality, science, efficiency, and profit reigned, but during leisure time or in domestic life, the rational businessman was allowed a sentimentality and a sensuality that would have been unthinkable at the office. It is the same type of polarity we find in the rational use of the productive landscape and in the romantic view of the nonproductive recreational landscape.

The problem is that nature came to stand for many different things for the Oscarians. Nature could symbolize the primitive and uncivilized forces in the world, as well as the unbridled animal urges that had to be repressed or disciplined. The whole upbringing of the nineteenth-century bourgeois was based upon a notion of moral superiority to the more bestial lower classes. He had mastered the animal within. At the same time, this cultural superiority was also based upon his highly developed sensitivity to the natural kingdom. He could take in the full aesthetics of a sunset or the sacred qualities of the wilder-

Rational and Sensitive

ness, but this highly developed sensibility also made it possible to stand emotionally closer to the animals.

The cultural contradictions in middle-class views of nature express an abhorrence for "natural ways" together with a longing and fascination for the "natural way of life." To return to the classic definition of culture quoted earlier, it concludes with a discussion of the problems of overcivilization: "Culture, which has resolutely turned its back on the crude state of nature in order to struggle toward a harmonious state of refined nature, thereby runs the risk of going astray on roads leading toward the unnatural and the artificial" (Nordisk familjebok 15:226).

The recreational landscape thus became a necessary antidote to the dangers of overcivilization or, to return to the ideas expressed in the yearbooks of the Swedish Touring Club: "Cultured man needs to be allowed out onto the grass now and then, returning occasionally to his role of natural being. Inside every human breast there burns an unquenchable yearning to return to the clear fountainhead of nature. Only in nature can one feel that one is a complete human being" (Améen 1924:x).

The recreational landscape is given a healing, cleansing, and compensatory function in contrast to the image of city life as fragmented, unharmonious, and stressful. Civilized man has lessons to learn from both the animals and the children of nature, the authentic, simple, and rustic folk in the fishing villages or in the wild mountain regions. They are real people, living a real life. In the cult of the authentic and natural, life in the peasant villages and in the animal kingdom can be used to construct middle-class utopias. The interest in the rugged life of fisherfolk or backwoodsmen, the free life of the birds, the love of pets, and the fascination with both wilderness and wildlife mirror dreams about a different or better world. As human society is experienced as more complex, more anonymous and difficult to handle, these dreams of another life have become more common. Today they

The Nature Lovers

constitute an important part of our cultural inheritance from the nine-teenth century.

· 3 ·

The Home Builders

The transformation of nineteenth-century society not only created a new perception of nature; it also rearranged the social landscape in which individuals, groups, and classes moved. The social landscape has more to do with social classification and cultural space than with the actual physical setting. It reflects culturally conditioned perceptions of closeness and intimacy, distance and estrangement, the feeling of being either at home or out in the unknown.

The following attempt by Fredrik Borelius to characterize the mental map of a rather isolated Lappland community about the turn of the century captures the ways in which peasants could experience the world:

> All they know about regions and countries comes from two
> sources: their own travels and the storytelling of others.
>
> Their own journeys have generally not taken them very far:
> to religious meetings, to market, to church and the district
> court; the men have traveled with transports and perhaps
> worked in other places, floating timber down to the sea. . . .
>
> The rest of their world view is based on hearsay. And these
> stories mostly cover the same ground. The storyteller may
> have been to the next parish or parishes, or perhaps even
> down as far as Haparanda; the younger men may have been
> to Boden for their military service; and the Lapps know a

The Home Builders

great deal about northern Norway. Then there are those who have been to Stockholm, or even further away, and letters from America have been read and commented upon. But the pictures they paint are rather blurred.

The world, their own world, . . . they know intimately. They know the roads, big and small, their length and direction, they know the location of the farmsteads, their appearance and size, people's names and ages, their peculiarities of shape, speech, and behavior, their private means, their ancestry and kin. And, not least, their religious views and their prospects in the world to come. Mark well! They know all these details, whether they have visited the place or not, whether they have met these people or just heard about them. . . .

The area I have called the familiar ground, the territory known through personal experience or oft-repeated stories, . . . in many ways constitutes the *whole* world. What lies beyond is in a sense unreal; it is perceived as a gray mist. They have heard some names: Boden, Stockholm, America. They are all situated at a roughly equal distance on the fringes of the world or, perhaps in reality, outside the world. Palestine is of course known and has its own reality. It is probably situated close to Stockholm and America, if it is not confused, wholly or partly with the heavenly land of Canaan. . . . The distance to these places may vary by a day's journey or two, but for the imagination, these day's journeys can be either on foot or by wagon, and they have in any case no clear ideas about any of that. It is all mist. Sun and moon may shine in those places, there may be trees and flowers just as here, but they cannot be entirely sure of it.

As it is with the alien world, so it is with the people of that world. It is not at all certain that they are like us in body and

Rational and Sensitive

soul. . . . Of course, they do get to see people from unknown territories, to be sure. Public officials and civil servants arrive, even clergymen, and ordinary people move in. They really do have arms and legs, just like themselves, but there is something peculiar and strange about them nevertheless. Nothing is known about their ancestors, they do not have brothers or sisters, cousins or second cousins, they cannot be the same sort of people. They do nothing, they do not cultivate the land or make hay, they get their money at the post office and live sumptuously every day, probably with fruit soup for dessert after every dinner. Their life is strange and frightening, they are probably both freethinkers and freemasons, which in the local speech means unbelievers in alliance with Satan. (Borelius 1936:156f., 163f.)

The mental maps of nineteenth-century peasants were frequently based on a notion of territoriality. The question "Who are you?" was more often put in terms of "Where are you from?" or "Who are your folks?" The basic categories of social classification into *us* and *them* were usually organized in terms of territorial units: the group of people on one farm, in one part of the village, in one parish. Sometimes this spatial identification could mask growing class differences in the villages. The social gap between farmers and servants, landed and landless was widening, but still young farmhands could side with the farmers' sons in village fights against "outsiders," those who lived in the neighboring village or the next parish. Identity was still very much based on locality (Hanssen 1952:36ff., 70ff.; Rooth 1969).

In the traditional Swedish conception of society as organized into four estates rather than into classes, the social hierarchies were very visible and often unproblematic. In early nineteenth-century life social mobility was low and social divisions clear-cut.

In a social system of this stability there is no need to devote much energy to activities and rituals designed to preserve the boundaries. In

The Home Builders

town and country alike the different classes could live in close proximity without the need for the upper class to communicate its distance. People knew their places, and the patriarchal relations between those in authority and their subordinates confirmed this stability.

With the growth of the new class society, however, social relations had to be redefined. Proximity was now seen as a problem, especially for the new bourgeoisie and the new agrarian upper class—the landed farmers. At the same time, the increased geographical mobility created the need for clear and simple codes by which to mark identity and class boundaries.

It is against the background of this social reshuffle that the new view of the relation of the individual to the collective, and the heightened distinction between private and public in everyday life, must be considered. In a quickly changing world the individual must find other social anchors than those previously provided by the neighborhood and the collective. This need leads to a greater polarization between the home and the outside world. The sharpening of the focus on the nuclear family as the natural center of social life—the phenomenon termed familism—is characteristic of the transformation of nineteenth-century culture. This chapter will examine some of the cornerstones of this family-centered life-style, namely the couple, parenthood, and the home, three concepts with a meaning for bourgeois culture and the new class of farmers different from their meaning in peasant culture.

The Loving Couple

The concept of the family had no self-evident position as the foundation of peasant society. The social landscape was based on the farm, not on the individual or the biological family (Löfgren 1974 and 1984b; Gaunt 1983:85ff.).

Rational and Sensitive

In the same way, there was none of today's view of the married couple. Marriage was of course a foundation for both production and reproduction in peasant society, but twosomeness did not have the same emotional and symbolic value it was later to acquire. The couple was simply a component of the economy of self-sufficiency. Old maids and bachelors had a low social status and were often figures of fun. Widows and widowers hastened to remarry, since farm production was based on a well-tried and efficient division of labor between men and women.[1] The importance of the couple was economic rather than emotional, and husband and wife did not together constitute a discrete unit.

If one looks at everyday life in peasant society—work on the farm or in the fields, meetings at the well or in the village street, feasts and holidays, churchgoing and trips to market—one is struck by the extent to which the two sexes acted as two separate collectives. There was, for example, a very strong spirit of community among the women, based partly on production (collective tasks and the need for mutual help in both work and child minding), but also on a sense of togetherness outside work.[2]

Although the married couple made an important production team, this does not mean that they lived together in intimacy. The cherished idea of the peasant family—mother, father, and children gathered together around the family hearth or constantly united in work—is nothing but a myth. Production in peasant society was not nearly so centered around work on the farm as the myth suggests. Work was mobile, taking the members of the household away to jobs far outside the farm and the village. The men often spent more days on the road than behind the plow, working at a variety of jobs scattered over a wide area. This tendency varied both regionally and socially, and was even stronger among the landless laborers of the nineteenth century. The fact that the man of the house was often away from home meant that the womenfolk had a greater responsibility for day-to-day work on

The Home Builders

the farm and also created a need for cooperation among women in neighboring farms and from different generations.

By contrast, the bourgeois homes of the eighteenth and nineteenth centuries provided a very different basis for marriage. The family became increasingly a unit of consumption, not of production, and the man took on the role of breadwinner, leaving the woman the role of housewife. The old work-based spirit of community between husband and wife, parents and children disappeared; what was left to hold the family together?

Bourgeois culture develops an ideology that emphasizes the importance of the emotional ties that bind the family together. Love becomes the cement uniting husband and wife, just as parental love directs relations between the generations. Intimacy is to be sought or created within the little family group.[3]

The cult of love became a major theme in bourgeois family ideology, but for us to understand this we must bear in mind that such words as love, tenderness, and intimacy, although they reflect universal human needs, are formed or deformed by culture. In the same way that culture guides our sexual desire, arouses it, represses it, or directs it into fixed social channels, so culture also shapes our need for love and intimacy.

The tangled history of love has been written and rewritten over the past decade. Many authors have described a development from relative lovelessness to Western society's focus on love in marriage, but such a line of argumentation tends to oversimplify, missing the fact that the concept of love does not automatically lend itself to transhistorical analysis.[4] Public expressions of tenderness were strictly rationed in Swedish peasant society. There was on the whole an antitactile tradition; man and wife were not supposed to walk arm in arm, or embrace or kiss in public, and the same went for courting couples. "Tenderness should only be shown between four eyes" was the rule one peasant remembered from his youth.[5] This does not mean that

Rational and Sensitive

people lived without love, but rather that affection and tenderness were expressed in a different cultural language from our own.

Love therefore had a place in peasant society, but this was scarcely true of the cult of falling in love; marriage was far too important an affair to be decided by such an ephemeral emotion. Common sense, not fancy, guided the choice. "Look at the lasses on the dunghill, not at the church door" and "The liking can come later" were two of the many proverbs expressing this attitude.[6]

The nineteenth-century bourgeois view of romantic love as the basis of marriage was part of an entire cultural complex that attached new importance to intimacy and emotions. This focus was reflected not only in youthful infatuations and marriage but also in a new cult of friendship. The new sincerity was also a weapon that the middle class could wield against the traditional prodigality of the upper classes, who, like the peasantry, had a more pragmatic view of marriage and a freer attitude to sexuality. The sensitive romantic is a product of this change.[7]

Courtship and Engagement

In bourgeois environments of the nineteenth century we can see how the romantic ideal of love enters the premarital game and comes into conflict with a more pragmatic view of marriage as a matter of convenience. This sort of love brought many a woman into conflict with narrow-minded parents and their intended "good matches." Contemporary novels are full of examples of heroines fighting for their love against an uncomprehending world. The same theme is found in the autobiographical literature, where the romantic passion struggles against proposed "rational marriages" (Löfgren 1969:42ff.; Gaunt 1983: 34ff.). This epoch may appear as a period of transition out of which

The Home Builders

love emerges triumphantly. Men too begin to expect romantic love to be the foundation for a marriage. It was no longer just a matter of persuading the parents. An uncertainty in the face of the new demands is seen, for example, in the description of the way Edvard Lidforss met his future wife when he was employed as a private teacher by her wealthy parents:

> Edvard Lidforss fell in love with this girl, six years younger than himself, but she does not appear to have returned his interest. He complained in letters that she always seemed so quiet and serious when he was there. He nevertheless summoned his courage, and one day in July, 1862, he set out from Uppsala to push his suit. . . . The daughter appears to have been hesitant, but since the parents had nothing against the young man, she said yes. Edward Lidforss returned to Uppsala in a state of confusion. That he was unsure of her affections is evident from a letter that he wrote to his fiancée, "Mademoiselle Anne-Marie Swartling" on July 6th. He begged her importunately to say in every letter "just once, but expressly, that you truly love me (just a little at this stage) and that you want to be my wife." (Vendelfelt 1962:9)

Love, however, was scarcely a revolutionary force on the bourgeois marriage market. We can observe the way love was domesticated in the nineteenth century, channeled into suitable forms. In her memoirs of her youth in Stockholm society, Alice Quensel has captured the important boundary drawn between infatuation and the stern reality of the marriage market:

> Girlish hearts fell for uniforms, the older the better, for a dashing posture, a chivalrous manner, and, above all, for superior dancing skills, a part of a cadet's education. . . .

Rational and Sensitive

It was . . . mostly a butterfly game for girls like us who were not "rich parties." For even if an officer was not greatly concerned about money, it was still the case that it was considered his duty to himself and his regiment to live as befitted his station, although this he could rarely afford on his own, at least not on his salary. There had to be some rich relative or a wealthy father-in-law behind him. . . . It was even said that when the taxpayers' directory, that advocate of the value of money, was lying around in an apartment, a young gentleman could be discovered leafing through it before joining the next dance. One's heart was not entirely insured.   (Quensel 1958:155)

The myth of passionate love, with its expectations of being swept off one's feet by the arrival of the one and only, was instilled from youth, but people were also instructed to fall in love not just with the only one, but also with the right one, in other words a person from a suitable background. The risk of falling in love outside one's own class was not great. Passionate love proved to be well programmed. Preparation for falling in love also included learning that romantic love and sexuality were to be kept distinct. Couples before marriage could engage in courtship and coquetry, but in etherealized forms.

Hugo Hamilton notes in his memoirs that flirting was not considered decorous in his youth. "If our hearts occasionally caught fire, as could happen, this was for us a sacred flame which we were very careful not to profane" (Hamilton 1928:143).

The boundary between courtship and sex, between proper and improper, was closely guarded and hedged by rituals and taboos. Young people in mixed company were always under observation. Lotten Edholm complains in her memoirs that as a young girl in the 1860s she was constantly chaperoned. It was not possible to talk seriously to another young friend even for five minutes without feeling that she

The Home Builders

had the eyes of the world upon her (Edholm 1919:105f.). The eyes of the world were those not only of the chaperon and the parents, but also of the entire social environment. It may be difficult for us to understand the amount of energy expended on the supervision of a young couple's behavior, in the whispered gossip about who was interested in whom, about who had been seen with whom, about whether those two were now courting. People were acutely conscious of the concept of the couple.

The rules for etiquette also stressed the importance of behaving in a manner that could not be misconstrued. The following quotation on the morality and hidden dangers of skating show that sex was always lurking in the background:

> Accompanying a lady home from the rink can naturally only be permitted for close acquaintances, and that only if they are in the presence of an older lady, a brother, or a relative. If a gentleman assumes this role himself he must, even if the lady to be escorted is his sister, remain at her side and offer her all the services she may demand. However, he should avoid putting on or taking off her skates, since not every onlooker may know that they are watching brother and sister; and the young lady might thus be the subject of unpleasant misconstructions.

We see from the memoirs that these rules of behavior were an everyday reality. There was an incessant discussion of what constituted propriety and impropriety. Was it permissible to walk in the company of a young gentleman? Yes, under certain circumstances; but it was, on the other hand, questionable whether a lady and gentleman could travel alone together in an open landau in Stockholm at the turn of the century (Alkman 1965:126; cf. Quensel 1958:156f.; Blom 1969:12).

The strictest supervision was naturally exercised at the most impor-

Rational and Sensitive

tant outlet of the marriage market: the ball, where all actions and thoughts could be colored by dreams of falling in love. Preparation for this came early through an important institution of nineteenth-century bourgeois culture: the children's ball, which was one of many means of educating the young in proper premarital conduct (Lundwall 1946). Letting children play adults was a way for the older generation to sentimentalize childhood infatuation while giving the young strict training for the ritual world.

Such effective preparations meant that the genuine balls the young people later attended were great events. Here was a chance to come into contact with serious love. This period in life is brought out particularly clearly by the female memoir writers. Alice Quensel's reminiscences are of a time with a "head full of dizzy thoughts of all the invitation cards at home on the bureau," countless consultations with the dressmaker, and long visits to the hairdresser; the ball season had begun. At the same time it was essential to bear in mind the rank order and to keep a properly organized dance card. It was important not to be compromised. "We were not even allowed to dance more than once with the same partner. I remember well my father's rebukes when at a ball at home I had danced three times with the same musical lieutenant" (Quensel 1958:157). Once again we meet the strict supervision of premarital contacts. Contact between two young people of the opposite sex always had to be in the presence of an adult chaperon who could decide whether an introduction would be proper.

The next stage in training for marriage was the engagement, which also had its many rituals. The whole game of secret engagements followed by festive announcements shows the importance of the transformation of two individuals into a couple. During the engagement period, which was often fairly long, the couple appeared as an indivisible whole, though of course they were accompanied by a chaperon in delicate situations. Although it was permissible to walk arm in arm, physical intimacy had to be limited. If a couple dared to transgress the

The Home Builders

boundaries, it had to be done in stealth; this very stealth reinforced still more the sense of being "we two against the world."[8]

During their engagement a couple entered the social landscape and created their own intimacy based on love, shared secrets, and a common destiny. This overwhelming intimacy between two people closer to each other than to anyone else in the world was communicated in a number of ways. Unlike married couples, engaged couples had the right to sit together at table—when they were out together they should ideally never leave one another's side. This tolerance, which was almost a requirement, gave a special aura to a couple in a culture where physical intimacy and tokens of tenderness outside marriage were often either tabooed or formalized into harmlessness.[9]

"It Caught on"

The cultivation of the couple's physical and spiritual intimacy was initially felt as something exotic by the peasantry. There is ample testimony to the wide-eyed amazement that met bourgeois couples who not only walked arm in arm but also embraced and kissed each other in public. One local comment was: "They must be fashionable people or they'd be ashamed to be kissing when others are looking" (EU 3639:343).

One sign of the new togetherness of the loving couple, which may seem unimportant but had great symbolic significance, was revealed in the altered seating arrangements in parish churches. Men and women had previously been separated, in a pattern that communicated a solidarity within each sex and cut across boundaries of kith and kin. Among the new urban bourgeoisie this arrangement was abandoned for a new one: the wife left the other women and came to sit at her husband's side. The first instances of this rearrangement pro-

Rational and Sensitive

voked strong reactions from the peasants. Usually it was visiting townspeople or local upper-class couples who introduced the pattern: "It was the quality folks that started this, like the gentry: anybody else would have been embarrassed to sit beside a man, but it caught on," one peasant woman recollects. Another remembered the angry reaction when visiting couples from the nearby town sat together: the older people took offense and said, "Those fine folks with their fancy manners!" (Gustafsson 1956:48ff.). Many women felt it was a betrayal of female solidarity when this practice slowly reached the ranks of farmers and farm laborers.

This symptom of the married couple's withdrawal into the new intimacy of the family was only one feature of the more familistic and class-oriented life-style that emerged among the farmers during the nineteenth century and at the beginning of the twentieth. This change cannot be explained in terms of a simple process of embourgeoisement, but must be understood against the background of the changing social and economic structure of the countryside. The household unit was split into family and servants, with the increased social stratification of the villages and with the more frequent tendency to recruit servants exclusively from the growing number of landless peasant families. On a superficial level the household structure remained the same on the farm, with the family and the servants living in a single domestic unit; but gradually a number of visible and invisible boundaries separated them. It is possible to follow in many peasant settings the way the family withdrew from the company of the servants: they no longer carried out the same tasks or shared the same bowl and table at mealtime, they built special sleeping quarters for the servants, and they kept their children from socializing with servants and cotters. With the growing accumulation of farm capital, kinship links became more important to the landed farmers. Village feasts that were previously open social occasions become segregated. Although landed and landless continued to live in the same village, two social communities were created (Löfgren 1980:208ff.).

The Home Builders

Husband and Wife

The ideal of twosomeness created a new model for the relation between husband and wife, between man and woman. The notion of romantic love in the family ideology of the Oscarians was based on a fictional definition of two equals in love with each other. In fact there was often a marked sexual division of labor in this love game. Marriage was based upon the two being united into one—the one being the man.

As in other European countries, marriages among the Swedish bourgeoisie were asymmetric alliances. First of all, we often find a great age difference between man and wife. A man could only marry if he had an income large enough to finance an adequate home and support a wife, children, and at least one servant. As an optician who married in the 1880s recalled, "In those days you had to be able to offer your wife a fully furnished apartment before there could even be talk of marriage" (cited in Gejvall 1954:142; cf. Stiernstedt 1946:190ff.). A residence to fit one's station usually involved as a minimum a dining room, drawing room, bedroom, and kitchen, as well as rooms for a maid and later for children.

For many middle-class men with a poor economy or slight prospects of promotion, this goal could not be achieved. The tragicomic figure of the humorous magazines, the old bachelor teacher or clerk who spends his evenings in the restaurant of the city hotel, was a sad reality, as is shown by the sharply falling frequency of marriage among the upper classes toward the end of the nineteenth century. Yet it was the daughters of the bourgeoisie who were hardest hit by this development. The unmarried woman had few opportunities to pursue her own career and acquire her own home.[10]

Ideally it was felt that a man should not marry until he was well established in his career. This often meant that he would be five to ten years older than his wife, already a man of the world, who had usually

Rational and Sensitive

lived by himself for some time and was firmly integrated into public life. The wife, on the other hand, who was often taken directly from the protected life of her parental home or a finishing school, knew little of the realities of life. The ignorance of practical matters is illustrated by Margareta Lindström, who grew up in a manorial setting just before the turn of the century: "I was abysmally ignorant. Cleaning and bed making were totally unknown tasks for me; I had never before washed a floor or learned how to make a bed" (1966:186). A girl's knowledge of public life, politics, and economics was often equally slight, and she would have had few opportunities to develop an independent identity.

A woman was often not yet fully adult when she became a wife; the older man therefore saw himself as provider and protector of a young and innocent wife, whom he regarded as a fragile creature, to be sheltered against the ugly realities of public life. For a girl who had been socialized into a longing for Mr. Right, a husband represented the only chance of freedom from the home and parental authority. Her entire quest for an adult identity was built up around this ideal of being united with someone else. While the woman fell passionately in love, the man mostly satisfied himself with flirtation and courtship. His goal was not really to fall in love, but rather to find a wife. The premarital game thus presupposes a distinction between the active role of the man and the passive longing of the woman. Love could mean different things for the two sexes, a fundamental difference that is maintained in contemporary medical books and marriage guidance literature. It is obvious that this pattern made marriage into a parent–child relationship rather than a partnership of equals; marriage for a woman meant replacing a father with a father figure.

Any discussion of equality must also involve a look at the classic theme of the double standard—the way men and women acted in different moral systems with different laws and taboos. It was something of an advantage if the man could enter matrimony with a certain

The Home Builders

amount of sexual experience, but it was unthinkable for a woman to do so. The man could operate in two different moral spheres. An upper-class girl was not a permissible sexual object, but it was possible to take advantage of the freer view of extramarital sex to be found in lower social classes, or to go to prostitutes. In rich bourgeois homes the maids could be fair game for the sons of the house.[11]

That people were fully conscious of cause and effect in the matter of the double standard is shown by a statement in a parliamentary debate on prostitution toward the end of the nineteenth century: "Would that the educated and wealthy Stockholm woman could learn to dress for festive occasions in such a way that her attire would not arouse emotions and passions in young men, driving them, after they leave the party, to go to places where they can satisfy their lust before they go home!" (cited in Michanek 1962:46).

Perhaps the clearest example of this situation is in that archetypal bourgeois man's society, the university. "A favorite sport among students in Uppsala was café flirtation. . . . There were also willing cigar girls, seamstresses, ironers, and maids. Finally, there were considerable numbers of whores engaged in organized prostitution."[12]

The double moral standard involved a corresponding double view of women. "Man has regarded Woman's body as a delicacy, but also as 'The Temple of the Holy Spirit,'" writes Carl G. Laurin in *Kvinnolynnen* (Women's moods), which appeared in a number of printings during World War I (1916:82). His chivalrous expositions on the essence of Woman make an excellent illustration of this ambivalence, making her both madonna and magdalen. The pure and innocent figure of the madonna/mother is contrasted with the sex object, woman as whore and temptress. The bourgeois male view of women often expresses this double nature in a combination of scorn and adoration. Repression is disguised in a cloak of gallantry, which conceals it even from the men.

This repressive chivalry is one of the most thoroughly internalized

In the life of the bourgeois male the stag party was an important rite
of passage that tells us something of the views of sexuality and
marriage. The high age of marriage meant that the participants
were often a rather gray-haired lot. Here some gentlemen are
gathered at the local hotel in Skurup in Skåne, where the future
bridegroom, a factory owner named Haker, has just been
adorned with a pair of lady's bloomers. (Photograph from
Folklivsarkivet, University of Lund.)

The Home Builders

components of the view of women, yet the interesting thing is that many men felt themselves at the mercy of women. Behind the façade of authority there was often hidden a sense of insecurity and inferiority with regard to the feminine. Since sexuality and biology were effectively tabooed during youth, this made the opposite sex strange and alien (compare the discussion in Chapter 6 below).

When Nils Lidman, superintendent of customs, got married in 1873, his detailed list of purchases for the wedding included a manual of female sexuality (Lidman 1952:27). The century saw an increased production of literature for men on the mysteries of the female sex and the art of pleasing women. Sexuality is made into both a mystery and a problem as never before, while also becoming a subject for scientific research.[13]

The interplay between husband and wife could therefore be rather complicated in a bourgeois family. The definition of a man's career also included expectations and demands to be cared for in the home sphere, to receive some of the woman's brightness, warmth, and sexuality. Such a structure also gives the man, the master of the house, a sense of dependence. Beside the favorite comic stereotype of the house tyrant there was another picture, the henpecked husband and the domineering, scheming termagant. The memoir literature suggests that the house tyrant has a better basis in reality than the henpecked husband, but it also shows the means of power available to a married woman in a patriarchal society.

If power belonged to the man of the house—the person who represented the family in the public sphere—the housewife, though in effect declared legally incompetent, had rather more subtle powers of sanction. Both the children and her own sexuality could be used as weapons in this struggle, but also her very femininity as it was defined by men. The view of the bourgeois woman as a charming but frail being, who had to be under constant protection not only from the hard realities of life but also from strong emotions, meant that this weak-

Rational and Sensitive

ness could be used in the struggle between the sexes. It is in the Victorian era that we meet women who swoon or become hysterical, who suffer from weak nerves and headaches (Sennett 1977:177; Cominos 1972; Ehrenreich and English 1973). This frailty could in certain situations allow the woman to have her way in the family, winning a silent war that was often waged on an unconscious level. The process had a reinforcing effect. As a repressed individual, the woman was forced to use such subtle, indirect weapons, which in their turn confirmed the man's view of the weakness of "feminine nature," or else they gave rise to favorite men's maxims such as "Woman's cunning is beyond Man's understanding."

Anthropologist Michelle Zimbalist Rosaldo has analyzed this form of struggle from an inferior position, her work largely based on sex roles in Mediterranean countries. She has pointed out another side of this conflict between the sexes: women can create a counterculture in which they define themselves as purer and morally superior to men (Rosaldo 1974:38f.). Something similar can be found in the Oscarian woman's world, and it is clear that the masculine ideology of the woman's double role as madonna and magdalen also brought about this sense of moral inferiority in men.

Parenthood

If the concept of the couple was the first building block of the new family ideology, the second was parenthood. It was in nineteenth-century bourgeois culture that the eternal triangle of mother–father–child took shape. Relationships within the nuclear family take on a new meaning and are more strongly marked in the social network. Not just the contemporary view of childhood has its foundation in this milieu, but also much of the pattern of good parenthood.

The Home Builders

Greater moral demands came to be made on parents, demands reflecting a new view of the significance of childhood and child rearing. A number of scholars have described the growth of this new child-rearing ideology in bourgeois society, a development that can be traced back to the rise of mercantile capitalism on the Continent in the sixteenth century. As Ronny Ambjörnsson has maintained, however, the great changes did not come until later:

> When the class structure of Western European society grew complicated in the eighteenth century, it naturally led to greater complications in the patterns of child rearing. If the roles were subject to change it was of course vain to attempt to fix them in set rules for how to live. It was no longer possible to imprint them mechanically into people; good sense had to be internalized as morality. (Ambjörnsson 1978:91)

This was the goal of the new pedagogical reformers, such as Rousseau, but it was only during the nineteenth century that this child-rearing ideology became general among the Swedish bourgeoisie.

One of the preconditions for the expansion and success of the bourgeoisie was a new programming of the individual, a new character structure, with the key words being self-fulfillment, self-discipline, and an ingrained sense of morality. A child-rearing program like this requires considerable efforts on the part of adults. Nineteenth-century bourgeois society created new groups of specialists for this purpose: governesses, private tutors, and a range of special teachers of everything from etiquette to ethics. An ever-greater part of the parents' time, effort, and interest was also directed to this end. The nature of parenthood in peasant society is strikingly different.

The problem is that the picture of child rearing in Swedish peasant society is ambivalent. On the one hand there is a picture of children as victims of thrashing and coercion, harshness and insensitivity, re-

Rational and Sensitive

flected in numerous Swedish proverbs on the theme of "Spare the rod and spoil the child." On the other hand there are many examples of intimacy and mutual respect in child–parent relations. Variations in time, place, and social milieu appear to have been great, but it is possible to discern some general trends.[14]

First of all, it was a matter of course that childhood was a time of training for productive work. Children were taught the importance of their role in the work of the farm from an early age. Communal labor welded the members of the household together and taught the children the skills they would need in later life.

Second, child rearing was not just a matter for parents; it was the concern of the collective. Children were brought up not only by the parents but also by the servants on the farm, the people on other farms, where many young children were sent as servants, and by neighbors and relatives. All these adults had a right to a voice in the correction of a child's behavior.

Third, the incorporation of children into the labor collective and the community created patterns of identification quite different from those found in bourgeois culture. Börje Hanssen has drawn attention to this fundamental difference:

> If we begin with the relation between mother and child in the preindustrial society under consideration here, we see that it was affected by the mother's commitment to hard productive labor. Care of infants and children was no onerous duty when compared with our own times. Apart from breast feeding and a summary removal of the infant's waste products, children had to a large extent to fend for themselves. . . . Children were also integrated quickly into the adult world, having to start working at a very early age. The adults created no special idealized children's world. . . .
>
> There was thus no room for any personality development of the sort we know, through identification with a lot of pos-

The Home Builders

sessions or with literary symbols in the form of princes and princesses, incarnations of strength and beauty, or distant, seductive ideals of what to be when one grew up. It was obvious that people stayed in the environment where they were born. . . .

The possibility that the child could develop a grandiose ego was therefore limited, since he was not exposed to any great amounts of tenderness and care, or love in the way we mean it today. There was nobody to treat a child as his or her own property. The child consequently was probably given no ideas about the value or significance of his own ego. His own limited possessions had to be shared with brothers and sisters. There was no chance for the imagination to create identifications, since existence allowed little time for reading or fantasy. Instead, the palpable human contacts were all the more numerous. They meant a greater range of people with whom to identify, as well as more safety valves in the event of emotional conflicts with parents or rival siblings, with the probable result that the childhood situation was colored by fewer real or imagined injustices and conflicts than those experienced by the modern child. By this I do not mean that conflicts did not arise, but that they could quickly be resolved without lasting investment of the ego and without consequences for the molding of the personality. (Hanssen 1978:16ff.)

In the nineteenth century there were many complaints about the way peasants reared their children. Interestingly enough, it is not physical cruelty that is the target for criticism. The problem is primarily that peasants are said to be unable to bring up their children in a spirit of discipline. The usual accusation is that the parents lack method and firmness (Öller 1800:131ff.; cf. Therkildsen 1974).

Such protests reveal more about the bourgeois ideology than about

Rational and Sensitive

the situation of children in peasant society, who were reared in a way that was unproblematic and lacked a conscious ideology. Children unreflectingly learned the skills needed in the farmyard or the fields, through participation and imitation; they understood that they had breached a boundary or broken a taboo when a parent reacted with anger and a scolding. It was a matter of course that the individual was subordinate to the collective. In the bourgeois family, on the other hand, this pattern was scarcely relevant.

Beating and cruelty were everyday features of childhood in many agrarian and proletarian environments, but this violence was more direct and manifest than the ritual, methodical corporal punishment that was administered in bourgeois homes in the nineteenth century. When toward the end of the century educationalists began to criticize caning, it must not be forgotten that new methods of punishment replaced the old:

> Father had acquired ideas about child rearing, probably
> through books, ideas that were rather more modern than
> those generally current at the time. One principle that was
> maintained unconditionally was that the children were not
> to receive corporal punishment. There was no beating, not
> even a slap on the ear or a shaking or a blow on the arm in a
> fit of anger. A tone of voice or a look were almost always
> sufficient to reprove us. As it happens, both Mother and
> Father had a remarkable ability to express wrath through
> voice or eye. . . . Father was angry quite frequently, but Moth-
> er's rare anger—when the mild features stiffened and the
> eyes turned hard and loveless—was even more effective.

This is how the newspaperman Herbert Tingsten (1961:25f.) describes his childhood around the turn of the century; the modern method by which he was reared was not as uncommon as he thought.

In his memories of childhood in a merchant's home toward the end

The Home Builders

of the century, John Falk records that he was beaten only once, but that it was rather more common for the delinquent to be locked in a dark closet until he was "a good boy" again (1946:15). Similar patterns appear in other bourgeois homes. Children are no longer beaten; the cane is replaced by the dark closet, and parents now play more on the child's sense of guilt. Mother does not hit, she does not get angry, but she can be sad, so it is the child's duty and punishment to reflect on his own guilt and once again behave properly and make his mother happy.[15] Punishment became less manifest but hardly less effective. This gradual transformation of child rearing had massive consequences not just for parent–child relations but also for the individual's identity.

Another result of this new breeding for self-discipline and self-control was an increase in repression and dissimulation. The child learned from an early age to restrain himself, to bridle spontaneous emotional reactions, not to act on every impulse. It was always a question of modifying the expressions of the body and the emotions. Self-discipline meant that violent outbursts of joy, anger, or sorrow had to be muffled and channeled into more civilized forms. The same applied to many bodily functions, from laughter to sexuality (see Chapter 6 below, the section "The Origins of Self-discipline").

The inhibition of spontaneity, with the demand for dissimulation and the repression of animal reactions, leads to insecurity and a view of other people as playactors. Does Mother really mean what she says, does she really love me, is Father happy or angry "for real"? What is going on behind the cultured façade? This insecurity about people's reactions and behavior must have played an important role in shaping social interaction in bourgeois culture. The need for absolute self-control combined with uncertainty about the reactions of others created a seedbed for many mental disturbances and illnesses, from everyday neurotic meditation about the self to hysteria and other common Oscarian complaints.

Richard Sennett has discussed this development in Victorian society

Children preparing themselves for the pair bond at a dancing school in Skurup in 1912. Dancing schools offered middle-class children some of the necessary training in body language and the etiquette of the people. (Photograph from Folklivsarkivet, University of Lund.)

The Home Builders

from a sociological point of view and has pointed out how conscious people were that their innermost feelings could be betrayed by body, gaze, or behavior. Such feelings were to be expressed only in the safety of the intimate sphere, not in public. The fear that drove many Victorians to mental doctors was a product of a childhood exposed to constant observation and correction. God and the parents saw everything, knew everything (Sennett 1977:172).

The insecurity was heightened by the fact that children had to be protected or excluded from so many things. Compared to parent—child relations in peasant society, the bourgeois adult world was further removed from the children, a tabooed area. Many memoir writers note the unease they felt about this distance. Marika Stiernstedt, who grew up in an aristocratic officer's home at the turn of the century, has captured the atmosphere:

> Children were not initiated into the concerns of the parents, and it would never have occurred to us to ask why Father or Mother looked sad or anxious. I developed a genuine terror of the occasions when my parents closed themselves in a room and had long conversations, which usually ended with Mother leaving the room with the household account books in her hands and traces of tears on her cheeks. (Stiernstedt 1947:169)

The adults' problems were taboo for the children, who therefore developed an exaggerated fear of parental conflicts—the quarrels behind closed doors, the hostile glances and sarcastic innuendos.

Many aspects of the children's life were likewise taboo, carefully avoided by parents and children alike. One such was sexuality, a field where the new child-rearing ideology created problems for parents and educators (see Chapter 6 below, under "The Ever Present"). Few other topics occasioned so much unease and discussion.

Rational and Sensitive

Michel Foucault has drawn attention to the paradox that sex was taboo and unmentionable, while the entire ideology of child rearing demanded that parents constantly monitor and actively intervene in the child's sexuality (1978). This need for supervision and control of the unmentionable is most evident in the battle against what was seen as the greatest danger to culture: masturbation. Throughout the nineteenth century and well into the twentieth, there appeared a wealth of expository and advisory literature on the subject. Here is a clear example of the way sexuality comes under the rule of self-discipline and self-control, partly with the assistance of the weapon of guilt. Child-rearing manuals and medical handbooks offer very concrete advice to parents, declaring even that it was permissible to break the taboo of silence in the struggle against masturbation, "the most shameful and terrible of all vices" (*Kärlekens hemligheter* 1844:22). It will be shown later (Chapter 6, under "Hands on the Blanket") that certain diseases were said to be caused by masturbation, and that advice was proffered to parents who wished to cure their children of the vice. One measure, suggested by Dr. Ruff in his popular medical encyclopedia, was to banish sexuality from the home:

> It is the habit of many parents to take children into their own bed to bring joy to themselves and the children. We recognize the sacredness of the parents' love of their children; we appreciate the rapture which father and mother feel when they clasp so fond a creature in their arms, and when the child embraces them so intimately; nevertheless, we most definitely advise against these expressions of love. Herein lie the seeds of sensuality. Who has not observed how quickly a child finds pleasure in the contact of his body with another person? It is enough if the parts of the body are touched with softness and warmth for the pleasure felt by the senses to lead to other things.   (Ruff 1893:555)

The Home Builders

The heroic self-control displayed by the parents gave the children an example to imitate. To understand the way this control of the self was assimilated by the child, it is important to look more closely at the techniques and contents of the new child rearing. We have already seen glimpses of it in the discussions of time keeping and the career mentality. Other aspects will be examined in the analysis of bourgeois discipline below. Some general features may be outlined here.

A striking characteristic of bourgeois child rearing is the asceticism described in much of the autobiographical literature. Children were not to be spoiled; they had to be taught to use all their resources economically, with their gaze directed toward the future. Self-denial was a moral essential. This ideology was given a clear and manifest form in the stress on simplicity in everyday life. Rich parents taught their children the virtue of eating ill-tasting *ölsupa*, a thin gruel mixed with small beer.

Ulf Pernö has discussed how well anchored the Protestant ethic was in child rearing:

> On the material level this is seen in the relatively simple everyday diet and in the restraint concerning toys and presents given to children. The rejection of indulgence, excess, and uninhibited enjoyment in favor of strictly disciplined conduct taught children through the example of their parents and the atmosphere in the home, where the watchwords were self-discipline and responsibility. All these expressions of an ascetic way of life were linked to the Protestant work ethic, which bred people for diligence and industry. The application of this attitude to work was rather important for the children of government officials. Their social status was not automatically bequeathed like capital to the new generation; it had to be reconquered by means of the training and competence demanded by social life and a professional career.

Rational and Sensitive

Dogged industry was obviously seen as a virtue by the children because it was preached and practiced by parents, relatives, and in the ambitious spirit of school. (Pernö 1979:31)

Another important facet of the imprinting of self-control was the daily training of both body and behavior. Mealtimes, for example, were lessons in etiquette, with parents supervising and correcting the children's speech and movements.

Child-rearing was not just exercise, it was also a game. Many bourgeois norms were learned unconsciously through play. Alice Quensel, daughter of a Supreme Court justice, has left us a fine portrait of the way a future generation of lawyers and civil servants organized their own disciplinary program in the nursery:

> "Nurseryland" was a wide-ranging concept, which eventually grew into an ordered legal state after my brother Gösta, who was to become a justice of the Supreme Administrative Court, took over the leadership of his younger brothers and sisters and all the subject toys. He drew up carefully written laws and constitutions covering all aspects of life in Nurseryland. Its inhabitants were ordinary toys and old hair-tonic bottles, paper dolls brought to life. Penalties were laid down for varying degrees of transgression, one of which was for flying through the air! The steepest fines were payable in the feathers used for Lenten decoration, after which came colored foil—the brighter the color, the greater the value. Parliaments were held, as were law-court sessions. (Quensel 1958:38f.)

What was the end product? The children of the bourgeoisie admittedly entered the world well trained in the arts of repression and dissimulation, but they also had a great deal of self-confidence, encour-

The Home Builders

aged by parental expectations. Many children felt these expectations
as a sort of natural, unproblematic security, the knowledge that they
had grown up in the best of all possible worlds. The memoirs of childhood reveal not so much the overt disciplinary training as the result-
ing internalization of bourgeois character structure and morality.

Safely assured of their own excellence, these confident children
wandered out into the world. Their mental map was engraved with
clear lines and fixed contours. (Paradoxes and inconsistencies did not
appear until later in life.) Herbert Tingsten has summarized this world
view:

> What were we raised to, what sort of people were we to be-
> come, what rules were established for our lives? It is not easy
> to answer these questions for that age, and perhaps it is as
> difficult for our present age. We were taught, in accordance
> with a religion in which the messianic kingdom was near, the
> virtues of selflessness, submissiveness, the insignificance of
> all things earthly; yet we also learned the duties of work and
> diligence, to stand up for our own rights, for our society and
> the nation. We learned that self-effacing goodness, not look-
> ing to its own interests, was the highest virtue, but also that it
> brought immediate rewards that made it smart policy. We
> were taught not to resist evil, not to kill, to turn the other
> cheek, but also that the soldier was heroic and that we
> should be prepared to die in battle for our country. We
> learned the holiness of poverty, yet we were also taught how
> to act if we wanted to obtain a good position with a high in-
> come. We learned that all men are equally good, but also that
> we should look to our own advantage and admire the rich,
> the distinguished, and the mighty. We were taught to forgive
> everything, but also that sin and crime must be punished. We
> were taught chastity, but also that we should people the

Rational and Sensitive

earth. We learned to worship heavenly love, but it was earthly love that shimmered in the books we read. We were told incredible stories that the adults themselves did not believe, yet we were also taught that truth was the goal and the quest for truth the noblest of all aspirations. A foundation was laid for the moral ambivalence that was to follow us through life. (Tingsten 1961:27f.)

The Beloved Mother and the Respected Father

The new family was based not only on love between man and wife, but also on an ideology of parental love and care for children. This is the message that appears with tiresome regularity in the autobiographical literature, which abounds in beloved parents and happy recollections of a childhood filled with eternal gratitude to father and mother. This homogeneity is partly due to the filtering out of unpleasant memories of early years, but partly also to the effectiveness with which the norms of parental love were imprinted. We are once again faced with the question of the relation between ideal and reality. How much of this is the ideal dream of motherhood and fatherhood; how much reality has been repressed and censored?

Let us begin with the picture of the parents as portrayed in the memoirs. Division of labor is firmly established, sex roles are stereotyped; father is respected from a distance, while mother stands for light, warmth, and love.

Love for the father is largely based on reverence and distance, but the picture of the father is ambiguous. Many descriptions of childhood show him as a figure to be respected, admired, and feared. Father was "stern but just," "charming but choleric," "dutiful but admirable."[16] Be-

The Home Builders

hind this ambivalent father figure is the double life led by the bourgeois man. Unlike the mother, the housewife, he moved freely in two spheres, home and the outside world. Every morning he disappeared into the world of production and his career, dutiful and eager to provide for his family. Many children found something mysterious and unknown in this double life. There were vague ideas about the father's other life. If he worked at home, he closed himself in the office or the study, where admission was forbidden. Father's office was part of the production sphere, a taboo area for the children.

When he returned to the bosom of the family after a day's work, he was transformed; the dark suit and the black leather boots were taken off and replaced by the velvet-smooth smoking jacket and the worn carpet slippers. The Oscarian child could thus observe the passage rite that transformed the efficient, distant professional man into the family father.

His time together with the children tended to be limited but spent in a spirit of efficiency, in sharp contrast to the mother's. Father *did* things with the children, reading aloud to them, taking them to museums, explaining the world to them.

The career father, even in the bosom of the family, could be troubled by the concerns of the production sphere. Even when he sat surrounded by his loved ones, he was not always present. Memories of situations like this are easily simplified into amusing episodes, like one anecdote about how a politician, absent-mindedly whistling as he pushed the baby carriage, wandered on unaware that little Claes had fallen out and was crawling around in the ditch: "He had combined the job of minding the baby with the solving of some legal or political problem, as the whistling suggested. When Father whistled he was always in his own world! But after that Mother never dared to entrust him with minding the baby" (Lindhagen-Kihlblom 1949:158). The moral of such episodes was obvious. Neither the mother nor the chil-

Rational and Sensitive

dren could be really sure that the father was present. This led to the early insight that the home was his proper place of rest and retreat: "Papa must not be disturbed, he has had a trying day."

As master of the house he defined the atmosphere that prevailed when the family was assembled. His moodiness, the sudden shifts from severity to gentleness, appear clearly in the memoirs. A classic situation is Father at the breakfast table:

> Sunday mornings at home. Conversations around the breakfast table. Father like a volcano liable to erupt at any moment. Mother's anxious efforts to make breakfast nevertheless pleasant, a poor reflection of the convivial rites of her own childhood home. . . .
>
> He is tired when he comes home, often has a headache and broods over how the money can be made to run to it. The office, his own consultancy, is something that everyone thinks of. It fills the air in the evenings, making it heavy and hard to breathe; it makes the morning nervous, irritable, sour. (Leijonhufvud 1978:23f., 51)

This is how one novelist has attempted to capture the atmosphere of a later bourgeois childhood in Malmö in the 1950s. Moving back in time over a century, we see that the pattern is identical. The novelist Emilie Flygare-Carlén writes in her memoirs that it took time before conversation got going around the table, because they first had to establish "what nuance the father's disposition had" (cited in Paulsson 1950: 1.144).

This house tyrant often had a Janus face, able to switch suddenly from dark to light, from anger, melancholy, heavy thoughts, and headaches to charm, boyishness, enviable confidence. A doctor's daughter writes of her father: "Father was in truth a house tyrant, a tyrant with charm and heart, and we loved him as much as we feared him. This is

The Home Builders

praise indeed, for we were terribly afraid of him" (Blumenthal-Engström 1947:41). Other memoirs portray the sudden change into a
playful father, clowning about as if in a second childhood.

The picture of the father is full of such contradictions. He symbolizes power and is the link with the outside world. As well as being the
outward face of the family, he communicates and filters much of the
family's knowledge of the big world, the exotic and the exciting.

When the father is criticized in the memoirs, it is usually with an ex-
cuse like: "He was a man of duty. He only wanted what was best for us.
Only later have I come to understand the heavy burden he bore." The
assessments often reveal a sense of guilt for not having understood
and loved the father enough. Only in later life do people reshape their
picture of their father, but there remains the distance, and the ritual
love is expressed in such words as respect, reverence, admiration.

The picture of the mother, by contrast, is quite different: "The most
primitive and yet the most noble feeling, which evokes the most spontaneous, most reckless self-sacrifice, the feeling that all men with few
exceptions have benefited from, is the maternal feeling. For the
woman as mother all men, except the most brutal, feel an instinctive
respect." Carl Laurin's definition of love of the mother (1916:83) is
echoed by many memoir writers. While the father was loved at a distance and with reservation, capitulation to the mother was total. The
maternal image is almost saintly and sacred. The adjectives describing
her are bright, warm, gentle, pure, radiant. She stands for love and
consideration, she is adorable, the indisputable emotional center.

Mother is portrayed as "our warming sunshine," "a living flame," "the
bright spirit of the home." Two accounts, one of a minister's wife, the
other of a managing director's wife, typify the radiant mother:

Mother mastered a thousand arts and knew everything best.
We scarcely noticed that she was busy, yet she managed
to do an enormous amount of work. Capable, industrious

Rational and Sensitive

people often have an aura of agitation and haste about them, but nothing of the kind was ever true of Mother. Mild and kind, full of humor, she spread warmth and peace. I never saw a cold or unfriendly look in Mother's eye, never heard a hasty or hard word. . . . Our "school household" in Gävle, where three of my brothers and I gathered around our beloved Mother, remains in my memory as a soft, warm nest in sushine and shelter. (Gawell-Blumenthal 1946:43)

Although we had five servants and a governess, Mother naturally had no time for anything outside the home. It was her world, which she looked after with a firm but gentle hand. What is now called social work and the like was not yet known by that name, but it existed, for Mother radiated goodness, and her hand filled the larders of the needy and clothed their children. (Göransson 1946:88)

This picture of motherhood must always be related to the father's role. If Father was a "powder barrel," Mother was the home's "rock of ages," the "bastion of the family" (Blumenthal-Engström 1947:41, 48). She was the mediator, the intercessor. If Father was in a bad mood at the table, Mother had the given task of ensuring

that pleasant conversation arises, to encourage the other guests at table by her tactful and cheerful disposition, to avert and brush aside as quickly as possible anything that can "stir up bad blood," and in this way *make dinner the most delightful moment in the day.* . . .

It is in everyday life in particular that this duty of the housewife must not be neglected. . . . She must banish anything that she knows can irritate him [the husband], ensure that his commands are carried out, his wishes observed, in a word, *she* must maintain peace in the home. (Langlet 1884:99ff.)

The Home Builders

This division of labor gave the mother the role of tactician in the home, along with the difficult double position of supporting her husband while being the ally of her children. If the age difference between the spouses was great, a girlish mother could feel closer to the children than to her husband. It was in such a structure that the complementary and opposing roles of father and mother were established.

Invisible Parents

Mother and Father overshadow everything else in the bourgeois memoirs, but occasionally other realities are glimpsed behind the family idyll.

Several writers, after effusive descriptions of the radiant, beloved mother figure, point out that contact with her was in fact rather limited, and that physical contact in particular was strictly rationed. "I never remember having received a caress from her, at the most a pat on the shoulder," writes one daughter (Wahlström 1946:241), and similar observations from the turn of the century occur in other memoirs (Quensel 1958:65).

In a number of cases the picture of the happy times with Mother is rather a yearning for a mother who was all too rarely at the children's side. This is most evident in the upper strata of the bourgeoisie, where the mother's duties as hostess left her little time for the children. Even the children in this social milieu had a given function to perform in formal entertainment, like props in a performance. They were led in to table, washed and cute, brought in for goodnight kisses, and shown off on family outings. Everyday contact and upbringing, however, was delegated to hired specialists, wet nurses, maids, and governesses.[17]

English anthropologists have drawn attention to the fact that the Victorian bourgeoisie was one of the few cultures in which the role of mother could be transferred to hired labor (Boon 1974; Gathorne-

Rational and Sensitive

Hardy 1972). Nannies were not as common in Oscarian Sweden, but the pattern was nevertheless similar. Children went to the servants to get their noses wiped, and it was from them they received consolation, attention, and scoldings. Children ate and slept with them to a large extent, and experienced with them most of their adult bodily contact.[18]

It is symptomatic that these surrogate parents receive only a modest amount of space in the memoirs, in the same way that Freud's discussions of the mother–father–child triangle usually ignore the fact that the child's early intimate contact with adults was rather more complicated (see discussion in Chapter 6, "The Subordinates," below).

The important position of the servants in everyday childhood life gave rise to conflicts. It was in the very highest classes that parents had least contact with their children, who instead were in close contact with another class. The memoirs reveal that people were conscious of this problem. There were those who wondered what was the use of parents and schools devising grandiose educational programs if the objects of the schemes, the children, were at the same time exposed to influence from the servants (Leman 1961:164ff.; Stiernstedt 1947:28ff.).

Below stairs, in the maid's room and the nursery, the children met a different culture and different child-rearing methods, which were not nearly as sophisticated and refined as the parents may have wished. Margaretha Posse was brought up in her manor house by a nanny, a children's maid, and a governess. Vava the nanny used her own unorthodox methods to make the children obey. When one of the younger infants refused to eat its porridge, Vava juggled with the Dresden dinner service which was used in the nursery, and when the child opened its mouth in surprise, she would stick in a spoonful of porridge. At the same time she sang "forbidden, rather risqué songs" (Posse 1955:52).

"Superstitious maids" were a concern for the adults and an everyday reality for the children. Many memoir writers recollect the secret and

The Home Builders

forbidden information they learned as they sat in the maid's lap or overheard the conversation in the kitchen. It went beyond risqué songs and other frank glimpses of life's realities. The children were also exposed to a whole world of folk belief. Most of the maids came from the country, the peasant world peopled with supernatural beings, dreadful ghosts, and spirits.[19]

It is obvious that the bourgeoisie at the turn of the century realized that the coexistence of children and servants had to be limited, or else the servants had to be morally rearmed. The best solution was the old faithful retainer who had come to identify herself with the goals and ideals of the bourgeoisie. The worst was the rapid turnover of saucy, unreliable maids. Exasperation with them became a classic theme in the twentieth century: "It's so hard to get good help nowadays!"

The Home

We have arrived at the third building block of the bourgeois family: the home. Chapter 2, under "How Nature Became Natural," has already addressed some of the moral and ideological connotations associated with the concept of the home; such expressions as home comfort, home-loving, and homemade were loaded with important values. Some of the implications of this concept can be glimpsed in the entry for *home* in an etiquette manual from 1930: "Fine furniture and expensive interiors do not create a *home*, but when the inhabitants of the house display tact and good manners, then we may talk of both a fine home and a *good home*" (*BVT:s Lexikon* 1930:86).

When considering the role of home in middle-class culture, it is not necessary to limit the discussion to ideals and norms. The actual layout of houses and apartments, their interior decoration, and all the material objects that make up a home reveal the ways in which ideals

Rational and Sensitive

were realized in everyday life. The study of homemaking thus becomes a key to understanding the way family life changed during the past hundred years and how ideology was put into practice.

Public and Private — the Home as Stage and Sanctuary

During the latter half of the nineteenth century, bourgeois homes in Sweden changed radically. Up to the middle of the century, dwellings were characterized by simplicity and austerity. The pieces of furniture were few and placed along the walls. The same room could be used for different functions: eating, working, entertaining, and sleeping. This traditional pattern started to change in mid-century. A totally new world was created inside the walls of the home. Austerity was replaced by opulence and almost a horror vacui. The floors were filled with bulging sofas and chairs; doors and windows were draped in heavy silk and smooth velvet. The walls were strewn with pictures and ornaments. Empty spaces were filled with plants, bric-a-brac, and souvenirs. Tassels and lace decorated everything.

During the period from about 1860 to 1910, different styles were boldly mixed, but the basic themes remained the same: romance, sentimentality, and fantasy characterized interior decoration.

When one looks at pictures of these overloaded interiors, their theatrical features are striking. As never before, families invested time, money, and a burning interest in designing their domestic tableau, creating impressive landscapes and special atmospheres in room after room.[20]

There was, of course, a material foundation for these displays and interests. The increased wealth of the rising bourgeoisie made investments in better housing and more extravagant interior decoration possible, while technological innovations made housing arrangements

The Home Builders

more comfortable and mass-production of furniture and ornaments feasible. The social transformation of Swedish society also produced another important resource for Oscarian homemaking: a growing rural proletariat from which cheap domestic labor could be recruited. The sweetness of home depended on the drudgery of numerous servants.

For the bourgeoisie, the home was both a showcase for the world and a shelter against it. The family home became the stage on which the family paraded its wealth and displayed its social standing, an important function in this period of rapidly changing class boundaries. Yet at the same time there was a development that stressed the significance of the home as a private domain and haven. The same economic class that administered the new production system under capitalism also created a compensatory world of intimacy, coziness, and warmth. The Oscarian home became a counter to the growing anonymity, rationality, and efficiency of the outside world. It is important to bear in mind this cultural contradiction.

The layout of the typical Oscarian home testified to this dual function of the home as stage and shelter. A number of spatial boundaries were drawn with the use of entrances, passages, doors, and sequences of rooms to separate public from private, servants from family, and children from their parents. For the first time, doors could be closed to guarantee the privacy of the individual. It was no longer necessary to pass through other people's bedrooms or to witness private activities. It was now possible to retire from the company of others.

This increase in the privacy of living arrangements had begun earlier in the upper classes, spreading rapidly in the nineteenth century.[21] A symptom of this developing interest in privacy is the way the bourgeoisie complained about the peasant's lack of concern for individual privacy. Guests in peasant homes could find themselves in embarrassing situations. Dr. Borelius brings out this sense of difference especially vividly in his recollections of journeys in remote northern areas around the turn of the century; he observed that the peasants saw

"Morning Reveille in Orsa" is the title of this drawing by Fritz von Dardel showing a farmhouse in Dalarna in 1893. It illustrates the lack of privacy and modesty that bourgeois visitors to peasant households found so revolting. (Nordiska Museet, Stockholm.)

The Home Builders

no difference between public and private—they quite simply have no private family life, all is public. Locks are never used in the isolated villages—night or day—and one never knocks when entering a house. One light summer night I came to a farm where they used to take in visitors. The main entrance to the farm was open, as well as the front door, but not a soul was in sight. I had to walk through the whole house until I found the family sleeping soundly in the innermost room. The mistress of the house woke and sat up in the double bed, and I told her who I was and asked for a bed for the night. Well, that was no problem! She just got up and made up a bed for me.

Ordinary middle-class people like us do not care to have strangers coming into the room where we are sitting down to table. The really old-fashioned peasants never worry about that. . . .

We do not like to dress in the presence of strangers. That does not embarrass the peasants I am talking about here, and they cannot understand that kind of feeling in others. (Borelius 1936:39f.)

One particular memory of this stuck in his mind:

During the famine year of 1902, an unusually tall woman traveled up to northern Lappland to help organize relief. It was in the autumn, so it was already dark when she came to the farm where she was to stay. She was tired from her travels and went to bed immediately. But on the farm they had never seen such a tall woman before; the sensation had to be shared with others, so the message was sent round. From all corners of the village came one family after the other: father, mother, servants, and children. For every new batch of visi-

Rational and Sensitive

tors the farm's only candle stump, stuck in the neck of a liter bottle, was lit, and people walked over to the bed in the corner to view the resting wonder. At midnight the lady had to say sharply that this was to be the end of the day's demonstration. (Borelius 1936:41f.)

The notion of a private and secluded room for sleeping was more or less unknown in early nineteenth-century Sweden. Peasants were accustomed to sharing both sleeping quarters and beds with others. Even in upper-class settings, the bedchamber was used for social entertaining and everyday activities (Paulsson 1950:1.121ff.; 2.353ff.; Gejvall 1954:198ff.). With the growing emphasis on the privacy and intimacy of the married couple, the middle-class bedchamber was transformed into the *sleeping* room—a good example of the rearrangement of social space. During the Oscarian era the bedroom was usually located as far away as possible from the entrance to the house, where it became the most private domain of the home, open only to the husband and wife. Its backstage atmosphere was underlined by the fact that it was often furnished with older, less fashionable furniture. The eyes of a visitor would never fall on it. Toward the end of the century, the new ideology of hygiene provided further arguments for this seclusion; bedrooms were to be kept well aired and practically sterile (Stavenow-Hidemark 1970:47ff.). The whiteness of the walls, the polished brass or shining mahogany of the large double bed stress that here lies the sanctum for the most intimate of all social relations, that between man and wife. It was the arena in which the only form of legitimate sexuality could be performed in total privacy, and a room to which the married couple could withdraw at night in order to discuss the happenings of the day.

It is hardly surprising that it was the parents' bedroom that was relocated and reconfigured in this way. At first the adults did not worry much about the sleeping arrangements of the other members of

The Home Builders

the household. In bigger apartments the maid could have a room of her own, but the servant girls usually slept in the kitchen or with the children. In new houses and apartment buildings, a separate room for the maid was included toward the end of the century. It was usually located next to the kitchen with space for a bed and a dresser, and with only one window. Maids were not given any great amount of privacy in middle-class homes.

Children also had a low priority in Oscarian housing arrangements. As late as the 1870s, separate nurseries were rare. Children usually slept with the servants in a small, dark room furnished with leftover furniture. For most children, the parents' bedroom was forbidden territory: "Beyond the dining room was a world I never entered, but where I supposed that my parents had their rooms," recollects one Oscarian (Hägglöf 1976:11). Another tells that he shared rooms with the servants above his parents' quarters, and that "what went on downstairs was largely unknown and incomprehensible" (cited in Gejvall 1954:216). In these upper-middle-class settings the sweet patter of tiny feet was to be heard only on suitable occasions.

When the campaign for bright and roomy nurseries with their own style in furniture started toward the end of the century, it was a result of changing perceptions of both the meaning of childhood and the role of children in family life.[22] It was also at this stage that parents started worrying about the unsuitable intimacy between children and servants, which had never been much of a problem for the aristocracy. New boundaries, both cultural and physical, were drawn between these two social categories in many middle-class homes.

The changing significance of the bedroom and the nursery illustrates the growing stress on intimacy and privacy in family relations. A private sphere emerged, a territory to which outsiders were denied access. At the same time that this backstage home life developed, the public part of the home was elaborated and differentiated. Visitors were sorted according to rank. Some had to go through the trades-

Rational and Sensitive

man's entrance or the kitchen door, others were only allowed to enter the hall or were told to remain on the doorstep. In larger apartments and houses there came to be an intricate system of social sluices: entrance, hall, drawing room, and sitting room were stations leading toward the heart of the home. The actual rituals of entering these stations became more complex. An analysis of Swedish etiquette books shows that the chapters on the art of visiting expanded considerably toward the end of the nineteenth century.

The drawing room became the main stage for greeting visitors (of the right social standing), so its decoration was an important concern. In a contemporary handbook of interior decoration the following rule was laid down:

> The drawing room is the place for entertaining visitors, the place for social contacts between the family and the outside world; the drawing room thus represents the house, which must therefore display here its most brilliant side. . . . Empty tables, naked walls, bare surfaces are nowhere as intolerable as in the drawing room, where a chilly atmosphere would counteract the warmth of the welcome, during which conversation should cover thousands of topics, all the time seeking inspiration from the surroundings. (cited in Paulsson 1950:2.524)

This consciously or unconsciously theatrical aspect of homemaking fits well with one of the main themes in the nineteenth-century bourgeois world view: "Civilized Man" as a polished and sophisticated actor, who maintains self-control and a pleasant but restrained façade toward others.

The interior of the home was also given a form that stressed its function as a place of retreat and rest. A cozy and comfortable world was created in drawing rooms and sitting rooms with the help of bulging padding and a multitude of cushions. The half-lit rooms had a quiet and restful atmosphere, and a muted sensuality radiated from the warm colors, the rounded edges, the soft materials. The home was not only a stage on which the family could perform, it was also like a snug and sheltered theater box, from which the family could observe the busy outside world. The feeling of homeyness was growing.

The Heart of the Home

"A real home-loving person is a kind of sun. Whether she sits in her own corner, smiling genially, or walks from house to house, spreading warmth, she is always at home, radiating comfort and coziness. Such a person is invincible" (Wahlman 1902:17). This is how a leading Swedish architect once defined the home-loving person, or rather the home-loving woman — it is quite obvious that the production of homeyness was women's work. During the Oscarian era the qualities of home became the qualities of woman. Notions of home and womanhood, privacy and sentiment were interwoven.

Other economic and moral rules were applied in the domestic rather than the public sphere. Home stood for emotions and warmth, for security, harmony, and coziness. While the Victorian middle-class male was defined through such qualities as rationality and efficiency, which were demanded in the sphere of production, his wife was supposed to be full of love and care, passive rather than active. In this new construction of gender differences, the career-oriented *homo economicus* is contrasted to the tender *femina domestica* (Cominos 1972).

The woman stands as the guardian of the home and its many virtues. In Victorian childhood memories, home and mother appear to have been an inseparable entity: "What was the lifework of my mother?" asks the daughter of a civil servant, who continues: "It was

Rational and Sensitive

the *home* she built for us. In this task she invested all her most pains-taking care and her warmest love. This was her calling" (Krook 1946: 117). Another author summarized the same feeling in the words "Home was, above all, Mother" (Beskow 1946:22).

The ideal existence of *femina domestica* was defined by men. Middle-class women were supposed to be spared heavy and dirty chores at home. Real productive work was not for them; they were expected to express their womanhood through other activities. It was up to the housewife to provide an atmosphere of homeyness. Inside her own home a woman was free to build her own fantasy world, she was able to paint and embroider, as well as plan and decorate. Her delicate piano playing and her warm smile were supposed to fill the house. The lovingly arranged bric-a-brac on shelves and mantelpieces symbolized the new womanhood. There were always a thousand ways to elaborate and ritualize the day, while daydreaming and waiting for the man of the house to return home from the outside world.

Female ambitions were expected to focus on making home a pleasant retreat from the stress of public life, or, as one of the new manuals for good housekeeping put it:

> A man who spends most of his day away from the family, who has to work outside the home, counts on finding a restful and refreshing atmosphere when he returns home, and sometimes even a little merriment or a surprise. A good man who not only provides for his family but also allows it occasionally to enjoy some of the delights of life, if his income admits it, has the right to expect this, and it is his wife's duty to ensure that he is not disappointed in his expectation. She must do her utmost to make his stay at home as pleasant as possible; she can thus continue to keep her influence over him and retain his affection undiminished.   (Grubb 1889:13)

The Home Builders

In order to understand the new images of domesticity, we have to relate them to the bourgeois reorganization of gender. Contrary to notions of gender in, for example, traditional Swedish peasant culture, the new conceptions were based on complementary emotional structures. The ideal of the rational and disciplined male operating in the public sphere was constructed with the help of a new femininity. A loving wife and the support of a good home became important assets for the man who wanted to conquer the world. But home was not only a female domain, it was also a cultural breathing space where men could act out the more emotional or even feminine parts of their cultural personality. In the secluded privacy and intimacy of the home, surrounded by his nearest and dearest, he was able to behave in a more relaxed fashion, showing emotions that were taboo in the public sphere.

The new construction of gender polarities was not a fixed set of male and female roles, but rather polarities of masculinity and femininity that had a more dialectical relationship. The *femina domestica* helped to underline the maleness of the man in the public sphere, but also created a private antipode to the outside world, a cultural space where men would be under the spell of female domesticity and intimacy.

When looking at the Oscarian era, however, it is important to distinguish male dreams and ideals about femininity from the actual everyday activities of women. The majority of middle-class housewives spent most of their time doing other things than playing the piano or producing needlework. They became homemakers in a more practical sense. Running a household in this period was a complex task, especially if the desired level of respectability, orderliness, and ritual elaboration was to be maintained. Even in urban households there remained a considerable degree of self-sufficiency, with the time-consuming preparation and preservation of food. The wives of civil

Rational and Sensitive

servants, factory owners, and clerks had few opportunities for idle daydreaming, and there was even less leisure time in the vicarage or the small manor house in the countryside. The discrepancy between ideals and realities was as greatly marked in this area as it was in many other fields of Oscarian culture.

The Lessons of Home

Yes, a home, a world in miniature—*is this not everything!* Joy and disappointment, upbringing and festivity, repression and liberation.
   The home, the bourgeois home, was by and large, in the lovely nineties, before Nobel's explosives and turbines, massive strikes and lockouts, before all the "isms" and inflation, radio and stink-chuggers—as old Jörgen called automobiles at the turn of the century—in the Good Old Days *the home* meant an existence of quite a different pith and strength and security than now.

Torsten Tegnér concludes thus his reflection about his childhood home (Tegnér 1947:205). For him and for many of his contemporaries growing up in the Oscarian era, home is transfigured in a nostalgic glow.
   Home was, however, more than a childhood memory; it was also a lesson. An analysis of memoirs of this period reveals how much children learned about social relationships and cultural rules from the physical arrangements in their homes, which became part of a silent and unconscious socialization. The walls kept talking to the children. This can be illustrated by quoting a few examples. The first is a description of a merchant's home in Stockholm, where the family dis-

The Home Builders

played its cultural ambitions in the pride of place given to the magnifi-
cently illustrated editions of obligatory Swedish classics that lay on the
table in the drawing room, which

was decorated entirely in red and mahogany. The Brussels
mat with its billowing, weaving pattern was red, the fine textile wallpaper with its sunken, silklike figures was red, and
the fabric on the curved-legged, fringed easy chairs, the up-
right chairs, and the long sofa with its hard, pearl-embroid-
ered cushions was red. But the red was broken by the pier
glass between the windows, which had a gilded frame and a
marble console table, and by the tiled stove, which stood opposite and also boasted a high mirror on top of the mantelpiece. I loved to sneak into the drawing room, where we were
never allowed on ordinary days, and stand between the two
mirrors to see how my figure was reflected to infinity, becoming smaller and smaller until it disappeared up at the edges. I
probably understood why this was, but it was nevertheless
mysterious. I still think so. . . .

The dining room had, of course, high, narrow-backed
chairs with cane seats; thick, lined curtains with lace borders;
and a magnificent flower table of woven cane in front of the
middle window. The girls' room was in blue, while the boys'
room was something of a hodgepodge, although a handsome
but abused drop-leaf table stood before the sofa. Every room
but the girls' had the characteristic piece of furniture of the
times, the spittoon, made of brass with a removable container
of porcelain or cast iron, filled with fine white sand, which
was raked every morning in an elegant pattern. It was probably only there mainly as a traditional showpiece. At least, I
cannot remember it ever being used very much.

Life in this Stockholm apartment, which was no doubt typi-

Rational and Sensitive

cal for the middle bourgeoisie, was quiet and peaceful, with few pleasures and little entertainment; that is my impression. The opera occasionally or the theater or a concert. Otherwise it was the traditional gathering around the drawing-room lamp in the evenings. Father read *Aftonbladet*, sometimes reading an article aloud. If it was not the free traders who upset him it was talk of a strike somewhere. Mother darned stockings, my sisters did handwork, as it was called, and my brother and I read or painted. It must have been the perfect family idyll, but unfortunately I came into the picture late, since I was the youngest, six years younger than my brother, and I did not have the opportunity to enjoy it long, because my sisters got married. The circle was thus broken.   (Swensson 1947:182ff.)

The second example comes from a manor house:

The large drawing room was always stiffly on parade. We were not allowed to enter it, and in the evenings it lay in an eerie darkness, so we scarcely dared to sneak in. Father's study next to the vestibule was the normal meeting place for the family, but in the evenings we gathered in a little room where time was ticked away by a beautiful white grandfather clock which was a family heirloom, and which now stands in my home. . . . In that room we gathered in the evenings, after homework and play were over for the day; about five o'clock a maid brought in a coffee tray and lit the fire; around the divan table sat Mother and the governess, the tutor and the masseuse—Father had once injured a shoulder down at the works—and the reading aloud began. Father often played solitaire, always the same game, and the ladies sewed, mostly Gobelin-style tapestries with foxes and birds and other lovely

The Home Builders

things in the patterns. We children had various things to pot-
ter at, drawing or, in the fall, making decorations out of silk
paper for the Christmas tree. The apples came in, and there
was a comfortable atmosphere of peace and tranquillity, far
away from all strife and conflict; this gave us children a
delightful feeling for our home, one that we fondly remember.
The times around the evening lamp—how can we ever re-
gain them? (Wallquist 1947:218)

Memory is selective; what it filters gives us important information
about what people want to remember. It is striking the way the scene
of the evening gathering is so often described as the center of the
home. Yet another picture, this time from the home of an industrialist,
shows how this family feeling was created and ritualized:

Otherwise, what I remember most vividly from my childhood
is the evenings gathered round the dining-room table, with
everyone reading silently, or occasionally Father or Mother
reading aloud. . . . The circle of light around the hissing kero-
sene lamp was concentrated on the table; farther away in the
room the shadows were thick, and in the adjacent drawing
room, the door of which stood ajar, it was normally pitch
dark. Ugh, when we had to pass through that room! . . . But
these evenings of reading were delightful times of tranquillity,
when we felt more than at any other time that we belonged
together, that it was a *family* sitting there in the lamplight.
Young people nowadays have largely lost such experiences,
without getting anything in their place. (Boberg 1949:35)

The important point here is not the quantitative intensity of the parents' and children's hours together, but rather the symbolic and moral
values with which they are loaded. Many of the children who grew up

Rational and Sensitive

during the decades before World War I had very limited contact with their parents, yet the unity of the home and the nuclear family stands out clearly in their memories.

Gunnar Hägglöf writes: "I can scarcely emphasize enough how strong the feeling for home was during the whole of my childhood. . . . The essential and the central feature was the home." His father, a circuit judge, said: "I am convinced that the family is the only proper foundation of a civilized society." This was the same father who visited the nursery only once during his son's entire childhood, but, as Gunnar Hägglöf points out, the intensity of feeling for the home was expressed "not so much in the actual times spent together as in the feeling of belonging together" (1976:178, 202).

This silent or indirect socialization of the home was perhaps more important than the stream of verbal admonitions and rules for behavior. The strict, musty colors of the father's study, with its impressive and disciplined array of books and its polished desk, communicated ideas about serious work and male responsibilities, just as the choice of colors and furniture for the boys' and girls' rooms provided pervasive comments on gender.

The many mirrors scattered about the house gave them a chance of observing their own behavior and appearance, and also reminded them how important it was to know how to "carry themselves" properly.

Above all, the silent socialization of the home kept bombarding them with one of the essential ground rules of bourgeois culture: there is a time and place for everything. The need to learn how to separate people, activities, and functions was taught with the help of the many spatial and temporal rituals that structured everyday life at home. Children learned to respect the boundaries separating various arenas of the home, never to enter their parents' bedroom without permission, and to be aware that they had to behave differently in the drawing room than in the nursery. They observed the difference between the atmosphere and language of the kitchen (where the servants set

The Home Builders

the tone) and the restrained behavior demanded in the dining room.

Each family meal became a lesson in the necessity for functional differentiation and self-discipline: "Be on time for dinner, wash your hands before sitting down to table, keep your elbows in and your mouth shut, answer only when you are spoken to!" The straight-backed dining-room chairs also reminded children not to slouch.

In their memories of these Oscarian childhood days, people reorganized and reinterpreted the past. The process of idyllic idealization suggests that actual experiences were often repressed or reinterpreted. It is interesting to compare what people want to remember with the way the cultural stereotypes of family togetherness and parental love were constructed. Although parents were, in reality, often distant and formal figures, it is the memory of the family gathered around the evening table, or the mother as a warm, radiant sun that is preserved. These memories are more of a symbolic statement about the way family life ought to be.

Home Improvement

It is evident that most middle-class children who grew up about the turn of the century left home with fixed notions about a proper family life based on the foundation of the marriage bond, the loving parents, and the good home. Their world view with its family rituals was the product of concrete economic and social changes in nineteenth-century Sweden, yet many of their values and habits are still part of our hidden heritage a century later. Our conceptions of sexuality and love, home and privacy, male and female are still perhaps more influenced than we care to admit by the culture that the Oscarians built. So effectively can these notions be internalized that many people still take them for granted as natural and may find it hard to understand cul-

Rational and Sensitive

tures or historical settings in which interpersonal relations are structured differently.

To what extent did this middle-class ideology of the family and the home come to attain cultural dominance throughout Swedish society during the early twentieth century? The Oscarians represented a colonizing culture, dedicated to the task of implanting their ideas of a good and proper life among the lower classes. In discussions of the development of family ideals in the twentieth century, this process of embourgeoisement is often referred to in oversimplified terms. It cannot, however, be explained as a wave of cultural innovation sweeping over the country and through the classes. Nor can the problem be dismissed with the trivial claim that it is only a question of a new economic and political elite imposing their ideology on a helpless working class. It is necessary to take a closer look at the manifold ways in which these ideals were communicated and to what extent they were turned into dreams and aspirations among the working people.

Toward the end of the nineteenth century, the old structure of Swedish society was crumbling. Traditional rules of hierarchy, loyalty, and social control no longer seemed to be functional. The rapidly growing working class was seen as a menace to the old social stability. There was an atmosphere of tension, of clashing values, which made those at the top frightened. If the old order could not be rebuilt, then a new moral cement was needed in order to keep society from disintegrating. For some, one answer to this problem was found in the importance of a good home life. If only the working classes could be domesticated, if only their unrest and ambitions could be directed inward, toward the home and family, many problems would be solved. The change should be moral rather than economic.

A government committee stressed the importance of state loans for working-class homemakers who wanted a small house of their own. In their report they state that "there is every reason to believe that owning a home will strengthen a worker's feeling for both his community and

The Home Builders

his fatherland" (Egnahemskomitén 1901:14). A homeowner's journal (*Egna hem*) was started, carrying the motto: "Goal: A home of your own on freehold land. Means: Industry, thrift, and godliness." A number of organizations worked to protect the values of the home and to increase love of the home in society. One of the most ardent missionaries of this ideal wished in 1910 that

> all good thoughts were united into a mighty wave to save our homes and protect our nation.
> *To make our homes pleasant and delightful and make our nation strong and healthy!* This would carry us forward, it would protect us from much evil and avert dangers. This would be a New Year's resolution we ought to make in every home, our hands joined in a closed circle as a symbol of our unity, our strength. (Törne 1910:28)

The virtues of a stable home life were echoed in parliamentary debates, newspaper articles, and pamphlets. The ideals were spread through many channels, such as housing and educational reform programs, welfare agencies, and campaigns for good housekeeping among working-class women. The happy family smiled from advertisements, popular prints, penny novels, and even, as was mentioned earlier, from zoological illustrations.

It would be wrong, however, to talk in terms of a well-planned attack with the explicit goal of pacifying the unruly working class. Many of the social reformers saw themselves as missionaries of "the good life," of modernization and development. They wanted to improve housing conditions, diet, and child care. Many of them were not aware of the fact that their reforming activities exhibited heavy moral overtones. Many of these reformers complained of the suspicion and ungrateful attitudes directed toward them by the workers, who resented these moral connotations.

Rational and Sensitive

Working-Class Homes

What about the realities of working-class life at the beginning of the twentieth century? There were great differences in life-styles in this heterogeneous class, but one thing they all had in common was the proximity to agrarian society. The workers of the turn of the century were the sons and daughters of the rural proletariat, the cotters and farm laborers. They came from families in which the home was not the rallying point that it was for the farmers, but rather a base from which the members of the family were sent out to earn money. The children left the home early, finding jobs with farmers and later as industrial workers. While the fathers often roved around in search of temporary jobs, the mothers had little time for the children; they did day-work, washed, sewed, looked after what little land they had and the few animals they could afford to keep. Conditions here were not of the sort to allow a stable life in the bosom of the family (Löfgren 1978).

A similar pattern existed in urban settings in the early twentieth century. Unlike middle-class children, for whom work was a distant world from which fathers returned in the evening, working-class children knew work as a constant companion and an economic necessity. In middle-class homes, work could be a moral lesson, rarely a necessity; the young prepared themselves for future work and career by being good and diligent children. For working-class children, on the other hand, work represented both prison and freedom. They had to spend a lot of time after school, on weekends, and in the summer, helping the parents or taking odd jobs. Until the 1930s, many urban households still lived in a kind of hunting-and-gathering economy. Periods of unemployment as well as low wages meant that all kinds of extra sources of income had to be sought, and even marginal resources exploited. Work took up much of the children's free time but also gave a certain amount of freedom, teaching them to earn their

The Home Builders

own money and to fend for themselves, in contrast to the more sheltered middle-class childhood.

A very striking feature of family life was overcrowded homes. As late as the 1930s, the majority of Swedish working-class families lived in a single room and kitchen, or just one room with a small stove in the corner. In both rural and urban areas, living conditions were poor and housing shortages made rents relatively high.

In these conditions, family life took on a different character from that evidenced in middle-class settings. A young middle-class boy whose family moved into a working-class neighborhood during the 1920s was surprised to find that the local children, when playing families, always had a bachelor along with the make-believe father, mother, and children. He gradually realized that lodgers were a normal part of working-class households. Single persons had to attach themselves to existing families in need of the extra cash (Nystedt 1972:68). Middle-class distaste for such living conditions was well expressed by Gustaf af Geijerstam:

The dwelling is the external and practical foundation of the home. No home is conceivable without a clean and healthy dwelling, where comfort is not spoiled by the necessity to have lodgers, and where health does not suffer through cold or damp. From the moral point of view no less than the sanitary, it is one of the cancers of working-class life that the lodger system is as important as it is in the home life of our working class. It leads to a moral coarseness and a mental savagery that no statistics can reveal. . . .

Finally, it removes from the dwelling the last residue of the feeling evoked by the word home, changing it to a place where men and women sleep together like animals, with no hope of any improvement in the future. . . .

"Give us better workers' housing," a philanthropist once

Rational and Sensitive

cried, "and within twenty years Stockholm will have a better working-class population." (af Geijerstam 1894:52)

Here social pathos mixes with bourgeois disgust and sexual anxiety over the physical intimacy of working-class dwelling conditions (see the English parallels in Wohl 1978).

It is possible to highlight middle-class ideals about family life by looking more closely at life in a fairly typical working-class urban setting during the period from 1910 to 1940, in the town of Landskrona in Skåne.[23]

Life in a single-room apartment meant that beds and various other sleeping arrangements took up most of the interior space. Home was not a place where people longed to spend their spare time. Socializing had to be carried on elsewhere.

A striking feature of working-class life before World War II was the relative unimportance of family togetherness. The men spent their time in male company, women visited one another, and children often looked after themselves, playing in backyards or roaming about the neighborhood. There were neither material conditions nor cultural traditions for a more family-oriented life-style.[24] The mother is often portrayed as the key figure of the household. The father was often a rather distant figure, the breadwinner who was given the best pieces of food and who came home tired from long working days, just to lie down or to go out and spend the evening with his mates. Mother was the unifying force and the mediator, who took the chief responsibility for the children's upbringing (Ek 1982:111ff.). The money children earned was usually turned over to her, since she was in charge of the family budget; her job was to make ends meet.

The social landscape of working-class children who grew up during this period was thus far less home-centered than in middle-class milieus. As in peasant society, "we" could mean more than "we in our family"; it also meant "we in our apartment house, on our street, in our neighborhood."

The Home Builders

One's social identity was to a great extent anchored in these territorial units. The boundaries between *us* and *them* were manifested in many ways, from neighborhood nicknames to gang fights. Local solidarity was also maintained through systems of reciprocity and sharing. Across hallways, backyards, and alleys there was a steady flow of cups of sugar, flour, and other necessities. This borrowing between households had both economic and symbolic aspects. Unlike middle-class families, working-class households lacked both resources and space for independent domestic budgeting. The constant borrowing was a part of working-class economy, like the weekly visits to the pawnbroker. Entering a network of reciprocity was also a way to manifest a sense of social belonging.

There is often, however, a note of ambivalence in the memories of these neighborhood networks. People talk about the constant borrowing between housewives and then add: "but in our family we always kept ourselves to ourselves," or "we always managed on our own." To fend for oneself, to be dependent on neither neighbors nor welfare, was an important mark of working-class respectability.

Most working-class families faced a life of very narrow economic margins and had to make a constant effort to keep the family afloat. In this life they were perpetually reminded that their behavior did not measure up to the standards of the official, dominant culture. Ideas about being an honest and respectable working man or woman can be seen both as a defense against an intruding middle-class moralism and as a boundary marker against those who had "lost control of their own lives," those unfortunates who "lived at the mercy of the welfare people," those who "could no longer fend for themselves," and thus had to subordinate themselves to the regulations and admonitions of the official institutions. This constant fear of losing one's footing in society was based on the knowledge that one's position was very precarious. Unemployment, sickness, a husband who started to drink, or children who got themselves into trouble could wreck the family.

Clear boundaries were thus established between those husbands

Rational and Sensitive

who took a drink on Saturdays and those who squandered their meager earnings in pubs every evening. There was the distinction between those who dressed up for Sundays and those who did not bother, the distinction between women who could keep a good home and those who lived in chaos. These ideas about respectability should be seen as cultural defense rather than as embourgeoisement. Working-class families fought a battle on two fronts, against both middle class and lumpen proletariat, and in this process of culture-building, firm rituals and rules of social life were created. Sex roles, drinking patterns, forms of socializing were often rigidly defined, which led middle-class intellectuals and progressive reformers to sigh about working-class traditionalism and inflexibility.

A number of detailed surveys threw public light on the poor housing conditions of the working class during the teens and twenties. Both conservative and progressive commentators could agree on the gravity of this problem, but both their analyses and their proposed solutions tended to differ.

Was the overcrowded home an economic or a cultural problem? An official survey from 1933 in the city of Gothenburg argued that overcrowding was not always a result of economic necessity; some families "prefer to use their income to cover other needs . . . in a way that is wrong from the point of view of social values." The social evil of "their self-imposed low housing standards" was said to be "caused by a lack of interest in hygiene and generally poor habits regarding the house" (SOU 1933:14.25). This moralizing attitude has a long tradition in middle-class discourse on working-class life: no long-term planning, wrong priorities, insufficient love of home. There is a total lack of understanding of both working-class culture and material realities.

Another argument found in the housing debate of the period is that working-class families used their living space incorrectly. The most blatant example of such bad habits was found in the use of the parlor. From Landskrona comes a typical description of the domestic scene from a cooper's son who grew up in the 1920s:

The Home Builders

We lived mainly in the kitchen. The room my parents used as parlor was meant for show, and you had to be very sick to get to lie down in there. When the doctor came to visit, you couldn't be bedded down in the kitchen, of course. Otherwise, all five of us lived in the kitchen. And the kitchen wasn't big, something like eight feet by eleven. It was heated by an iron stove, but when times were real hard we had a miniature burner on top of it. It was warm enough and we had a good home. . . . Nearly all of us shared one bed in those days. When I got a little bit older, I was allowed to move over to a bed which Ma and Pa made for me on top of a couple of boxes. We all slept in the kitchen and the other room was kept neat.

The phrase "and the other room was kept neat" is echoed in most other childhood memories from the period: "We had a parlor too, it was so neat that you were barely allowed to touch the doorknob. . . . It was always like that. No matter how little space you had, there had to be a parlor." For middle-class intellectuals, it seemed a strange and wasteful way to live. They found it hard to understand that working-class wives fought hard for their parlors. To have one silent and well-kept room where no one was allowed to sleep was well worth the nuisance of an overcrowded kitchen. The parlor with its plants, mantelpiece clock, and lace-decorated sofa was not a pathetic attempt to imitate bourgeois life-styles; instead, the room had its own symbolic meaning in working-class culture. It was a cultural space separated from the drudgeries of everyday life, and to enter it meant being ritually transformed. It had an atmosphere all its own.

Many working-class women came into contact with middle-class standards of housekeeping through their first wage-labor experience as domestics. This did not lead to a surrender to middle-class values and habits, but rather to a much more complex reaction. On the one hand the working-class women could show that they had incorporated middle-class ideals of orderliness when the time came to set up

Rational and Sensitive

homes of their own, but on the other hand the insights into bourgeois life could lead to a contempt for the striking difference between ideals and realities in these settings, where the double standards were so evident behind the scenes.

Any discussion of the hegemonic spread of middle-class ideas and standards must therefore be carefully balanced. There is always a risk of romanticizing life in urban working-class settings, where tough material conditions certainly did not create idyllic home situations. There is also the risk of overemphasizing the efficacy of middle-class cultural colonization. It is important here to distinguish between form and content when discussing working-class appropriation of middle-class life-styles. Elements may be borrowed, but they are often charged with new cultural meanings.

The Threatened Family

"We seem to be living in a time of crisis for the home—not only because of the rapidly increasing number of divorces, but also because of the new style of life, if one can call it style: parents play bridge and go to the cinema, they go to the seaside without their children and let their little ones grow up in kindergartens or boarding schools." These reflections are taken from the introduction to a collection of childhood memories (Söderberg 1947:1), but they could easily be matched by more recent complaints about the sorry state of the modern family. Let us, however, hear one more voice from the heated debate of the 1940s, from another collection in which thirty-three authors examine the problem of the Swedish home:

> The rapid development of our society during the recent generations has created many and difficult problems. The insti-

The Home Builders

tution that more than any other has been damaged in this
process is *the home*: discussions about its future existence
are not only of academic interest; this is a question that concerns us all. At the same time that the conditions for a survival of the home have deteriorated—the minimal dwellings,
work that splits up the family, the strong forces that lure the
young in particular away from home—all this has confirmed
us in the understanding that the home is the indispensable
foundation for human happiness and the healthy evolution
of mankind.   (Hedström 1947:9)

This type of literature, mourning the death of the family and the disin-
tegration of home life, has existed as long as there has been a family-
centered life-style in Swedish society. It is very much a nineteenth-
and twentieth-century genre of public discourse.

What was the reason for all this worry and concern? Looking back
on the 1940s, one can argue that during no other period of Swedish
history has the family had such a strong and clearly delineated position in the social landscape. At this time the old collectivity of working-
class neighborhoods had started to disintegrate, and a much more
familistic life-style was emerging among workers. The fact that one in
sixteen marriages ended in divorce in 1937 was a cause of grave concern for some observers at that time. Today, when the Swedish divorce
rate is one in four, these figures seem less menacing.

The notion of the disintegrating family becomes even more difficult
to understand if one looks at the history of household formation in
Sweden. A century earlier, 43 percent of all children were born outside
marriage, while only 26 percent of all women of marriageable age were
married in the city of Stockholm. These figures were something of a
European record.[25] In that urban setting, the nuclear family household was not a dominant cultural form.

Rational and Sensitive

It is important to ask why the family is portrayed as a threatened institution at any particular time, who is supposed to threaten it, and who feels threatened. In order to understand the debate on the future of the family in 1900 or 1940, such concepts as home and family must be seen as powerful symbols and metaphors. The family may appear in our view to be a fairly stable social institution in the 1940s, at least compared to the situation a hundred years earlier. The image of a disintegrating family system should rather be seen as a metaphor for other social anxieties. It mirrors the self-conception and the worries of the middle class, which felt itself threatened during this period of rapid social change and working-class mobilization. It is not so much the family that is changing as the whole of society. The same tendencies are evident in the Oscarian debate on the family.

Different social groups and classes will for different interests use the image of the home or the family as a cultural weapon. In this process, the past will often be reorganized for the present. The Oscarian middle class extolled the virtues of family life in traditional peasant culture. The picture they painted of a stable, home-centered life, of obedient children and loving parents, tells more of their own aspirations and ideals than about historical realities. Their homage to the mythical "extended family" mirrored the longing for a more stable and patriarchal structure in a rapidly changing society.

In the same way, critics of the welfare state in the 1940s created their picture of the sound and happy family life of the Oscarian bourgeoisie, using it to prove their point that the family was going under quickly. Contemporary radicals turned history the other way around and talked about the double standards and pretensions of Oscarian family life.

A historical approach may help to put this ongoing debate on the fate of the family into perspective. Family historians have shown that the nuclear family is no invention of industrial society. It was a common household type in earlier times (Löfgren 1984b). It is not so much

The Home Builders

the composition of the family and the household group that changes in nineteenth-century Sweden, but rather the emotional and psychological structure of family relations. This was the time that the family began to stand out in the social landscape, built on the triple foundation of the loving couple, the caring parents, and the good home. It is in the middle-class home that the triangle of father–mother–child develops as an emotional ideal, if not as a reality in everyday interaction. The isolated nuclear family was a rather rare phenomenon in nineteenth-century middle-class settings, where it was common to find numerous domestic servants, as well as an array of close kin, lodging aunts, and visiting cousins.

This discussion of the new family ideals has simplified a more complex middle-class reality. Family life did, of course, differ in the various subcultures grouped together under the label of the middle class. The aim here has been to illustrate some general traits and point to the more-or-less conscious cultural heritage still encountered in both the ideals and the praxis of contemporary family life and public debate.

There are many contradictions in this debate, some of which can be traced to the paradoxes of family ideals that were part of middle-class culture building. At the same time that the importance of a private family life was stressed and the boundaries between home and public life became more marked, there were also arguments for a closer supervision and control of what went on inside the home. As the good and healthy family life became an important middle-class remedy for social ills, the sanctity of private life became too important a social activity to be left to people themselves. The family became the building block of the nation, and parents needed help in their task of turning children into good citizens. Privatization was thus encouraged, and at the same time the privacy was penetrated by admonitions and counseling. It is now no longer certain that mother knows best.[26]

Clean and Proper

BODY AND SOUL THROUGH PEASANT
AND BOURGEOIS EYES

Jonas Frykman

The civilized and the primitive. A student doing fieldwork in a backward rural area in Skåne, 1928. (Photograph from Folklivsarkivet, University of Lund.)

· 4 ·

The Cultural Basis
of Physical Aversion

It is an oft-repeated truth that most of today's Swedes have their roots in rural society. The ancestors of today's city dwellers are to be found among the nineteenth-century farmers, cotters, agricultural laborers, and craftsmen. In recent years the image of this society has slowly started to change.

There was once a perfectly understandable sense of relief that Sweden's days of poverty were a thing of the past. Many could testify to the fact that country life involved more misery than well-being. The nineteenth century was seen as a time when people were forced to endure hunger, disease, and poor living conditions and had to earn their daily bread by the sweat of their brows. The immediate descendants of these people had little time for nostalgia for the old days, for rustic Romanticism or back-to-nature movements. Today, however, those who know from the depth of their own experience what the good old days were really like are becoming fewer and fewer. When grandparents and parents are no longer around to tell how it was or to correct today's view of past reality, then dreams and wishful thinking begin to take over. The children and grandchildren of the welfare state now have a rosier conception of bygone conditions. The past is coming to be seen as a time when people lived near one another, lived in contact with nature and animals, when everyone had his or her given place, when old and young alike were needed.

Clean and Proper

In order to understand our changed view of the past, we must be familiar with the background against which it has emerged. Pessimism about the future, the claustrophobic feeling of being surrounded by cars, concrete, and asphalt, all this can make the dream of peasant society especially seductive.

How well does this dream bear comparison with reality? If we could experience the negative side of everyday life in the past, down to earth and close to nature, we might perhaps find it less rosy. The filth and the stench of people and animals do not, of course, come across on television or in books, in music or song. But the dirt was there, constantly making its presence felt.

In a tape recording made at the end of the 1960s, the daughter of a stonecutter tells of her childhood on the island of Tjurkö in Blekinge. The time she refers to was about 1910. She gets onto the subject of cleanliness and gives some concrete examples of everyday problems. The little cottage where they lived had its fixed depositories for dirt. There was the slop bucket under the kitchen workbench, the spittoon with its tobacco saliva by the kitchen door, and the pot under the bed. Apart from these permanent depositories, there were those which were of a more temporary nature. One such was the father's snuff, which he normally spat out behind the sofa, another was the youngsters' handkerchief, which they kept in the bed, and which was used by everyone. There were bugs behind the wallpaper, and all the children had lice. So did the adults, but they often combed their hair assiduously, thereby removing the lice eggs from the scalp. The lice thrived because washing was a rare occurrence. There was a basin in the cottage, used for washing hands and faces. It was used regularly before Sundays and church holidays, but probably not otherwise. The body was never washed. Little babies were kept clean, however, even bathed. On occasion, too, even the grownups might take a bath indoors before Christmas, but it was no general rule. The absence of bodily hygiene made itself felt inside the cottage, the informant recalls. Sweat and dirt and unwashed genitals give off smells. The odor of

The Cultural Basis of Physical Aversion

clothes and bodies pervaded the atmosphere, together with cooking fumes, the smoky downdraft from the chimney, and the stench from the dirt depositories.

As I listened to her story I could not repress strong feelings of nausea over this aspect of human life. I thanked God for cleanliness, for all the progress that has been made in hygiene, for the shower, the deodorant, and the vacuum cleaner. Such sharp deviations from today's standards of cleanliness are hard to accept. They provoke so much of the concealed disgust and repulsion that obviously exists in our minds but rarely needs to appear openly in our neat and tidy everyday lives. Perhaps our picture of the past would be truer to life if the smells were documented as thoroughly as the other aspects of the human condition that are considered suitable for the drawing room.

The fact that certain sides of human life are unpleasant for the modern reader is intrinsically interesting, since it also testifies to modern ideals of cleanliness. The contemporary Swede has become obsessed with hygiene, convinced of the value of keeping everything clean and tidy. Bygone generations of Swedes living in the countryside and in the working-class areas of the towns were comparatively indifferent to such concerns. Even if this were not the case, the practical conditions for cleanliness were less favorable then than today.

The past hundred years have seen a thoroughgoing change in this area, which will be the focus of interest in this section of the book. The concept of cleanliness as viewed in nineteenth-century Swedish peasant culture will be discussed, along with the circumstances of the many landless and impoverished groups in rural society. Their attitudes will then be contrasted with those that prevailed among the bourgeoisie in the towns around the turn of the century and a little before. The links between this bourgeois culture and the present are particularly strong.

The modern conception of hygiene, the cultural history of disgust, and accounts of the disagreeable must be part of a wider context if they are to be more than mere curiosities. What we take to be natural

Clean and Proper

and instinctive feelings are in fact intimately bound up with our culture. Concepts such as "disgusting," "dirty," and related terms are not intrinsic qualities of things; it is we who give the spittoon and the snotty handkerchief their power to disgust us. Revulsion as an emotion exists, of course, but we have to learn which things evoke this feeling.

Emotions can be an effective defense for a particular social order. What is overtly or covertly felt by people to be unpleasant is part and parcel of their social identity, and it generally functions as a barrier between social classes. The differences between peasant and bourgeois attitudes to dirt are therefore revealing, but their study requires two preliminaries: a reflection in general terms on what dirt actually is; and a caveat about the nature of the available evidence.

Suppressed Evidence

It is a difficult task to paint a picture of the ways the peasantry and the bourgeoisie viewed dirt in the nineteenth century, because the research material is comparatively diffuse. Folklife archives are usually brimming with information about more "respectable" topics such as folk dress, house construction, seasonal festivities, riddles, legends, songs, and games; but when it comes to dirt, the researcher must be grateful for each scattered piece of testimony, each description, each illustration. This is because the suitable subjects for study have not included cleanliness, nor the names of parts of the body and the activities associated with them. This applies in particular to the more physical rituals of lovemaking and the routine evacuations of the body. These are areas in which scholars in the past practiced an unconscious censorship. The topics discussed by the farmhands and the language in which they were discussed remained confined to the farmhands' quarters.

The Cultural Basis of Physical Aversion

It must be reiterated that the neglect of certain subjects was unconscious. The many fieldworkers and folklife scholars had little opportunity to tear off their blinkers. In their own culture, which was generally middle-class, the nastier side of human existence was strictly taboo. It was these people, with their distinctive ideas about what could suitably be recorded as a monument for posterity, who made the selection, not the men and women they interviewed.

There are numerous examples of ethnological records that were considered unsuitable, because they contained foul language or accounts of improper things, and were therefore under a publication ban. I occasionally came across material like this during my research for a book on the position of the unmarried mother in rural society (Frykman 1977). In scholarly circles it was even common to view with suspicion anyone who paid particular attention to cleanliness, hygiene, and sexual matters.

With regard to bourgeois culture and its attitude to dirt, the source material situation is equally difficult, partly because this social group has not been subjected to the same sort of systematic research as the lower classes. This does not mean that information about bourgeois culture is lacking, but the information is provided on the informant's own terms. To illustrate this statement, take an invaluable body of source material, the autobiographical literature. It is the narrator himself who chooses what to remember in his memoirs, as well as what to suppress. No inquisitive fieldworker sits on the sofa, notepad in hand, beside a Supreme Court justice, asking him about life and death, meals and table manners, clothes and festivities in the old days. The material is not produced primarily for research purposes, although the memoirs can very well serve as a subject for research.

During the Oscarian period, many sides of human life were not considered proper conversation topics. What memoir writers had been taught all their lives to bridle and conceal would naturally not be included in their life stories. The past as met in these memoirs is therefore often idyllic in the extreme—totally lacking smells, urges, and bodies.

There are, however, isolated examples in later literature, as will become evident from quotations in the following chapters, but we are largely forced to paint a picture of the reality from vague hints, comical episodes, and interpretations of the material environment and the clothing of the day.

The correctness of the analysis cannot be judged just by the wealth of the source material, but should also be assessed on the logic of the reasoning. It is therefore only proper to state my theoretical premises —to describe the lens through which I view the problem.

Dirt Is Disorder

A good basis for the analysis of the cleanliness concept is provided by the social anthropologists' theories of taboo and ritual uncleanness. It may seem rather far-fetched to consider our culture from the viewpoint that anthropologists adopt when studying non-European peoples of the sort sometimes designated as "primitive." From our elevated position as "civilized" people we may find it too easy to see other people's culture as categorically different from our own. Yet concepts like taboo and impurity are universal human ways of thinking and looking at the world.[1] To put it very simply, our intellect can be compared to a computer constructed on binary principles. We are constantly making the distinctions right/wrong, good/bad, acceptable/repulsive; the things we repudiate are described as dirty, disgusting, impure. How this computer is programmed depends on the culture in which the individual grows up, the experiences he has undergone, and the knowledge he has been fed. The consequence of this theory is that our clean/unclean polarity is in principle the same as that of

The Cultural Basis of Physical Aversion

nineteenth-century Swedish peasants and the tribes of central New Guinea, but it finds expression in different ways. To use another metaphor, we can say that ideas of dirt and impurity are our minds' policemen; all that does not fit into our world and which is against our established laws is arrested and locked in a prison with walls built of our own ideas about taboo and dirt. Different cultures have different views of what should be arrested. As Mary Douglas says, absolute dirt does not exist—dirt is simply in the eye of the beholder (Douglas 1966:2).

An examination of one of the most socially despicable jobs in Swedish peasant society, that of the knacker (*rackare*), will exemplify the way ideas of impurity are associated with people whom we for some reason perceive as dangerous. This man looked after dead horses, flayed them, and disposed of the carcasses; in addition, he was usually called on when a horse had to be killed. He was recruited from the dregs of rural society and was considered unclean. Decent people would refuse to eat in his presence; his company was for obvious reasons avoided; and when he entered a house he was not permitted to come beyond a beam known as the "beggar's beam." He was not allowed to take communion from the same chalice as the righteous; his children were baptized at a different time and according to a different ritual (Egardt 1962).

Impurity imparted a stigma that shut him out effectively from full membership in society. The same form of exclusion affected many individuals on the periphery of peasant society. A woman of loose morals or an unmarried mother was ascribed properties that similarly made association with her impossible. Among other things it was believed that she could infect children with rickets simply by looking at them or by entering the room where they lay sleeping (Frykman 1977).

Other people such as gypsies and vagrants were viewed the same way, being considered anything from generally repugnant to directly ill-omened—but always as dirty. The common factor for all these people was that they stood outside society, either because of some crime that they had committed or because of their social or racial origin. The stamp of impurity functions here as a police force protecting the honest from the dishonest, the establishment from the outsiders.

Exactly the same social mechanisms operate today. Individuals who for one reason or another are on the fringes of our existence are classed as dirty, perhaps repulsive, often suspect. The fundamental difference is that we lack the fixed, institutionalized concept of impurity prevalent in peasant society. There is no generally held opinion that gypsies smite children with disease, or that it is dangerous to eat with an Assyrian, or that Poles are especially dirty. Yet thoughts like these smolder in many people's unconscious minds, ready to flare up if the wind blows strongly enough. Such attitudes lead to jokes that immigrants plant potatoes in their bathtubs, build saunas over the kitchen stove, store meat in the toilet, and keep goats on the balcony. Ideas about dirt commonly spice our prejudices about people who are unusual in one way or another.

Peasants lived in a feudal society with clear boundaries between different groups of people. The nobility, the clergy, the burghers, and the peasantry were God-given classes, each with its own functions. Individuals who did not fit the pattern, coming far down or at the very bottom of the social ladder, were kept at a distance as if they were ritually unclean.

Toward the end of the nineteenth century, however, the boundaries between the layers in the social world became more fluid, especially as a new class began to make its voice heard—the workers. At the same time the middle class was growing ever stronger, feeling the need to define its distinctiveness from the layers above and below in the hierarchy. The consequent increase in the exploitation of various ideas of impurity is an important part of today's culture. The ways that some of these ideas found expression in Oscarian culture, and also the way generations of children from the lower classes have been imbued with feelings of insecurity and shame, will be examined.

The Cultural Basis of Physical Aversion

People are branded as unclean because their behavior is somehow in conflict with the order that the majority is accustomed to viewing as the only correct one. An example can be taken from the current controversy over the ordination of female priests in the Church of Sweden. The vicar of a Stockholm congregation explained in a television debate that it would be impossible for him to allow a female minister to officiate in his church, since she was not permitted, according to traditional biblical teaching, to perform the offices that have been entrusted to men. It would, he said, defile his church. The norms of society are symbolized by persons. If the church can be defiled by a female minister, this fact reveals important details of the religious system that is threatened by the intruder. Impurity or dirt results from the overstepping of a boundary. This example corroborates Mary Douglas's observation that where there is dirt there is also a system (1966:35). By provoking cries of "unclean," a person who breaks a norm shows where the boundaries are drawn.

The system need not be based on religion. Earth becomes dirt when it gets on the drawing-room carpet, but not when it is in the garden plot. Unwashed saucepans are acceptable in the kitchen, on the cooker, or the drainboard, but many people would probably find it repellent to have them in the bedroom. Underpants can be neat and tidy lying in their drawer, but they take on a new meaning if they are found lying around on the sofa or the piano. As long as everything is in its place, every person where he or she should be, there is little probability that people will start thinking in categories of dirt. By classifying the world, organizing it according to the system one has learned, one sorts out the things that do not fit. Dirt is consequently the by-product of this systematic arrangement. Every act of ordering involves some things falling outside the system.

To remain for a moment in the household milieu, with the examples of the earth, the pans, and the underpants, the act of cleaning can be seen in a new and interesting light. By restoring order, which is the

Clean and Proper

goal of cleaning, we reorganize our immediate surroundings and define the world as we want to have it. Cleaning has thus both a practical side and the symbolic function of satisfying our need for a fixed point in existence. It is common to clear one's desk, get rid of the piles of papers, and put the books back in their place, to vacuum clean and dust at home, as a counter to the feelings of instability that can occasionally arise in private or working life. If only the little part of the world over which one has control is neat and tidy, this is enough to instill some security. A similar security comes from the confidence of personal cleanliness, with hair, beard, and nails well trimmed. The battle against dirt, impurity, and disorder is the classic struggle against chaos.

The Taboo Theory

By focusing on dirt it is possible to learn a lot about the system, the society, or the culture that ascribes the property of impurity to certain acts, persons, or things. It is from this observation that Edmund Leach proceeds when he shows the ways we use the concept of dirt in our way of thinking. As a covering term for dirt and the like he uses the word *taboo*. According to his theory (Leach 1964), taboo is necessary to divide verbal categories into well-defined units. To put it another way, the so-called objective reality around us is in fact subjective in the extreme. With the aid of words and a general consensus as to what they mean, we name the world, dividing it into units, deciding what should belong in each category. The categories or systems do not, of course, exist as such in the world, but only by virtue of the fact that we have named them into existence. There has to be a general consensus about what is to be called chair, table, flower, man, woman, child, rich, poor, and so on. Our categorization must also be consistent, so that we

The Cultural Basis of Physical Aversion

The natural continuity of the physical world

The physical world divided into named categories

Named "things"

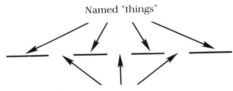

Taboo areas, "nonthings"

A schematic presentation of the taboo theory. Culture provides the discriminatory grid we impose on our world. The world is divided into named things and non-things, which are tabooed. Such things are often designated by nicknames or euphemisms, known as noa names. Based on Leach 1964; cf. Hastrup et al. 1975.

do not include in one category flowers, tables, and women, and in another category chairs, men, and old people. Chairs belong to the category of furniture, and people are distinguished from plants and dumb creatures. Shared values concerning the meaning of words and the reality they signify is a precondition for communication.

It is in this categorizing process that ideas of taboo are most useful. What falls outside the scope of a word or a category becomes taboo. The socialization of children is a good example, according to Leach. The little child has not yet learned to divide existence into the compartments established by adults, but adults will teach it the language it needs to do so. Existence is a continuum with no clear boundaries. There is at first no clear distinction between the child's own mouth

Clean and Proper

and the mother's breast, between the breast and other parts of the body, between the child himself and the world around him. The differences between mother and father, brother and sister, friend and relative are as unknown as those between books, cookies, and cigarettes. These experiences await the child.

In his discovery of the world, the child is not only assisted by his own experiences but also by the words for people and things that he learns. He is taught to see existence as composed of clearly distinguished entities, each associated with one word. The world consists of objects with different names. Things without names do not exist and are therefore tabooed. Taboo is therefore all that falls outside the established categories, all that finds no place in the system of words and concepts.

Some taboos are strong, while others are less pronounced. The strongest are those that concern the way a person draws the boundaries between the self and the world. For this reason the boundaries of the body are the focus of so many concepts of taboo. Consider, for example, all the things that belong to the body but leave it: hair that has to be cut at intervals, nails that must be kept short so as not to get ragged or troublesome. Ideas of taboo grow in intensity when it comes to things that are on the boundary between the individual and the outside world: excreta and urine, blood and sweat, saliva and mucus, breast milk and semen. These things are considered repulsive and disgusting, charged with power and danger, because they are on the boundary. As soon as they leave us we have to define them as not-us. The same applies to similar matter discharged from other people.

The next step in examining the way ideas of taboo and impurity function is to observe that what falls outside, between the categories, is especially interesting. This interest explains such things as the power that all cultures have ascribed to blood and the strong sexual symbolism of hair. People who have been branded as unclean are not just deserving of scorn, they have also been ascribed special powers.

The Cultural Basis of Physical Aversion

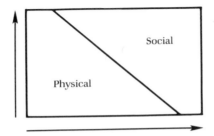

The physical body is the individual's link with nature. The social body is shaped by culture and society. Increasing social and cognitive control of the individual leads to a greater effort to discipline the physical self. The horizontal arrow in the figure shows the proportion of the physical and the social, while the vertical arrow shows the degree of social and cognitive control.

Old gypsy women knew how to cure rickets, and the same disease, often known as *horeskäver* (whore-rickets) could be cured by a drink from a whore's shoe (Frykman 1977:33). This aura of ambivalence—danger, excitement, and remarkable powers—can still be seen today. In a heterosexual culture, there is an excitement about homosexuality; particularly exciting is lesbianism, since women are considered the proper sexual object of those who dominate our society—the men.

It may be said as a general rule that the stronger the sense of taboo and the stronger the feelings of revulsion and nausea, the greater will be the degree of dirt and impurity that people perceive, permitting a clearer view of the fundamental values of the culture and the society. Some of these taboos concern relations to animals and nature. For example, spiders, insects, and rats are terrifying for people who have grown accustomed to viewing nature as a place of recreation inhabited by friendly and useful creatures. Other taboos concern our role as social beings.

Clean and Proper

The Body as a Bridge

Right from infancy we learn the importance of distinguishing us from not-us. One way to make such a distinction is to taboo physical functions, excretion, perspiration, and sensations.

This demarcation, however, does not have the same importance in every context. It goes without saying that we feel freer within the bounds of the family than outside. It is possible at a pinch to use one's spouse's toothbrush, but the thought of using a workmate's toothbrush is somewhat distasteful. It may be all right at home to belch after a meal—or at least it is allowed to pass with a giggle and a mild protest—but in public it would be extremely embarrassing. The same is even more true of other natural sounds that are harder to conceal.

Physical intimacy, together with an escape from the morality and etiquette police who patrol public life, makes life at home less demanding, but in public and when entertaining, the body has to behave itself according to the rules of good breeding. The boundary between home and the outside world is marked by the reduced number of taboos and by the slighter risk of reactions of disgust and impurity.

The home has its due place in the prevailing social hierarchy. There is a difference in the degree of the liberties one can take at home, depending on whether one lives in a castle or a cabin. The degree of bodily control depends on the social position a person is born into and on the culture of the class in question. It is therefore possible to make the somewhat oversimplified statement that the picture of the body and how it functions is a reflection of society. A sufficiently penetrating analysis allows us to trace our view of our bodies back to social factors.

The higher up the social scale a person climbs, and the more he feels himself to be in the grip of society, the tougher the control he will have to exert over his own body. This principle is described by Mary Douglas as the "purity rule," the rule of distance from physical origin (1973:12).

Which members of society are forced to behave most strictly, to bear

The Cultural Basis of Physical Aversion

themselves with the greatest self-control, to modulate their speech most carefully, to restrain their laughter so that they do not sound silly and vulgar? Who chooses his words with the same solicitude as he selects a hat or a necktie, and knows how to behave at table in the company of other people? Who can communicate by speech and gestures the fact that he has succeeded in bridling the coarser side of his nature and has learned how to conduct himself in a cultured way?

These questions cannot be answered by pointing to any particular group. Instead, the need for such control grows in proportion to the height at which an individual stands on the social ladder. Yet the increase of control does not follow a linear progression; a person who has a confident mastery of the social codes may show his status by ignoring the rules of etiquette.

This self-control is internalized during the period of primary socialization, in other words, during the first years of a person's life. It seldom happens as a direct and conscious process perceptible to the intellect, instead proceeding via control of the body. That is one reason why class differences are so clearly perceived—they sit in the backbone.

Ideas of impurity defend the status quo. People who cannot master the life-style of self-control, those who have not learned the code, risk ridicule and ostracism. Scorn from above and shame from below guard the social boundaries on either side. For the sake of clarity, it should be added that this does not mean that the stratification of society is a result of these taboos. Their role is to defend what already exists. An individual's position on the social ladder depends, of course, primarily on economic factors.

It is important to be aware of the subtle indoctrination that is a part of the interplay of body and society. Society gives us a picture of the body, which in turn reinforces our view of society:

> The social body constrains the way the physical body is perceived. The physical experience of the body, always modified

Clean and Proper

by the social categories through which it is known, sustains a particular view of society. There is a continual exchange of meanings between the two kinds of bodily experience so that each reinforces the categories of the other. As a result of this interaction the body itself is a highly restricted medium of expression. The forms it adopts in movement and repose express social pressures in manifold ways. The care that is given to it, in grooming, feeding and therapy, the theories about what it needs in the way of sleep and exercise, about the stages it should go through, the pains it can stand, its span of life, all the cultural categories in which it is perceived, must correlate closely with the categories in which society is seen in so far as these also draw upon the same culturally processed idea of the body.   (Douglas 1973:93)

Nature and Culture

Rules of cleanliness have a simple message: they are concerned with the triumph of culture over nature. This way of thinking permeates all societies and can be recognized directly by every individual.

Mankind sets as the goal of his existence the mastery of nature, which provides the external framework of existence—birth and death. We try to create order in nature by forcing our way of thinking onto it. The Linnaean botanical taxonomy is a fine example of this effort. Order is a creation of culture. We try to influence it directly by ritual and religious practices.

To bring up children is to transform them from their natural animality to the stage of cultured humanity. The taming process includes getting them to stop behaving like animals. They have to be trained not to slobber, burp, fart, or gobble their food.

The Cultural Basis of Physical Aversion

In better homes in the old days, children could not eat at the same table as the adults until they had been trained to eat with the skill demanded of a civilized being, which was usually accomplished by the age of seven. Before that they had to eat with the servants.

Just as children were subordinate to adults, so people closer to nature were subordinate to those who were more civilized, or cultured. This authoritarian relationship between culture—manmade—and nature has been used to explain the worldwide subordination of women to men.

Women's physical functions have made men view them as the sex that is closer to nature. Through her body, woman is bound to the reproduction of the species; each menstrual cycle is a reminder of her biological self; the birth and suckling of each child is a link between her and nature. The man's role in the biological process of propagating the species is only transitory. It is generally the woman who performs the transformations between nature and culture. She transforms raw material into food, rears children to human beings, and cleans away traces of nature's disorder in the home. She is defined as more emotional and more "natural" than men, and so forth. This transitional position occupied by woman as an intermediary between nature and culture can, according to anthropologist Sherry Ortner, explain her role as the second sex (Ortner 1974).[2]

Woman's role also serves to show the authoritarian relationship between nature and culture. People who behave in a "cultured" way have a better position in society than those who appear more "natural." By taming the animal within—emotions, organic functions, sexuality—a person becomes cultured.

Peasant Views of Purity and Dirt

It is difficult to free oneself from the conviction that the ideal of cleanliness that grew up during the nineteenth century was rational. The past hundred years not only saw technological and economic revolutions but also witnessed breakthroughs in hygiene and medicine. Doctors and public health boards managed to combat many of the epidemic diseases that had previously led to permanent invalidity or premature death. Many of these diseases were the direct result of insufficient personal hygiene and the general dirt of the environment.

The elimination of tuberculosis is a clear example of the achievements of enlightenment and hygiene. It used to be the practice among workers and peasants to bring children up on "chews" from the mother. She would first chew the food and mix it carefully with her saliva before giving it to the child. If she herself was infected with tubercles, which was not unusual in the poor living conditions of the day, then the child also received a dose of the bacteria. Informing the mother of the mechanism by which infection spread was enough to save the lives of the children at least. Tuberculosis was eliminated by means of better living standards, regular washing, and intensified medical control. Today the disease is rare to the point of extinction.

It is, however, too simple to believe that ideas of cleanliness were nothing but a result of increased knowledge about the origins of disease. It is also too simple to believe that the war against bacteria was waged solely for medical motives. At issue is rather a question of a profound distinction between the way peasantry and bourgeoisie,

Peasant Views of Purity and Dirt

workers and professors categorized the world and drew the boundaries between themselves and others.

It is important first to examine the social position of those who represented the various cultures, and how this influenced the way they
drew boundaries according to the clean/unclean principle. The current view is that the peasantry were filthy and the bourgeoisie were
clean. This view is well attested in all sorts of value judgments as well
as in more sober and objective descriptions. The eighteenth-century
academic Pehr Högström, dean of Skellefteå, could observe that the
upper and lower classes "smell equally bad to each other" (Wikmark
1979:285). The upper classes of the nineteenth century, geared toward
reform and progress, took a different view. In 1850 the Norwegian
Eilert Sundt wrote that the dirtiness of the lower peasantry was in-
jurious to good morals and deepened the gulf between higher and
lower classes, "because a person used to better circumstances will not
willingly tarry in a dirty house among its filthy inhabitants" (Sundt
[1869]1975:25).

Cleanliness was thus a moral problem, an obstacle to equality and
improvement. The same attitude is evident almost a century later,
when Ludvig Nordström made his celebrated tour of Sweden in search
of remains of filth in the countryside, with a view to dealing it the coup
de grâce. The year was 1938, during the tricentennial celebrations of
the colonization of New Sweden (now Delaware). He found Sweden
civilized but with a few blemishes:

> The lovely spring sun shone on the fresh, dancing, green
> grass and on the singing pink and white blossoms of the fruit
> trees, the sea spread out in what seemed like an infinity of the
> National Bank's latest tricentennial silver coins all the way to
> America, in what I took to be a celebration of our wealth, our
> model society, our model people, our model system. The
> whole of nature was like one huge Delaware celebration.

Clean and Proper

There in the center of it all, like the dot on the *i*, was the modern housing for industrial workers. A bright sunshine of white houses in functionalist style. Paneled porches, studies and living rooms with large windows admitting the entire light of the world, the blue sky and the scent of flowers and the glitter of the sea; water closets, central heating, stainless steel sinks, everything. Bedrooms on the second floor. A villa to suit a director general.

I saw it there. I found what I was looking for. The answer. There was the crux of the distinction between Sweden-the-civilized and Sweden-the-filthy. What was it? The answer is that off the kitchen was a little room, a dining room, a work-room, a general-purpose room.

And—it—stank! It—stank!!

This was the last trace of Sweden-the-filthy. The way from Sweden-the-filthy to the civilized Sweden of the future passed through the so-called best room of the poor, which was to be a charter of nobility for the democratic workers' state. Sweden's working class was to be ennobled by passing through here.

This was to be a nobility not based on birth or wealth, but on one thing alone, which was to be strong enough to tear down for all time the old walls separating the classes: *cleanliness, absolute cleanliness.*

When this foul-smelling room off the kitchen has disappeared forever, only then will Sweden-the-filthy be a memory, for only then will Sweden-the-civilized have won its final victory and achieved its final goal. (Nordström 1938:172f.)

Cleanliness brought liberation. The way from the old Sweden with its class distinctions to the new classless society could also be described as the road that led away from dirt. One of the most important

Peasant Views of Purity and Dirt

steps in civilizing Swedish peasants and workers was to arouse in them the insight that they lived in filth and lacked proper standards of personal hygiene.

Now that the results of a century of training in cleanliness are visible, it is possible to be wise after the event, querying what was once considered self-evident. Medical experts are beginning to talk about diminished resistance to disease as a consequence of reduced exposure to bacteria. The Swedish National Board for Consumer Policies, in a booklet entitled "Clean at Any Price?" (Konsumentverket 1978), has appealed to people to cut down on the cleaning, pointing out that it takes a lot of dirt to constitute a health risk. It cannot be taken for granted that clean and tidy homes are happy homes. In the sphere of personal hygiene it is beginning to be accepted that people can smell like people, whereas until recently it was considered best not to smell at all, or to smell "nicely" of deodorant, body lotion, or toothpaste. It may now be possible to look back at Sweden-the-filthy and its dirty peasants with less emotion and disgust than previous generations of Swedes could.

It is necessary to look quite a long way back in time to get an idea of how peasants viewed themselves and their environment, how they divided up things, persons, and activities according to their degree of cleanliness. During the nineteenth century, people in the countryside were exposed to a systematic barrage of propaganda aiming to teach them better morals and hygiene, to bring them up to be citizens pure in word, thought, and deed. This message came from the schools, the social organizations, and the mass media. Additionally, more and more country people had firsthand contact with the living conditions and the hygiene institutions of the towns. The message of cleanliness was broadcast in an environment where it could take root and grow to strength. Social differentiation in the countryside enabled many to see themselves as closer to the better people of the towns than to their rural neighbors.

Clean and Proper

To find out how things were when the older view of cleanliness still prevailed, an environment must be sought in which the class differences between those with and those without property were still small and in which class boundaries had not been drawn or reinforced according to new criteria of cleanliness. Fortunately, some such archaic areas still survived to the beginning of this century, providing much of the material on which our knowledge is based.

For the sake of simplification, the many regional differences may be smoothed away. (Peasants in Skåne in the south and Jämtland in the north were radically different in these matters, as in many others; farmers and fishermen in the same coastal tracts often had widely differing views of dirt, in particular of the dirtiness of the other group.) Since, however, the focus here is more on principles than on precise ethnographic description, this representation of peasant culture will be very rough-hewn. The idea is to show the fundamental differences between two cultures by sharpening the contrast between them.

The 1970 edition of *Fataburen*, the yearbook of the Nordic Museum in Stockholm, with the unconventional and therefore valuable theme of Sweden-the-filthy, contains many useful accounts for present purposes. Another excellent description comes from Levi Johansson's narrative of life in the old days in his home of Frostviken in Jämtland (1927). His unabashed directness makes the account unique. That it happens to be the peasantry of Jämtland who are exposed might make one suspect that people there were filthier than elsewhere in Sweden, but this is not the case. It seems on the contrary as if dirtiness increases the further south one travels. In Skåne, a stratified and feudal province, conditions seem to have been worst. The farms of Skåne "were whited sepulchers, concealing all manner of filth," observed Ludvig Nordström (1938:164). Jämtland, by contrast, is well known for its social homogeneity, which probably made it a better seedbed for cleaner living standards.

Peasant Views of Purity and Dirt

Man and Beast

Animals were a means of agricultural production. From them came meat and milk; oxen and horses provided the power needed to cultivate the earth. Farmers lived close to their animals both in the physical sense and in a symbolic sense. Animals were useful, they were the resource that was essential for producing food from the earth.

Peasants from the old days would be amazed at the modern farmer. He may live off his animals, but he certainly does not live with them. To avoid getting the smell of the barn on his clothes, the Swedish farmer of today pulls on his nylon overalls, protects his hair with a peaked cap, and wears wooden clogs. He has one set of clothes for his dirty, manure-smelling jobs, another for inside the house. Ritual changes of clothing such as this underline the difference between man and beast. Eighteenth-century peasants wore the same clothes in the house and in the barn. At that time it was mostly the women who did the milking and mucked out the cowshed. To avoid getting dirty they might hitch up their skirts, but it would have provoked ridicule to give themselves airs by wearing special clothes around the animals. People wore the same shoes all the time, if they had shoes at all; it was cheaper to go barefoot. A girl saved her shoes for dancing and churchgoing.

Today's self-evident practice of distinguishing the dwelling house from the barn would have seemed strangely impractical to farmers a century ago. The advantages of living near the barn were obvious. It saved a lot of walking and capitalized on the warmth from the cows' stalls. The nuisance of living near the smell from the manure was of little importance. Manure was a source of prosperity, not of pollution.

Traditional architecture in Skåne built the farm around a square courtyard, which functioned as an animal pen. People coming to the dwelling house had to cross the yard, across which cows were driven in and out every morning and evening. In the middle of the yard stood

Clean and Proper

the pride of the farm—the dungheap. The farmer could observe it with the satisfaction of knowing that it ensured good harvests in the future.

The stableboy also slept with the animals in Skåne. Winter and summer alike he slept in a stall beside the horses, with the additional possibility in the summer of sleeping in the hay. In the winter the heat of the horses was necessary to keep the sleeping place from freezing.

In central and northern Sweden, north of the Dalälven river, it was also the custom for the young to sleep out in the barn. Sleeping in the barn was considered neither an unpleasant necessity nor a banishment to a dirtier part of the farm. It was in fact preferable to the stuffiness of the house. Under the ceiling there was a shelf wide enough to lie on. It could be warm enough, especially if there was a fireplace in the barn. Not the least attraction of this sleeping place was that it gave the young people a degree of freedom that they would not have had in the house with their elders. There was nobody to ensure that they went to bed early, nobody to check what they were up to. It was in this part of the country that the practice of night courtship, bundling (sleeping together fully clothed), persisted longest. Boys and girls had greater freedom to get to know one another on the shelf in the barn than they had in the house.[1]

In Dalarna the barn was used for linen spinning. Anders Nyman has given examples of how they were the scene of "sitting-up evenings," which rotated round the various farms in the village. The women came with their spinning wheels under their arms and passed the evening in work and conversation. The barn was carefully cleaned and decorated for the occasion (Nyman 1970:146). If people could sleep with the animals at night and work with them during the day, there was no reason not to perform certain household tasks in the barn.

The farmer was concerned for the safety of his animals, protecting them from any kind of danger that might threaten them. Danger did not, however, include the dirt surrounding the animals. This caution

Peasant Views of Purity and Dirt

about the world outside the barn and the farmstead must be contrasted with the physical neglect that affected cattle in particular. A
dead snake could be buried at the threshold of the barn to protect the
cows inside from evil forces. A dead bird could be set up over the door
to frighten off the night-mare. People who were believed to have the evil
eye, such as gypsies and knackers, were totally banned from the building, since it was thought that they could steal the beasts' courage, dry
up their milk, or make them sick. When the animals were let out in the
spring they had to pass over a sharp iron edge to be able to withstand
harm from supernatural forces or envious neighbors.

On the other hand, grooming cows would have been regarded as a
complete waste of time. In the winter, when the animals were confined and badly fed, when they could not keep themselves clean, they
became shaggy, ridden with vermin and filth, their udders encrusted
with dung, but they were not cleaned (Szabó 1970a:164). The relationship between man and beast was based mainly on utility; there was no
clear boundary that made people view animals as especially dirty, or
to view their excrement as impure. People were less concerned with
protecting them from dirt than from the threat of magic and the evil
influences of nature or neighbors. From the peasant's point of view,
fear of the supernatural was more rational than fear of bacteria and
dirt. Using old-fashioned value judgments, it would be possible to talk
here of the difference between superstition and knowledge.

To claim that the boundaries drawn between nature and culture explain why people were unconcerned about the dirtiness of the cows
may seem overtheoretical. It might be thought obvious that if people
were dirty themselves, they would not be worried about whether their
animals were dirty. To show that the argument is nevertheless sound,
one must only look at the care with which horses on the farm were
looked after. People did not live off horses in the same way as they did
off cows, sheep, and goats. Their meat was not eaten—it was taboo
—and those who slaughtered horses and handled their bodies were

outcasts (Egardt 1962). Horsemilk is no part of the Swedish peasant diet. Horses worked, pulling the plough and the haycart out in the fields, but they were also used for public representation, being harnessed to drive to church or into town to shop. Horses were associated with the men, cows with the women. Horses belonged to the public sphere, shown off with pride to the neighbors. Cows, however, were a part of the private sphere of home, the women's world.

One consequence of the position of the horse, closer to culture than to nature, was that it was carefully groomed and fed the best hay.

> The possession of a well-groomed horse was something of a status symbol. Horses were given the best fodder, though they were not as useful as milch cows. The horse got the best meadow hay, while the cow was given sedgy hay or bog hay, or even had to content herself with straw, foliage, or other surrogate fodder. This differentiation of the value of the animals could also be observed in the way they were cared for. "A good grooming is half the horse's fodder," says an old proverb, known throughout Sweden and elsewhere in Europe. A well-groomed horse was a credit to a farmer, especially when driving to church or on other ceremonious journeys. The horse was expected to shine, immaculately clean and healthy. (Szabó 1970a:156)

The difference in the care of horses and cows epitomizes the peasant's attitude to cleanliness. The more utilitarian the relationship with the animals—in other words, the closer they were to nature—the less effort was expended on their care. The more publicity, prestige, and culture associated with the animals, the more important it was to keep them clean. The difference between the well-groomed horse and the shaggy cow is an interesting expression of this distinction.

Sharp boundaries between man and beast were first drawn when

Peasant Views of Purity and Dirt

animals were taken out of production. This happened relatively late in bourgeois culture. Many eighteenth-century town dwellers, in order to maintain a living, had to have a farm in the town to keep them supplied with pigs, cows, horses, and poultry. This group was known as *åkerborgare*, meaning roughly "farmer–burghers." During the nineteenth century, however, as the bourgeoisie became further removed from this business, they started to develop an interest in the things that made people different from animals; they began to erect barriers, in the shape of ideas of dirt, between what was human and civilized and what was animal and close to nature. (Compare the discussion in chapter 2, under "Our Animal Friends.")

Indoors

The dwelling house was not just for people; it also served as a shelter and a breeding house for numerous smaller farm animals. This intimacy between people and domestic animals occurred of course at an earlier stage than the practice of building special barns for animals.

The first good description extant of the way peasants lived in Sweden comes from the sixteenth century. It was written by a German merchant, Samuel Kiechel, from Ulm. He traveled during the winter and spring of 1586 through the south of Sweden to Stockholm and Uppsala. He has left such a remarkable account of the peasant farm milieu that he deserves to be quoted at length. On the journey up from Helsingborg he spent the night at "Ruy" in northern Skåne, where he observed the following interior:

> When it was time to go to sleep, we made our beds on the
> floor; in the wintertime it is not only the men with their wives
> and children who sleep in the house, but also dogs and cats,

Clean and Proper

as well as young livestock like lambs, calves, goats and pigeons, and most unpleasant of all, young pigs, who give off a
strong smell and generally lie in the middle of the room,
come up and lick people's faces in the night, with the result
that for a negligible fee the appetite is sated with nasty smells
and tastes faster than by the best of dinners.   (Kiechel
1866:58)

On the return journey south, he had another opportunity to renew his
acquaintance with this way of living. Before he left Sweden, he collected the following impressions:

To begin with, the houses are usually built square, of unhewn
logs jointed at the corners, only one story high, the roof
monotonously covered with logs. As for the interior, there is
no boarding inside the rooms, the spaces between the posts
or beams instead being filled with mud or cow dung. The
roofs are generally thatched with turf, upon which sheep and
goats get some of their summer grazing, and the underside of
the roof is the only ceiling in the room. They usually have in
the room no more than a single little window or skylight, half
an ell square, covered with parchment or glass. They do not
have any other windows. The doors into the rooms are so low
that one must bend low to come in. At the same time, the
thresholds are so high that it is not easy to get over them, like
getting into a byre. This is because of the young domestic animals (about which more later).
   Furthermore, in the house they have a table, usually as
long as the house is broad. In the winter this room serves as
kitchen, bedchamber, and everything to do with the household, and instead of a fireplace they have an oven; a big fire is
lit here some three hours before daylight, so that this room is

Peasant Views of Purity and Dirt

so warm the whole day that the woman of the house, along with the children and the servants who have nothing to do out in the cold, go around the whole winter in nothing but their linen chemises, even if it is so cold outside that the animals freeze in their stalls.

As for sleeping, every person has his own place: there is usually a sleeping place beside the table, with some few bedclothes but mostly made up of straw. This is for the farmer and his wife. Around the oven, where it is nice and warm, sleep the children: those so young that they still need to sleep in a cradle are laid in a little round-bottomed chest made of a hollowed-out log: this chest is suspended by a rope from a beam, hanging about an ell over the floor, where it swings to and fro. On the benches, which are covered with straw, sleep the farmhands and maids, guests sleep on the floor; but if the hosts wish to show them special favor, they are allowed to sleep on the table.

As for the young animals, apart from dogs, cats, hens, and pigeons, which do not matter so much, they also keep in the room with them calves, lambs, goats, and even young pigs. . . .

Furthermore, the master of the house is generally the first to seat himself to dinner, at the head of the table, his wife at his side, and he may during the meal emit a strong belch, or sometimes a succession of such, as do his wife and children. I believe it is intended to amuse guests instead of talking to them; if a visitor has brought food and drink for himself and enough to treat his host, he is welcome; moreover, the peasants know to ask guests for nutmeg, cinnamon, cloves, ginger, and such things; but it is rarely possible to extract anything from them, even for money. The drinking vessels which they set on the table consist of a large broad wooden dish or bowl which it takes two hands to lift.

Clean and Proper

> As for the women, they are by nature beautiful, slender, and white-skinned, and keep their clothes clean, tidy and noble; I believe they often wear the same chemise for a quarter of a year. Otherwise in their innate morals, virtue, and beauty they are not unlike gypsy women. This applies to the peasantry, who live here and there in the forests and wilderness and never go anywhere else; for the rest, the towns are not without their beautiful women.   (Kiechel 1866:81ff.)

Samuel Kiechel is describing the living conditions of a sixteenth-century culture that drew the boundaries between the physical and the cultural according to principles other than those he was accustomed to, and definitely different from those that apply today. Such living conditions as these persisted largely unchanged until the beginning of the eighteenth century. Dean Öller describes how the parishioners of Jämshög in Blekinge rear pigs in the house, "which is rather unpleasant in view of the stench and dirt they occasion" (Öller 1800:120). Kids, lambs, hens, and calves also shared the dwelling house with the people. The custom of keeping the animals indoors was due as much to economy as to tradition. "He who scorns the pig dung smell, can live without the pork as well," was a proverb recorded from Skåne in the 1770s by the dean of Bara (Lönqvist 1924:6). It appears to have been the rule to have animals indoors, from Skåne in the south to Lappland in the north. Exceptions grow in number, however, during the nineteenth century, and toward the end of the century the practice is rare. It survived longest in the poorer section of the population, who had inferior buildings for both people and animals.

Cohabitation with animals also had a regional aspect. It was most common in the area where Kiechel had encountered it in his day: southern Sweden. In northern and central Sweden, various factors made people more anxious to keep man and beast separate.[2]

Cleaning the House

Cleaning is a creative act. To begin with, by keeping chairs, tables, walls, and floors clean, one defines how they are to look. Clean objects are those that bear no trace of other activities and do not reveal any failure to keep categories separate. Dust and soot and dirt give us endless opportunity to create order from chaos. Cleaning also means putting everything in its place, organizing things in the right relation to one another. However clean things might be, they must still be arranged in culturally meaningful patterns (Douglas 1966:2).

For bourgeois culture at the turn of the century, dusting, sweeping, and washing up were part of the daily household ritual. But the farmer's wife in the first half of the nineteenth century was scarcely interested in waging an active war against dirt. To begin with, she lacked the necessary motivation. Dirt was everywhere, with the animals and on the people. It was a part of everyday life, not viewed as any threat. In any case, the farmer's wife had other things to occupy her than the role of housewife. She was needed for the economy of the farm, with labor being her prime function. If the farm happened to be large enough to need and support female servants, they were needed for work in the barn and the fields and sometimes also for household duties. Their primary duty was to help in the production of the necessities of life, not to look after the appearance of the surroundings.

To make the household function, it was essential to keep everything in its right place, but the house was cleaned very rarely. This was not due to laziness, for the women's day was full of household tasks, but to lack of interest. The house was the place where food was cooked, where people ate and slept, where animals ran around on the floor, and where children played. During the winter it was also the setting for the work that had to be done. In the evenings they sat around the fire doing by its light any jobs that could be done indoors.

Clean and Proper

The floor was cleaned only for the two great holidays of the year, Christmas and Midsummer (Sjöqvist 1970). The dirt between the floorboards was important for insulation—it reduced floor draft. Levi Johansson relates the following from a wintry Jämtland:

> It happened once on a farm in Jorm that the mother felt induced "to wash off the room floor," although it was in the chill of winter. She was expecting visitors and thought that the floor looked rather too grubby. When she had finished the job the old man from the neighboring farm came along. When he saw the new-cleaned floor his face took on a highly worried expression and he said: "Now you've done it! You can be sure that you'll have a cold floor from now on." The dirt that had filled the cracks in the boardless floor was now gone.
> (Johansson 1927:133f.)

Cleaning the house meant hard work, not just day-to-day fussing about dust. Cleaning was part of a larger program intended to transform it from its everyday to its festive appearance. The walls were decorated for Christmas, proclaiming the holiness of the season. In southern Sweden this transformation took the form of the entire inside of the house—ceiling and walls—being draped with woven cloths and painted hangings. A whole school of southern Swedish painters catered to this need to dress up the house for the Christmas holiday. Biblical motifs were hung up, and the holy season showed its presence in every way in the dwelling.[3]

The cleaning of the peasant house had a practical goal, but it was above all intended to mark a break in the weekly routines and an interruption of profane time (Leach 1961:134). Keeping the house clean was not a hygienic but a practical and ritual act. When cleaning later became a more regular occurrence, it was still a weekend task. The house had to be well swept and tidy for Sunday.

Attitudes to the Body

To describe the way the peasant viewed the body is also to describe the role of the body in the society of the day and thus to expose the peasant world view. Central values in the peasant's life and work are revealed by important properties such as physical strength, endurance, the ability to ignore minor pains and injuries. Every theory that people have about their own and other people's bodies also includes a social dimension: it is a more-or-less obscure reflection of society. Ideas about what the body can endure, how it gets ill and can be healed, how it should be cared for through exercise and hygiene — these ideas are filtered through the individual's social experience (Douglas 1973:93).

How did the peasant view the organic processes of the body, the familiar signs of physical life? Kiechel's belching host suggests that the attitude to the physical was fairly free in this environment. But how free?

The simple message of the purity rule is that, the more an individual seeks to bridle himself, his feelings, and his body, the more firmly he is held in the grip of society. If he feels that he is in a closed, formal situation, or if his position in society is restricted, exposed, or under threat, then he becomes anxious to define his boundaries clearly. Personal cleanliness is a well-known and much-used way to satisfy this need to keep categories apart and mark boundaries clearly.

Today it goes without saying that cleanliness goes hand in hand with hygiene. Peasants of the nineteenth century could hardly conceive that it might be dangerous not to wash. To go straight from the barn to the dinner table caused no sense of revulsion, at least not for hygienic reasons. People went around with visible traces of their work on their clothes and bodies. Fishwives smelled of fish and farmers smelled of the cowshed. Dirt was even viewed as something positive. It

Clean and Proper

was good to be dirty. Not washing too often meant that you did not feel the cold so easily; dirt and secretions afforded the body extra protection. The farmer knew that dirt gave life. A saying recorded from Västergötland goes: "A farmer's hand should be so dirty that if you put a seed in it, it will grow" (Eriksson 1970:10).

Country people thus displayed constant signs of their work, dirt that could be smelled and seen, revealing in unmistakable and undisguised forms the physical life of the body. There was little of the modern fear of bad breath, body odor, or the smell of dirty clothes, and little need was felt to wash in order to remove traces of the animal in man—to conceal or eradicate smells or exudations suggesting an organic life. The distance between the physical self and the social self was not strongly marked.

For the peasant, washing the body had a ritual character. Men, women, and children washed for particular occasions—but not because of the dictates of hygiene. "People washed as a rule only once a week, on Saturday [for which the Swedish is *lördag* 'bathday'], or on Sunday morning before going to church," writes Marianne Eriksson. "Anyone who washed more often could be considered haughty. As a rule it was only face, hands, and arms, neck and ears that were washed, rarely the genitals and feet" (Eriksson 1970:10).

Only the visible parts of the body were washed, and only for those occasions when one appeared in public. The same principle that we saw in the house recurs here: cleaning up for holy days. The explanation lies partly in the peasants' perception of time and the rhythm of their working week. Eilert Sundt has observed in his description of the state of cleanliness among the country people of mid-nineteenth-century Norway that the week constituted a single working "shift." During this shift the same working clothes were worn, clothes that were seldom cleaned, to be removed on Saturday evening, when people washed and put on their Sunday best (Sundt [1869]1975:290). The same applied to the rural people of Sweden. The following account il-

Peasant Views of Purity and Dirt

lustrates the fixity of the view that washing served to distinguish everyday life from holy days:

> In the 1890s there were still many who considered it almost
> crazy to wash more than once a week. An elderly man who
> had become more than usually sweaty from mowing a boggy
> meadow was urged by his daughter to take off his clothes and
> wash. He exclaimed in surprise and indignation: "What on
> earth! Wash in the middle of the week! How is a man sup-
> posed to know when it's Sunday?" So he refused to wash.
> (Johansson 1927:122)

Christmas brought ritual ways of marking the holy season through
cleanliness. In addition to sweeping and decorating the house for
Christmas, people too had to be newly washed, taking their Christmas
bath whether they needed it or not, as the saying went.

Samuel Ödmann has left a classic description of this Christmas bath
from Vislanda rectory in the eighteenth century:

> At two o'clock in the afternoon the bathhouse was heated up
> with birchwood, making a real Finnish sauna. The farmhands
> bathed in the first heat, which was considered less whole-
> some. Then came the dean with his curate and myself. We
> took off all our clothes, which we laid outside the door in the
> open air. Each of us took a bench as close to the heat as he
> found bearable. Pails of cold water were poured on the red-
> hot oven, which gave off a boiling hot steam, compared to
> which the fiercest sirocco would appear as a refreshing
> breeze. After a few minutes the naked bodies stretched out
> on the bare boards began to sweat profusely. Then each of
> the bathers was given a leafy birch branch dipped in luke-
> warm water, which he then proceeded to scourge himself

Clean and Proper

with more furiously than a Capuchin friar, until the skin became as red-hot as a boiled lobster. Then we stepped down
and sat on a board, where a lad set about washing us from
head to foot with his barbaric hands, and finished by pouring
a dipper of warm water over our heads. This was thus no
Turkish bath with its celebrated soothing and pleasant sensations, but literally a bath *à la tatar*. Finally, our clothes were
brought in from the cold, which was often some twelve to sixteen degrees [Celsius], and we put them on with not the
slightest displeasure. We returned home to made-up beds, in
which we lay with our clothes on. The after-effect was a slight
perspiration, which was refreshed with old March-beer,
sweetened with honey and spiced with aniseed, consumed
with crumbled Yule bread. Finally, the daughters and servant
girls bathed in the same way.   (Ödmann [1830] 1957:21f.)

When it comes to the customs of the people, Ödmann stresses the exotic rather than the everyday. A sauna bath before Christmas was not a
widespread practice. Saunas had been common in the towns during
the Middle Ages, but they had disappeared when they were seen as
sources of venereal infection. Saunas appear to have been common in
the countryside only in areas of Finnish settlement. Sauna bathing has
a medieval character, writes Ilmar Talve, but it is doubtful whether the
sauna was a normal mode of bathing. The usual Christmas bath was
probably in a wooden bathtub (Talve 1970:58f.).

The order of precedence at the Christmas bath in Vislanda shows
how the boundaries were drawn in the household. The first to go into
the dangerous heat were the farmhands, followed by the dean, his cu-
rate, and Samuel Ödmann, a student and relative of the family. Women
and maids bathed last. The ministers of the Word are scrubbed by
barbarous hands before it is time for them to go to bed—with their
clothes on.

Peasant Views of Purity and Dirt

Such distinctions according to sex and rank were also customary in Norwegian bathing, according to Eilert Sundt. He describes the practice from Søndfjord, where bathtubs were the rule. People bathed in order of age and dignity, first the master of the house and last the servants. For the initial washing, which included washing and combing the hair, the women helped the men who were at the same level in the household as themselves: mistress helped master, sister helped brother, maid helped farmhand. When climbing into the bathtub, the boundaries between people were not so strictly drawn as to necessitate changing water. The water must have become rather dirty, especially if a year had passed since the last general wash (Sundt [1869]1975:318). However, it obviously did not appear in any way strange to use the same water as other members of the household with whom one was in close contact during the remaining 364 days of the year. An interesting question is whether the Christmas bath could be stretched to include people from outside the household. Where were the boundaries dividing people who could and people who could not share the same tub and bathwater? All the extant descriptions refer only to bathing by household, but the available information is not very plentiful.

Eilert Sundt described the strictly private bath. One by one the members of the household went into the bathhouse to wash. This suggests that the well-known intimacy did not go so far that people were not modest about their own bodies. Total nudity was in fact considered particularly shameful. "Not even husband and wife appeared naked before one another," says Levi Johansson. This modesty was the reason why people in Frostviken bathed one by one out in the cowshed, not in the house, where it was harder to hide from other people (Johansson 1927:122).

For peasants, washing the body was a way to show where the boundary between the physical and the social was drawn. Cleanliness was not an everyday concern. Personal dirt was no enemy to be constantly

Clean and Proper

fought, so other people's dirt was not easily recognized. For everyday work it was permitted to reveal that one also had a physical self. The dirt that work left on the body and the clothes could sit there until a holy day came around.

For most people, holy days were a time for socializing and also sacred days of rest. The parish church was a place to hear the latest news, meet friends, arrange marriages, and conduct business. The boundary between everyday and holy day was the boundary between the private and the public. The need to appear clean was naturally greatest in the public sphere.

Exudations

In my native area of Kind, Västergötland, they had ... a board in the wall until recent times. My cousin Eskil Ollonmark, born in the parish of Örsås, Kind hundred, has told me how he met Emma Andersson of Böttnebo in the parish of Ambjörnarp in 1953. He had brought up the subject of an eccentric old man called Kalle of Älvshult, whose proper name was Karl Andersson, born in 1818 in Älvshult, where he had spent his life and, despite poverty and hardship, reached the great age of almost one hundred years. When asked if she remembered him, she replied: "Sure I remember the ugly old fellow, sitting there on his board." It was evidently not considered disturbing or embarrassing that the board was visible to the neighbors when the old man was obeying the call of nature. (Tilander 1968:16f.)

Gunnar Tilander, in the popular work from which this is quoted, has given us many examples of the principle of publicity that governed ru-

Peasant Views of Purity and Dirt

ral toilets in the old days. The needs of nature were discharged without a second thought on the dunghill, in the cowshed, or sitting on a board protruding from the wall of the house or between two buildings. As natural as these facilities were in the peasant's view, they appeared repulsive to visitors from the bourgeois or the academic worlds, who refused to use the plank which was good enough for the people on the farm.

For an observer like Ludvig Nordström, these filthy toilet habits decisively distinguished country people from civilized human beings. The board in the wall was for him a symbol of an inferior life-style forced upon the oppressed lower classes, associated with social unfitness, poverty, and moral laxity. He has left the following picture from a fishing community in western Blekinge:

"The most remarkable thing here are the toilets!" said the chairman of the sanitation committee.

"In what way?" I asked.

"Well, you just can't use them."

"Why not?"

"You can't, you daren't sit down there. As you know yourself, there are three sorts of toilet in Sweden: the W.C., the B.C., and the B.W.—the Water Closet, the traditional Backyard Closet, and the Board in the Wall."

"Which is it here?"

"The B.W. To be more exact, a single teetering plank, which is smeared so badly that no civilized person would risk sitting on it. Yet I've seen it used by young girls in high-heeled shoes, powdered and made up, with silk stockings and silk blouses! And then they go off dancing. I'd like to know how they behave——?"

"In both places, you mean?"

"Well, we know how they behave on the dance floor. We

Clean and Proper

hear plenty about that on the local council. Especially when it comes to these housing loans. You see, there are two classes of people, and the way the state assesses them seems very peculiar to me, to say the least. The ones that are decent enough and find a home of their own before they get married, the ones who behave properly in every way, do they come looking for handouts? No sir! Why not? Well, they just can't afford the repayments. But the others, the ones who run around, straight from the john to the dance, breeding like rabbits without ever thinking ahead, in neither of the two places, why *they* get the loans. The local council takes them to their hearts and rewards them. What can you say about that? What sort of people will that produce in the long run? No, we should really let a little morality have its say too." (Nordström 1938:145f.)

The same toilet habits had been typical of the peasantry for centuries without people worrying about them or reading moral considerations into them. The attitude to the needs of nature was more pragmatic than moral. Human excrement was known to make poor fertilizer, so it was not valued as highly as cow or horse manure. Once again, it was practical considerations that colored the peasant approach to the matter. For example, when stone was first quarried on the little island of Tjurkö in the Blekinge archipelago, the peasants welcomed the arrival of the quarrymen who swelled the local population. Apart from the income from quarry concessions, the numerous quarry workers meant a welcome addition to the poor supply of fertilizer; the limited number of animals could not provide the desired amount of manure. For this reason, when the farmers rented out sites for quarry workers' houses, they ensured that the contract gave them the right to use the waste from the outside toilets. The quarrymen and their employers did not have the same utilitarian view of the stuff, for which there was consequently no competition.

Peasant Views of Purity and Dirt

Cleanliness in conjunction with the necessities of nature was taken care of with the same undramatic approach as was taken with feces and urine. Levi Johansson records from Jämtland that the wiping material used after discharging natural functions was whatever was at hand: grass, moss, or snow for wiping, wooden shavings for scraping —all depending on the season and the supply: "Not so many decades have passed since the death of the old woman who, in answer to the finicky modern habits in this sphere, boasted that throughout her long life she had never used anything other than her index finger. She was surely not alone in this" (Johansson 1927:132).

On many farms in Norrland it was the custom to have a small rubbish heap outside the front porch onto which household refuse was thrown. Children used the heap as a toilet, and adults went there to urinate. In the spring it was carted away, because it had by then grown too high and would start to smell if the sun heated it. The public use of heaps like these shocked even a fieldworker with the experience of Levi Johansson. On a journey during which he learned that this practice was not restricted to his own parish, he learned too how indifferent people could be about mixing the physical with the social; they did not care in the least that anyone could see them answering the call of nature.

This *lillkasa* (little heap) was not unique to Frostviken. As late as the summer of 1918 I saw quite a good many similar heaps in northern Ångermanland, some of them in the form of well-tended compost heaps covered with fresh spruce branches, but others simply dungheaps. Here they were known as *brokasa* (porch-heap). On one farm where I stayed, I happened to surprise the daughter of the house, a lass of seventeen or eighteen, on her hunkers on the edge of the stoop, from which the heap had recently been carted away. The girl did not seem in the least put out. She got up calmly, wiped herself in exactly the same way as the old lady in Frostviken,

Clean and Proper

and went into the house. It was not without some hesitation that I followed her in, since I was afraid that the girl would be embarrassed by my presence, but her expression showed not the slightest sign of anything of the sort. (Johansson 1927:132f.)

The same observer records how adults showed the same lack of modesty regarding the act of urination:

As far as I remember, the women wore no underpants, neither winter nor summer, but had thick, warm skirts and long sturdy stockings. It was in many ways a convenient arrangement. I remember an old woman who squatted in the middle of the yard, artfully and without embarrassment. Nobody would have noticed what she was doing if she had had a little potbelly, but in the absence of such she had to hold her skirt out a little, which betrayed her. Afterward she pressed her clothes between her legs and wiped herself dry, with the result that she constantly had a strong smell of old urine about her. (Johansson 1927:126)

It is unlikely that this sour-smelling old woman was treated as a social outsider; the people around her probably did not react to the smell.

Urine had its medical purposes. People knew from experience that wounds healed faster if one urinated on them immediately. Urine is sterile, and therefore a suitable cleaning agent. The smell was part of the bargain. Selma Frode-Kristensen has related in the story of her youth among the poor of the Österlen region of Skåne how often this method of washing wounds was applied. Along with her mother she helped with the sugar-beet harvest. In November the haulms of the beets froze and cut the wet hands and arms of the harvesters:

Peasant Views of Purity and Dirt

We knew no such luxury as wearing gloves. Anyway, it would have been regarded as silly. . . . Grandmother and I were wretchedly cold. Our hands and arms became red and sore.

What did we do about that? Skin cream? When I think back, the very thought of that appears ridiculous. Nobody knew of such a substance. Nor was there any money to buy it with. No, we had a venerable medicine to relieve sore skin: warm urine! Nothing else. As soon as we got home we washed until we were really clean. Then outside to "do a little errand." Over the hands and arms. It stung terribly. But it helped.   (Frode-Kristensen 1966:18)

It was only during the nineteenth century that it became common for farms to have special houses or separate rooms with the sole function of affording privacy to people discharging their natural needs. Earlier, however, the urban and rural gentry had had their privies; the most famous privy in Swedish history is the one in Ornäs, Dalarna, used by Gustav Vasa (the king who liberated Sweden from Danish rule in 1523), when he was fleeing in desperation before the pursuing Danes (see the photograph in Tilander 1968:103). Medieval castles had privies built either projecting from the wall or inside the wall, with drainage to a place where the sewage was collected. In the countryside, however, such facilities came much later. To draw the social consequences of the new-fangled invention, it can be said that the privy reflects changes in the structure of village life and family relations. The novelty was first adopted in the better-off homes, in precisely those homes where people were becoming careful in drawing the boundaries between themselves and their animals and between household members of different ranks. When farm owners developed into masters instead of workers sharing the collective tasks, when the servants could no longer dine at the same table as the master and mistress, and

*There were places where both the better off and the poor did not
object to company. It was customary to build the privy with several
holes. This nineteenth-century drawing shows a gentleman on
the estate of Säfstaholm who has retired to mend his trousers
with a needle and thread. It is this needlework that surprises his
fellows, not the fact that he is caught with his trousers down.
(Nordiska Museet, Stockholm.)*

Peasant Views of Purity and Dirt

when the common sleeping area was replaced by separate bedrooms, then it was essential that bodily functions become a private matter.

It should be stressed, however, that the degree of privacy on farms never reached the same heights of perfection as in bourgeois culture. When privies were erected, they were built as collective rather than one-man establishments. As a rule there were two holes, but larger households could have even more. There are examples of buildings with twenty holes for the adult members of the household, and in addition a separate bench with a row of holes for the children.[4]

These communal closets offered an intimacy that had its natural attractions. Here was a place where people could be close to their own bodies in the company of others. Perhaps this sense of community was easier for children to establish, since they had not yet assimilated the idea that the physical had to be separated from the social. "Coming to the closet?" was a common invitation among children in the area of Roslagen where my mother grew up. Since the children were not wholly unaware of the requirements of decency and modesty, the "coarse" wording of the question was disguised in the noa abbreviation "CTTC." The invitation usually met with a favorable response. The closet had three holes, a window that looked out over the fields, and walls decorated with color prints of flowers cut from books and magazines. The decorations were intended to evoke pleasant associations with nature and to stimulate conversation among those who had come in company. Rural closets like these could not be transformed into today's clinical hygiene centers, where people well trained in cleanliness separate themselves from their waste products in privacy.

Country people in the nineteenth century had received no systematic training in cleanliness and hygiene. The lack of care that they showed about the natural needs of the very young illustrates this fact. In bourgeois culture, early pot training was an essential part of child rearing. If we follow Sigmund Freud's theory of the stages of infantile development, pot training is also the way to civilize people and make

Clean and Proper

them pillars of society. In the first phase, the oral stage, the child lives near the mother, sucking her milk and having tactile contact with other people. The child has few opportunities to draw boundaries between himself and other people or between himself and the material world. He lives in a continuum. The child begins to draw boundaries at the end of the oral stage, when he is weaned and enters the anal phase. In this stage, when the child learns to objectify himself, defecation and the accompanying pot training play a central role. The child finds it pleasurable to defecate. The delighted reaction of the parents—provided he does it in the pot—reinforces the sense of pleasure. Yet while the child is rewarded for his performance, he must learn to distance himself from the product. What lies in the pot has suddenly become not-me and is hedged with prohibitions and revulsion. The child learns to put a distance between himself and his own body. These discoveries happen while the child is learning to walk and talk, and he is thus amassing information about the world in many ways.

This elementary lesson in the art of cleanliness had no real counterpart among the peasantry. It is true that the peasants used pots (cf. Lindström 1970), but it would be wrong to claim for these utensils a parity with their bourgeois counterparts. There were none of the strong emotional overtones with which pot training in the nursery was invested. Little wooden commodes were a common item of furniture, but chiefly because they were practical places to set the little babies, who were thus prevented from crawling around on the floor, hurting themselves and others. This was a part of the peasant's rich arsenal of prohibitive measures designed to keep children inactive and in their place.

As soon as children could move about on their own, they were dressed in a sort of frock, a garment that had the advantage that the child had the freedom to urinate and defecate without dirtying the clothes. When it is remembered that the household also included

Peasant Views of Purity and Dirt

four-legged members who were more difficult to train in cleanliness, it will be obvious that a little bit of child excrement on the floor was really neither here nor there. If the house had an earthen floor, much of the dirt was tramped into it. Boarded floors had holes and cracks, which took away at least the liquid waste. Child excrement could be picked up off the floor with a pair of sticks and thrown on the fire, unless it was too runny, in which case it was wiped up with a handful of hay and then thrown on the fire—even if food was being cooked there (Johansson 1927:132). Of course, none of the adult members of the household could behave with the same liberty as the young children.

Children's waste matter caused less concern than that of adults. Mother–child contact was of the kind that allowed the mother to wipe the child's nose with her mouth. "Whether this was then spat out or not, I have not been able to obtain a definite answer, but the latter course is not inconceivable" (Johansson 1927:123). As soon as the child had grown, this sort of care naturally came to an end, and children were then frequently told to keep their noses clean themselves. The nose could be wiped with the hand or blown by closing one nostril with the thumb. If necessary, the nose could then be wiped on a sleeve, and snot could be detached from the fingers by rubbing them on one's clothes. Handkerchiefs were used, but only for decoration, not for wiping the nose. Eilert Sundt observed how handkerchiefs were used in church by a group of candidates for confirmation in Søndfjord in Norway:

> At another stage of the confirmation ceremony I saw the row of pretty girls in a state of profound agitation: some of them sobbed, and all of them were weeping. They dried their tears with the sleeves of their homespun tunics, which stained their cheeks blue; they wiped their noses between their fingers and then, showing the utmost care not to clean their fingers on their fine new dresses, lifted a foot and wiped them

Clean and Proper

on the sole of a shoe. And all of them held a hymnbook and a checked handkerchief in their devout hands, but not one of them used the handkerchief, for they were not in the habit. (Sundt [1869]1975:305)

Nosepicking is nowadays a solitary pursuit; if performed in company it is probably out of absentmindedness. This privacy was not so important in the peasant world of a century ago. Eating one's own snot was not tabooed, and was therefore not regarded with disgust by observers.

Dried-up nasal mucus was prized out with the nail of the index finger and—eaten. Perhaps not everyone did this, but at least many. The author remembers quite a few snot eaters, but even then it was considered filthy, and the practice is still not eradicated, although it is carried on only by ancients, and in greater privacy. But in the old days people were not in the least embarrassed by the presence of others. (Johansson 1927:123)

Other bodily exudations involved the same pragmatic attitudes. Sweating was perfectly natural, healthy, and certainly not harmful, as was often maintained by the bourgeoisie. Sweating cleansed the body from within, it was imagined, and consequently left people as clean as after a bath. Women were likewise purified by their monthly bleeding, and there was no shamefaced secrecy about sanitary protection. It is quite a different matter that women were regarded as unclean during their menstruation. They could, for example, bring bad luck to hunters, turn beer bad, or make dough fail to rise. The impurity associated with women can be explained by the fact that during this period they were socially and culturally anomalous. The ideal state for a married woman during her fertile years was to be pregnant. It does not appear, however, that menstruation was invested with any hygienic aspects or considerations of cleanliness. Menstruation was a sign that a woman could become pregnant. By suckling children for a long time she could delay the resumption of menstruation, with the result that prolonged breast-feeding has been viewed by many as a form of birth control. There is indeed a wealth of folk belief about the contraceptive power of breast-feeding. However effective it was, the same principle of publicity prevailed about this as about other bodily secretions. Babies were suckled long and freely, with none of the feeling instilled in bourgeois mothers that there could be anything socially offensive about this form of child care and this exposure of the mother's body. The taboo surrounding breast milk, which has given generations of nursing mothers a slight sense of repugnance, was absent from peasant society. In fact, breast milk was used for medical purposes; children's cuts and scurf were washed with it.

Sex Life

It might be thought that physical love was an area of peasant culture that was not at all taboo-loaded. While everything to do with sexuality was strictly tabooed in Victorian culture, the attitude of the peasant was more straightforward and uncomplicated. Prohibitions were fewer and freedom greater. Modern scholars have characterized the peasant as more sensual, more open, and more natural with respect to the pleasures of the flesh. A commonly expressed theory of peasant sexuality at the turn of the century was that the young people's practice of night courtship was a relic of primeval promiscuity; another theory was that they wanted to test the girls' ability to conceive.[5]

It is hardly surprising that there is so much speculation about rustic sex life; factual information in the form of authentic accounts is scarce,

Clean and Proper

while the interest of the academic world has been great, and general theories of sexuality are legion. It was not until Wikman (1937) described premarital customs in their cultural and social framework that it became clear that the sex life of country people was not one of happy-go-lucky promiscuity. It was on the contrary highly institutionalized, directed by shared norms and rituals. However, the discovery that there were rules for what had hitherto been seen as normless does not alter the fact that attitudes to sex were radically different among the bourgeoisie and among the peasantry.

It is often said that everyone in the country had the opportunity to learn about the mysteries of reproduction by personal observation. People lived in an environment where they could witness fertilization and birth frequently. Cows and mares on the farm had to be covered when they were in heat. The fertility of the domestic stock was a focus of interest for the whole family, discussed freely in the children's presence. If the children were big enough they could help to hold the cow, or to lead it by a rope to the neighbor's bull. Insemination went on without embarrassment in the chicken run, the sheep pen, and— above all—among the goats. It is therefore easy to draw the conclusion that children could absorb the information necessary to work out the causes and effects of the human reproductive process. This conclusion is perfectly correct, but only if the children had the motivation to translate what they knew of animals to human terms. A survey of sexual life in Sweden made at the end of the 1960s showed that knowledge of sex and reproduction was considerably less in the country than in the towns and cities (Zetterberg 1969:32).

The parallels between rural people of the 1960s and those before the turn of the century may not suffice to allow us to draw any safe conclusions. It is improbable that knowledge in the countryside then was inferior to that in the towns, but this is not to say how much country people actually knew. The information available strongly suggests that reproduction was a matter about which people were relatively igno-

Peasant Views of Purity and Dirt

rant. There was a huge gulf between their demonstrably wide knowledge of animal reproduction and their rudimentary ideas about human reproduction.

Cows were led away when they showed the outward signs of heat, but how was a man to go about making a woman conceive? Informants who have touched on this sensitive subject say that the best time to fertilize a woman is during menstruation. "Intercourse during a woman's monthly period is effective," according to a witness from Värmland, "but it has to be frequent, every day. And then the woman has to pinch her thighs together afterwards, so that the dose she receives can take root before it runs out" (EU 51278).

There is a good deal of peasant common sense in this. A woman's period has always been regarded as a time of particular potency, and this may be why fertilization was recommended during menstruation. At all events, this is a commonly recorded prescription, which reflects the peasant attitude to and knowledge of conception. "If you wanted a baby, the best time was during the woman's period, because she had the best chance of conceiving," said a woman from a cotter home in Blekinge (LUF 13449). If the marriage was cursed with barrenness, there was no better cure than intercourse during menstruation, according to an informant from Lappland (NM 51414).

The peasant's incomplete knowledge is further illustrated by records of ways by which it was thought that the sex of the baby could be determined. According to one report from Västergötland, boys could be begotten during the first five days after menstruation, and girls between the fifth and eighth days (ULMA 1991). Another informant says that boys could be conceived during the first few days after the end of menstruation, while girls were begotten during the last days of the menstrual cycle (LUF 13037). These statements say more about the world view of the people and their ideas of the relationship between the two sexes. One may ask, then, why they knew so little.

A few simple preconditions are necessary if people are to build up a

Clean and Proper

bank of knowledge. One of the most important is that the knowledge can be transmitted: in other words, that people can talk about it. If this possibility is not open, one must be in a position to make one's own observations. What was the situation of the peasant in this respect? Did they talk about sex? Were there opportunities to make one's own observations?

It is often said that children in peasant homes came into early contact with the realities of life. By being sufficiently observant they could see or hear their parents engaged in sexual intercourse. After all, parents, children, and servants slept in the same room, which was at once kitchen, dining room, and workroom. People were conceived and born there, and there they died. This is a gross oversimplification, since it ignores the fact that Lutheran morality had permeated people's views of sex within marriage to the extent that it was felt proper to conceal it from the other members of the household. The sources describe peasant sexual activity as something carried on outdoors: in the barn, in the hay, on the ground, or wherever opportunity allowed. To beget a child, it was generally thought best to try in the spring and summer months. The probability of conception was increased, according to some, by lying on a hard surface, or according to others, in hay. People could observe the signs of nature, from which they deduced that there were times that were especially favorable: when the juniper bushes or the rye became dusty with pollen, when the alder leaves were as small as mouse ears, when the moon was new, and so on. Intercourse is only rarely described as an indoor pursuit.

Mats Rehnberg once told of the suprise occasioned when certain films were shown in rural districts in the 1930s. When Swedish peasants saw the bedroom farces in native and imported films, they were amazed and bewildered at the antics perpetrated in and around the bed. For them the bedroom had no immediate erotic significance. "The Swedish peasant used his bed for sleeping, not screwing" (personal communication).

Sex was consequently something done in seclusion. It was not care-

Peasant Views of Purity and Dirt

lessly performed in company, not even in the presence of the intimate family circle. The parents, therefore, did not show the children, but did they at least tell them about sex? All the collected material on the subject of sex education shows that people actually said very little about it. Even in the matter of childbirth, they strove to keep the truth from the little innocents. Everything to do with sex was taboo, according to Ellida Ohlsson, an informant from Skåne. Mothers could sit together swapping stories about the labor pains they had suffered or heard tell of, but they told the children that the stork had brought them: "Even as a three-year-old I didn't believe that about the stork, and I still remember how, when the neighbors had a baby, some local women tried to make me believe that the stork had fished it up out of a turf ditch. 'No,' I said, 'that's not true, for Mrs. Lindoff (the midwife) had it in her bag, she told me so herself'" (LUF 12981). Keeping it secret from the children thus applied to the whole reproductive process, including childbirth. The mother's confinement to bed was explained by her need to lie down and warm the little baby. Although childbirth was an accepted and perhaps popular topic of conversation among women together, conjugal life appears to have been a forbidden subject. The same informant tells us that women of the older generation never mentioned anything to do with intercourse. "That was something which concerned only the partners themselves, and even they could be fairly modest and reserved in each other's company, and I'm sure there used to be lots of men who had never even seen their wife's naked body" (LUF 12981).

An informant from Värmland, born in 1844, confirms in an interview that children used to have no idea about the sexual relations between men and women. Adults tried to keep this secret from them as long as possible (IFGH 2310). "There were girls who thought 'they had some sort of ache' when they started to long for men. . . . You didn't talk about things like that in the old days," says another Värmlander, born in 1855 (IFGH 2305).

Sexuality was straightforward, probably lacking the sensual aspects that our modern culture has taught us to associate with the sex act. Caressing and cuddling occurred in nonsexual relationships—between parents and small children; kisses were reserved for children, not adults. The peasant village never witnessed caresses in public. Relations between the sexes were nontactile (see Chapter 3, under "The Loving Couple").

It is important to understand this strictly regulated sexuality before understanding why there was such secrecy in front of the children. The silence was not occasioned by verbal modesty. Peasants, like workers in general in former days, used four-letter words unblushingly. Even everyday tools and articles were called by local words for sexual organs. For example, stonecutters had to wrap a "drill-cunt" around the drill-bits to keep stone chippings and dust from spattering up at the man holding the drill, while the boom that sat on the quarry crane was called a "prick."

The names of sexual organs were commonly used as terms of abuse. A stonecutter with a reputation for being particularly sluggish was known as "trudge-balls"; a man who worked at a leisurely pace earned the nickname "dung-cock"; and the last to get his clothes on after bathing was called "tub-cunt" (LUF 10600, 6710, 8515). The names were an integral part of their daily lives. They were constantly heard, both in referring to the people concerned and as colorful ways of addressing them. Even the midwife—who was normally from outside the village community—was given affectionate names like "Mouse Mother" and "Auntie Long-Cunt."

Sexual references were a common feature of the great collective task of the year, the harvest: equivocal jokes and names came thick and fast (Eskeröd 1947:156f.). As late as the beginning of the present century, the making of blood sausage involved the use of incantations where obscene similes were used to represent the strength of the sausage skin: "Hard as horn and tough as cunt, you must hold and never split" (Bringéus 1975:41).

There is no contradiction in the fact that people kept sexual intercourse a secret from the children as long as possible, while nevertheless talking openly about sexual organs. They are two sides of the same coin. The peasant's view of sexuality was based on the utilitarian function of reproduction. Unmarried adults and sexually mature young people were permitted to have sex, provided they were betrothed or planned to marry. Since sex was reserved for these people, it had no relevance to children. They could not beget children, which was the whole point of sex.

To clarify the peasant approach further: as long as the formal requirements were satisfied—that the couple was married or engaged—sex was legitimate. There is therefore little sign of shame or guilt about sexuality, except when unmarried girls had children. It is harder to show that there was any shame about intercourse or the sexual instinct. It is not surprising, then, that the fines demanded by the church in atonement for premarital intercourse were a source of amusement and pride; people paid their "rump tax" willingly.

Prosperity and the Smell of Poverty

The peasant view of cleanliness centered around the notion of presentability. They tried to be clean for the great festive occasions, careful to be washed and nicely dressed in the presence of other people. There is a proverb that expresses this peasant attitude: "Clean and wholesome makes the best show."

The decisive difference between peasant and bourgeois views of cleanliness at this time hinges on the concept of hygiene. For the peasant, dirt was shameful and dirty people were treated with suspicion. But dirt was not dangerous. You could not hurt yourself by picking your nose, by coming to the table with unwashed hands, or by visiting the parish whore. Such behavior might involve loss of prestige and respect, but it did not endanger health.

When the new concept of hygiene began to take root in the country-

Clean and Proper

side, when peasants adopted it, there was a good seedbed to nourish it. The peasants were less tormented by the dirt that surrounded them than were contemporary visitors from the bourgeois world, but they were far from carefree in their life among flies, lice, and other vermin. Cholera, tuberculosis, rheumatism, scabies, and other diseases, which went hand in hand with the poor levels of hygiene and housing, plagued them just as much as, if not more than, the town dwellers. What they did not know was that many of these torments could be eliminated by elementary improvements in sanitation.

In addition, cleanliness became fashionable. A world without smells was an elegant, aristocratic world. "You have the world in your nostrils," says the high constable to Didrik of Lillvattnet, a farmer's son in Sara Lidman's novel *Din tjänare hör* (Thy servant heareth).

> "The world in my nostrils?" he said, puzzled.
> "That's a metaphor. When I say 'the world' I don't mean to equate 'the world' with 'sin' the way the pietists do. When I say 'the world' I mean Sweden, our native land, the Crown if you like. The same as what you mean when you talk about the railroad. *You* only need to read a bit out of the newspaper to feel Sweden like a scent in your nostrils. But the others! Like the boys from Vällingträsk, Blankvattnet or Tallheden— they need a real smell in their nose to kindle a thought in their brains and to make them set the ax to the root."

Didrik has realized that the railroad meant improvement in this inland parish in the far north of Sweden in the late nineteenth century. It would bring the new times with it. He sniffed what that would involve in the high constable's residence.

> Apart from the tobacco smoke, which Didrik liked, what fascinated him most in the high constable's drawing room

Peasant Views of Purity and Dirt

was the absence of smell. The smell of sheep, horses, cows, leather, hay, ashes, baby shit, tar, sweat—which combined to give the *reek* that filled the common people's cabins and hung like a pious cloud over the congregation in the church, and which it was wonderful to yearn for on a winter's day two hours away from human habitation—all this felt less attractive in July when the flies buzzed in the stench of the cabin. This was a time when a house like this, far from any barn, was so edifyingly clean. (Lidman 1977:217f.)

For many a peasant girl it was possible to gain firsthand knowledge of the way people in the other culture lived. The bourgeois home required a lot of work, which had to be done by servants. For most country girls the years between confirmation and marriage automatically meant a spell as a maid on a large farm or in a town house. A girl who had spent years of her youth dusting, cleaning, scrubbing, and washing in a town house would naturally bring ideas of order into her own home. If she had wiped the noses of middle-class children, taught them to come to the table with clean hands, and monitored their behavior, she had obviously acquired ideals of child rearing that would be significant when she brought up children of her own.

The countryside had many homes that could serve as a closer link with the bourgeois pattern of culture: the homes of the gentry and persons of rank—the clergy, the military, and the industrialists. "People learned cleanliness from the homes of the gentry in the neighborhood. Farmers' sons and daughters served in these mansions, and when they came home again, they tackled the dirt around them in an effort to imitate the mansions" (Sjöqvist 1970:135).

Before the new ideas of the beneficial effects of hygiene and cleanliness for health and home comfort could become general, there had to exist the right economic circumstances for their realization. Most important of all, they had to have some relationship to people's social ex-

Clean and Proper

perience. Was there reason to discipline the self and draw boundaries between the self and the world at this time? A sharpened focus on cleanliness and discipline is, as has been shown, one expression of the increased demands made on people as social beings (chapter 4, in the section "The Body as a Bridge").

The nineteenth century was the era when the large-scale Swedish farmer began to emerge. Land reforms, new methods of cultivation, new crops, and a plentiful supply of labor combined to shatter the homogeneity of the peasant villages and allow the establishment of a well-to-do class of landowner. In the village as a whole and in the individual households in particular there arose a need to draw boundaries between people of different origins and from different economic backgrounds. This social differentiation can be deduced from the new living habits on the farm (chapter 5, under "Exudations"). Masters and servants no longer slept in the same room. The old multipurpose room disappeared, to be replaced by a number of separate rooms for eating, sleeping, socializing, cooking, and so on. Whereas servants had previously eaten together with masters, it became customary on many better-off farms during the course of the century for them to eat in separate quarters. "There had been no clearer example of the communal spirit than around the peasant's table, where everyone ate from the same dish, with equal rights to the food. . . . The serving of food on separate plates meant that this primeval communion had to give way to the individualism of the new age" (Bringéus 1970:17f.).

There was also a redistribution of roles in the household. The master could distance himself from the physical toil of production, taking on the role of a "squire" who organized and managed the work of the farm. On larger farms a foreman was appointed to distribute the master's orders to the subordinates. The farmer's wife assumed the role of housewife, with the responsibility for looking after the home and directing the work of the female servants; she herself no longer participated in the work of production. The housekeeping bible of the 1880s

Peasant Views of Purity and Dirt

was addressed to "the housewife in town *and country*" (Langlet 1884). The employment of special maids for indoor work also increased the housewife's chances of realizing the bourgeois dream of a beautiful, clean, and orderly home.

When country people came into contact with town life and the ways of the bourgeoisie, they began to display an interest in cleanliness. The dirt of the barn was consigned to the sphere of production and was therefore not to be brought indoors. Any animals kept in the house were there as pets, not as livestock. Dust and dirt were kept at bay through daily sweeping and weekly scrubbing. The boundaries between the individual and the people around him were marked by greater personal cleanliness.

The schools taught cleanliness to high and low alike, to rural and urban children. Whether or not the children could put the rules into practice, they had to learn them. The children plowed their way through their *Elementary School Reader*, with its rules for good health stressing the need for clean, dry clothes, for clean, airy rooms, and for moderation in pleasure and rest. Rule number 11 in this book preaches that: "Violent emotions such as anger, envy, hate, and the like are dangerous for the health. Unchastity greatly undermines the strength of body and soul." The preceding rule says, "The skin should be kept scrupulously clean. Dirt is the source of many diseases. Wash daily in cold water, bathe frequently in the summer, but be careful! Never enter the bath while you are out of breath or overheated, after exertion or immediately after eating. Do not bathe more than once a day, and do not stay too long in the water" (*Läsebok för folkskolan* 1901:89).

The increasing prosperity of the landowning peasantry was accompanied by a greater destitution among the landless. The nineteenth century was the great age of proletarianization, when more and more people were forced to make their living off the shrinking land available after improvements in agriculture and its by-products. It was among

Clean and Proper

these poverty-stricken inhabitants of rural Sweden that it was hardest to change the norms of cleanliness. Dirt and poverty went hand in hand, accompanied by bad housing, disease, high infant mortality, and short life expectation.

Landless farm laborers and cotters continued to cohabit with their smaller animals as late as the turn of the century (Erixon 1947:118). The houses built by the cotters of Skåne and those who owned diminutive farms of the sort known as "cow places" usually incorporated an animal house. This proletariat, uncultured and hydra-headed, did not display the same vigilance as the landed farmers in guarding the boundaries between people and between animals and people. When agitators from the agricultural laborers' union traveled around Sweden in the 1920s and 1930s, they encountered a rampant rural slum. In a review of Ivar Lo-Johansson's proletarian novel *Pubertet* (Puberty), Gunnar Sträng, then finance minister in the Social Democratic government, recalled the gray existence of the landless laborers:

> The smells still linger stubbornly in the author's nostrils after all these years. He smells the impending decay of the old generation. Long years of toil and sweat have permeated the floorboards and the wall panels. Daily contact with domestic animals brings their particular smells via clothes and shoes into the house, where it mixes with the cooking fumes. This combination made up the lifelong atmosphere of the landless laborer. I can bear witness to this, having worked as a house agitator for many years. (Sträng 1979:11)

When in 1937 Ludvig Nordström visited the cottage of a laborer's family in Skåne, he was struck by precisely this gray, monotonous, and paralyzing hopelessness:

> No more filthy, wretched, hopeless, heartrending home did I see on my entire journey. They lacked even a best room. The

Peasant Views of Purity and Dirt

kitchen was an old entrance hall without even proper windows. Nothing but two panes on either side of the door, as is
usual in porches. A chimney wall, which was like nothing so
much as a blacksmith's sooty forge, and then a group of small
rooms without even curtains, where the seven sickly-pale
youngsters swarmed and crawled about amidst dirt, rags,
and leftovers. They were all coughing so much that it hurt my
own lungs. People talk about wartime cannon fodder, but
these were cannon fodder for Sweden-the-filthy. They would
grow up to be cheap labor in the lowest of agricultural ar-
mies. . . . And the smell! The stench! And the mother—the girl
who just kept on struggling! With her green face, eyes swollen
with weeping, eyes which no longer wanted to look out on
life but which stared backward, inward, with her rotten teeth,
her thin, worn hands and her dirty, ragged nails, with her
skeletal arms, which appeared to have almost exhausted
their entire power as she pressed the smallest of the children
to her dry-sucked breast.   (Nordström 1938:172)

Ludvig Nordström liked to paint with strong colors and undoubtedly
wrote this account with great pathos, yet there is no disputing the fact
that large groups of people stood outside the community of the settled
and the landed. These were people whose misery was frequently re-
newed by the way they moved from place to place; change did not
mean improvement. Dirt and vermin were links in the chain that held
them forever at the rock bottom of society.

Industrial workers were also recruited from the propertyless class.
Admittedly, working-class men and women had also felt "the world in
their noses," but they had little opportunity to make the ideals they
met into their own reality. The housing available to them usually
meant overcrowding and social destitution. Above all, it was scarcely
possible to move away from the stench of poverty, which sat in the
tenement walls like the mark of Cain. Gustaf af Geijerstam has de-

Among the poor the kitchen was the place for cooking, eating, sleeping, and casual visits. Often there was also a parlor, saved for ceremonial occasions and acting as a focus for order and respectability. The photograph was taken in the 1890s. (Photograph by Gunnar Lundh, Nordiska Museet, Stockholm.)

Peasant Views of Purity and Dirt

scribed the living conditions of some of Stockholm's working class during the 1890s:

> The first thing to be noticed in the poorer working-class housing is the putrid air, which does not appear to be due solely to the overcrowding and underventilation of the apartments. It hangs also on the stairs and in the corridors and the cellars—in short, everywhere, even where there are no people living. One warm summer's day as I was being driven in a cab past one of the worst buildings, I noticed in the scarcely half a minute that I spent in the vicinity that the whole of this poor people's barrack gave off an indeterminate smell of appalling nastiness. It came with the atmosphere of need and misery, from an entire barrack full of people, the house filled with poverty from the foundations to the rafters. (af Geijerstam 1894:57f.)

The indignation expressed here over the living conditions of the agricultural laborers and the stench-ridden poverty of Stockholm's tenements comes from people who represented bourgeois culture, but how did the people who lived in such misery view their own situation?

Students of the world view of the early industrial workers have pointed to the insecurity inherent in working-class attitudes to cleanliness and hygiene. People knew objectively the norms that applied, having read the rules in the *Elementary School Reader*, and they had also internalized the middle-class values of cleanliness and order. Yet at the same time they found that this life-style was difficult to realize in the environment in which they lived. Their economy and external circumstances proved an obstacle. There was the insight that the workers lived like animals, that the world of poverty was chaotic and dirty. This world has to be rejected by anyone who strove for the genteel world in which people were disciplined and clean. "[The worker] sees

Clean and Proper

poverty . . . as depriving men of the capacity to act rationally, to exercise self-control. A poor man, therefore, *has* to want upward mobility in order to establish dignity in his own life, and dignity means, specifically, moving toward a position in which he deals with the world in some controlled, emotionally restrained way" (Sennett and Cobb 1972:22). Cleanliness, self-control, and discipline go hand in hand as particularly important tools in the historical process commonly referred to as the domestication of the working class. The working class adopted middle-class values via ideas of hygiene, and they applied them in their own lives. This process not only made them conscious of their own failings, it also taught them the technique of self-control. They thereby became better workers in the industrial nation with its new norms. Dirty people are rebellious and hard to manage, while clean and wholesome people with a scent of the world in their nostrils become decent members of society. To consider the process from the workers' own perspective, the working-class struggle for respectability and recognition demanded the assistance of soap and water. They knew that only by being orderly, disciplined, and irreproachably clean could they offer a credible alternative to the bourgeoisie.

· 6 ·

Bourgeois Discipline

Words that were permitted in the peasant's house were considered embarrassing and unbecoming in the drawing rooms of their betters. Habits of personal hygiene that caused no comment in one environment did not fail to provoke reactions of distaste and repugnance in another.

In the discussion in the preceding chapter on the conditions in which people lived on the quarry island of Tjurkö, an everyday life was portrayed that was permeated with dirt, vermin, odors, and poor bodily hygiene. The carelessness the quarrymen's families showed about this purely physical order also made itself felt in their speech and thoughts. Like the peasants, they called things by their proper names, with no euphemisms or circumlocutions.

A description from a bourgeois home of the same period will show us how practically everything that was permitted and physically present in the working-class home was tabooed and absent here:

> We, Father, Mother, and all those we knew, were prudish in a
> sense that has now become rare. Prudery meant first and
> foremost the complete prohibition of all talk of physical and
> sexual matters. We must have learned this taboo so early that
> I have no recollection of it. I suppose I must at some time
> have asked my mother why there was a difference between
> boys and girls, and she must have answered somewhat eva-

Clean and Proper

sively, and then such questions were forgotten or concealed. But prudery was not just sexual. It affected many things that were considered disquieting or sensitive: people's characters, actions, and feelings: God, love, and death, the meaning of life, or whether there was no meaning. What surprises me about this is that the upbringing, with all its mildness, could be so effective that I failed to question or doubt openly so many things, out of a shyness that felt natural and instinctive. The fear or consideration or shame that more-or-less consciously forced the adults into silence was quickly adopted and practiced by the children, who refrained from embarrassing their parents out of anxiety and concern over their reactions—just as they felt anxiety and concern for the children—and who spared them surprises, pain, and offense. . . .

To take a ridiculous little example: Mother considered the tail end of the pike to be the best part, so she liked to divide it between Father and myself. Occasionally during this operation she would say, proud of her outspokenness, "Yes, I call it the tail end. Can you imagine, I once had an aunt who always called it the stem, to be really proper." The story worried me for two reasons. On the one hand I thought that Mother's speech seemed somewhat too free, while on the other I wondered what was so secret and dangerous about the tail end. But I never asked about this; that would have been beyond the bounds of what was permitted. What applied to the tail of the pike also applied to Aunt Lalla's "accident," Uncle Salle's suicide, why Uncle Carell's divorce was so terrible, where children came from, why we must die, and the remarkable relationship between God and Jesus.   (Tingsten 1961:56ff.)

The prudery described here by Herbert Tingsten took in much more than the human body and its physical processes. For Tingsten the eu-

Bourgeois Discipline

phemism for the tail end of the pike was condensed information on where to draw the boundaries between what could acceptably be discussed and what could not, between the decent and the indecent. These reflections of his are typical of the children of the Oscarian era. The human body was frequently used as a metaphor for society, the family, the home, and the way people related to one another and to life's great questions. The body has probably never had such a central role as a metaphor and a reference as it had in bourgeois society. The danger that charged the naming of the pike's tail made a whole series of connections clear to the young Tingsten.

In the following pages there will be a continuous stream of similar body metaphors, and their relations to one another and their dependence on the social structures will be considered in greater detail. As a preliminary to this discussion it is important to establish a stronger and more comprehensive empirical basis on which to build the theories.

It could be said as a broad generalization that bourgeois culture was like an organism with a hidden body. The body was there, to be sure, but its existence was persistently denied by the head. Bourgeois culture was spiritual, not physical. Even the embarrassing fact that men and women, children and adults possess bodies like other animals —or like people from the lower classes—was concealed as much as language allowed. These remarkable circumstances provide both a challenge and an obstacle for the student of this epoch and its people. When the physical is made private and withdrawn from the public light, the amount of information about it is naturally reduced. The words, or rather circumlocutions, that one meets are therefore particularly interesting, valuable, and sometimes also entertaining. Here are some examples of typical euphemisms.

People did not have a body but a *figure*, a more neutral word that suggested the body's function as a clothes-hanger rather than an organic being. The various parts of the figure included the upper and visible parts that were mentionable, like the head, forehead, and hands.

Clean and Proper

Anything below this was immediately more dubious. One of my father's uncles had a potbelly which sat unusually high, a deformity which he referred to as his "high breast." A high breast almost certainly gave him the increased personality that a potbelly could not have afforded him. Women also had a breast, in the singular; the plural form suggested more than just physical contours, and consequently could not be used outside medical descriptions. To be entirely on the safe side one could use the neutral word *bosom*.

The lower extremities of the body were likewise subject to taboo. One could not admit to having feet, although mention of an individual foot might be permitted. In one of Annette Kullenberg's interviews with the Swedish upper class, a member of the aristocracy gives a brief insight into the anxiety experienced by an acquaintance who broke both her feet and was forced to refer to the accident by saying that she had broken "the right foot and the left foot" (Kullenberg 1974:174f.). The plural form was too coarse, since feet should preferably not be mentioned collectively.

In the days when ladies wore long dresses, it was forbidden for the gentlemen even to imagine that they had legs, as Hugo Hamilton says in his memoirs. *Leg* was an unmentionable word, and it was quite improper to see or to show a leg. A walk in the forest in the company of ladies could bring awkward complications when the party had to cross a fence: "As if at a signal, the young men rushed over the fence and stood conscientiously with their backs to it while the girls climbed over. Then we would walk in silence and mild embarrassment for a while, for we knew that something highly improper had just occurred" (Hamilton 1928:157).

To suggest that one had a stomach was also improper. Any pain suffered in this tabooed part of the organism was described as "pressure below the heart." The heart was a noble part of the body, suitable for use as a point of reference. A person who withdrew to "pass water" could also express a need to "relieve the heart."

Bourgeois Discipline

Control of such bodily functions was used by the bourgeoisie to mark their distance from the lower classes. Samuel Kiechel's belching host had felt no need for such control, and of course farmers have continued to emit wind without embarrassment—a well-known literary example can be found in an autobiographical novel by the poet Harry Martinson (1935:158). Bourgeois etiquette books mention the need to muffle natural sounds such as coughs and sneezes, but belching and the like are silenced to the extent that they are not even mentioned; by definition and tacit convention they did not exist. Only in the most intimate situations could one complain of the embarrassing "visceral air" that resulted from pressure below the heart.

We could work our way through every type of bodily function and see how it has been hedged with cultural prohibitions; how the bourgeoisie have been taught to bridle their instincts, emotions, and impulses; how language and culture have become a straitjacket that effectively restrains all earthiness and joy of life. Many of these examples of social control are curiosities that serve to provoke amusement. People appear prudish, reserved, and somewhat ridiculous when seen, from the standpoint of a few generations later, seeking to distance themselves from the solid, deep-rooted Swedish peasantry.

This view of our bourgeois predecessors is, however, both misleading and unscientific. Modern scorn for Victorian prudery is no more justified than was the bourgeois dismissal of the peasant system of belief as superstition, the product of unschooled minds unable to perceive the right connections between cause and effect. Yet if the peasant's world view is considered on the basis of the conditions in which he lived, it appears logical, useful, and—for the outside observer—comprehensible. The same applies to the middle-class view of the body and to bourgeois ideals of order and discipline. If such ideas are seen in the light of the everyday experience in which these people lived, their rationality should also be clear.

The attempt must therefore be made to set the numerous taboos in their social context. This involves seeing how they came into being and functioned, both within the family and in society as a whole, in order to understand certain features of bourgeois culture, based on the scientific study of culture and society. This is one line to be followed.

The other is to consider the bridling of man's physical and animal self as the result of a long historical process. The schooling of each individual in a culture—the process of enculturation or socialization—is similar to the development undergone by the culture as a whole, what we call civilization. The fundamental feature of this process is training in self-discipline and control of interpersonal relationships.[1] For present purposes it will be sufficient to trace the roots of this process to the eighteenth century.

Legitimacy and the Beginning of Life

It has been shown how peasant children were deliberately prevented from learning of adult sexuality. In bourgeois homes this secretiveness was taken to its logical extreme. The pure world of the nursery was not penetrated by the pollution of the outside world. Children were by definition innocent and would remain so as long as parents had the power to filter the experiences to which children were exposed. In order to know how bourgeois culture aligned boundaries of class, culture, and gender, one may well examine how a world view took shape in the nursery.

Only well into the present century did it become common for women to give birth in the hospital. Childbirth took place at home. If there already were children in the family, there was thus a concrete risk that children could gain insight into the facts of life. Pregnancy and childbirth therefore gave rise to a rich array of evasive answers and fictions. It might be cautiously intimated that the mother was expecting a baby, but her dress and behavior seldom declared this openly. Contemporary books of advice for housewives warned of the displeasure that could be aroused by a pregnant woman's ostentatious display of her coming joy (Norden 1913:438). She should await the happy event in discretion and privacy.

"The birth of a child was shrouded in profound mystery," writes Ann Margret Holmgren. This suffragist tells of how even her aunts were not told that one of their sisters was pregnant. "They could only infer it when Grandmother cut out material for baby clothes for them to sew. They were not told which of the sisters it was for" (Holmgren 1926:78). It was only when they married that the daughters of the upper class learned the facts of life.

The children were informed of the arrival of a little brother or sister by the maid. To explain how the baby had arrived she could say that it had been let down on a rope from heaven, or that the midwife had brought it with her in her bag. "In those days the word midwife was never mentioned. At most the ladies could among themselves whisper the name 'Mrs. Necessary'" (Holmgren 1926:27).

Children were ensnared in a "conspiracy of silence" (Elias 1978:176). The right names of things were too hard and brutal for parents to utter. Only laboring men called a spade a spade. The parents, lacking a direct language in which to communicate with their children, were forced to use medical terms; these were culturally acceptable, although they might be used only reluctantly. The boys had to wait many years until they were old enough to understand what their father had to tell them, in hesitant and forced tones. As for the girls, the necessary enlightenment came at best immediately before the inevitable moment, just before marriage, although there are numerous accounts of the bride's complete surprise occasioned by the husband's wedding-night activities.

One of the most widely read good-housekeeping books also touches the question of the extent to which children should be informed of the

facts of conjugal life. In a manner typical of the age, the authoress rec-
ommends parents to try to sublimate children's curiosity about sex by
making them think in the more ethereal terms of birds and bees.

> Chastity is the growing child's most natural of feelings, but it
> must be heightened and reinforced to withstand the assaults
> of crudity and sensuality. It is best to treat the sexual rela-
> tions and reproduction of all living creatures as a part of nat-
> ural history, a continuation of plant propagation; children
> will then give the matter no thought and will not even under-
> stand when they hear unsuitable hints and allusions.
> (Langlet 1884:1003)

This was a clever way to resolve the conflicting demands of honesty
—children had to be informed of the reproductive process—and the
denial of sensuality and sexuality.

The result of this silence was that the children were free to specu-
late on the mysteries of life on the basis of incomplete knowledge. Ulla
Lidman-Frostenson tells how she (or Charlotte, as she calls herself in
her memoirs) constructed her own theory of where children came
from. She accepted that they came out of the mother, but not the manner of the exit:

> One day Blenda told of how children came out of their moth-
> er's body when they were born.
> "Ugh!" exclaimed Charlotte indignantly. She recoiled as if
> this were something shameful and degrading. To think that
> she had once been born in that way, helpless and with no say
> in the matter. How could God, who had created everything,
> have devised such a stupid arrangement?
> "Why must they come out there?" she cried."If I had my
> way, the breast would open just by the heart and the child

Bourgeois Discipline

would come out there, because that is a noble place."
(Lidman-Frostenson 1963:37)

The same writer recounts also how the girls could use their supposed
ignorance to score points off the adults. It was not considered proper
to know what people looked like under their clothes, and especially to
know which physical features made up the difference between boys
and girls:

> Boys and girls were different. Charlotte had seen that. She
> and Margaretha were sitting talking about that one day.
> When Grandmother came into the room, Charlotte realized
> that she could be considered well-bred if she did not admit
> to knowing what the difference was.
> "I have no idea what the difference between boys and girls
> is," she said loudly.
> "Yes of course you do," said Margaretha provocatively.
> "No I do not," maintained Charlotte.
> Grandmother came up and rested her hands on the edge
> of the table. "Calm down, children," she said. "Charlotte is a
> very good little girl, a very good little girl." (Lidman-Frosten-
> son 1963:36f.)

The child knew that according to the adult definition of the world it
was improper for a young girl to know certain things, although it may
not have been fully evident to the girl why this should be so. Alice
Quensel mentions how one of her aunts frightened her mother by
confiding in her that she was worried about having children. The girl
was in her teens, and the mother probably suspected an impending
scandal. The cause of the anxiety, however, was simply that the girl
had heard how terribly improper it was to have children (Quensel
1958:131).

Clean and Proper

The many bastions erected to protect the innocence of the nursery will be elaborated later, but consider for a moment the insecurity of the child's relation to the mother that could result from the denial of sexuality. Elise Ottesen-Jensen, founder of the National Swedish Association for Sexual Information, has shown how the mothers' hush-hush attitude to childbirth could lead children to doubt their legitimacy. When the mother denies that children grow inside her, feeding the myth that they come in the midwife's bag, or that they are let down through a hole in the clouds, or even that they were found in a trash can, the children are given a wrong view of their physical connection to the mother. She recounts an illuminating episode about a mother's mental block to the knowledge that Ottesen-Jensen and other pioneers of sexual enlightenment communicated to the children: "The poor, clumsy mothers are often filled with feelings of anxiety and guilt about the wonderful way life begins. Guilt to the extent that one mother, when her daughter came home after a sex education class in school and said "Just think that I grew inside you," replied: "You can tell your teacher from me that she might have grown inside her mother, but you did not grow inside me" (Ottesen-Jensen 1945:7). In her opinion, a secure relationship between mother and child could be attained by tearing down all such dusty curtains. A girl who had grown up with the story of the stork as the explanation of her origin was once present at one of her lectures, to which she listened wide-eyed.

> That afternoon the mother told me that I was allowed to be present when little Britta came home from her first ever lecture. The girl had rushed up to her mother and thrown her arms round her: "Mummy, Mummy, I'm your own little girl, I grew in a little egg in your stomach!" All sense of being abandoned had disappeared, and the foundation was laid for complete confidence between the girl and her mother. (Ottesen-Jensen 1945:6f.)

Bourgeois Discipline

Uncertainty about the biological ties to the mother was often reinforced in child–parent contact. The mother was a distant figure who
represented moral upbringing rather than physical presence and contact. It was by virtue of her character that the mother was the central
point of the home, as Alice Quensel says: "Only the very smallest children, the babies, were cuddled, and even that happened rarely"
(Quensel 1958:65).

There has been almost total agreement among the memoir writers
cited here when it comes to depicting the author's mother—she is a
radiant, angelic madonna (chapter 3, under "The Beloved Mother and
the Respected Father"). Some of the writers who look back to the turn
of the century recall their anxiety, even fear, that their mother would
be taken away from them or not love them enough. Herbert Tingsten
analyzes with great honesty the strong attachment he had to his
mother. He describes how he used all the tricks of a gifted child for the
emotional blackmail of his mother. She indulged her eldest son in
every way, showing by her actions that she really loved him.

The withheld knowledge about how children were born was one of
the building blocks of this attachment to the mother, this person who
had to be ensnared and won since there was no certainty that she was
bound to remain as a parent. Yet this was only one detail in the whole
physical masquerade.

The Hidden Body

We can once again turn to the children of the peasantry and their educational opportunities to explain the background of the circumstances
in which bourgeois children grew up. The former were surrounded by
potential information. If they were mature and receptive enough, they
could draw their own conclusions about animal reproduction, perhaps hear a couple of servants groaning together in the hay, and al-

Clean and Proper

most certainly learn how calves were born and suckled, how babies were tended and nursed. The mother was always present and could be seen in many different situations and in varying degrees of dress.

Almost everything was different in the cultural environment of the bourgeois home. There were no animals, of course, but that in itself was not the decisive factor. The mother and the women in the household were dressed to the teeth, as it were, with no chinks in their armor. Breast-feeding, which the mothers did not hesitate to do, was a private affair that concerned only the mother and the baby. The public displays of the peasant mother were unknown, and the babies were generally weaned off the breast after a few months. This pure maternal joy was private and brief.

It is perhaps a reflection of the uncertainty mothers must have felt about suckling that the arrival of feeding bottles was met with such satisfaction. The English saw one of the great advantages of this innovation in the way the bottle could be used to train young children in good habits at an early age (Robertson 1974:411). From the point of view of discipline, it was a greater risk to let the child indulge his oral wishes, whether at his mother's breast or with a wet nurse. It was moreover a social misalliance to allow the child to feed from the breast of a wet nurse of questionable background. The notion was still current that moral characteristics could be transferred to the child via breast milk. Reactions to wet nurses in Sweden were also colored by the view that the mother should not let a paid employee share the child's first smiles and signs of love (Langlet 1884:963).

There were few situations in which the children in the family could satisfy their curiosity about what women looked like (or men, for that matter). Sven Lidman has given us a sharply observed picture of himself and his mother in an intrinsically embarrassing situation, namely, in the bath:

> I am alone in the bathhouse with my mother. There is a little, cramped, wooden-ribbed bathtub. Steps lead up from it to a

Bourgeois Discipline

little, cramped changing room with a bench and a mirror. My mother stands on the top step. She is wearing a peculiar garment which I only now realize was a typical, standard Victorian bathing costume. A cap on her head, a sort of blouselike garment sitting tightly round her neck, and a skirt, both trimmed with white ribbons, and below the skirt black pants reaching to her ankles. The plank wall of the bathhouse appears terribly high to me, and the space on the steps down to the dark green water seems confined. There is something dark and deadly serious about the black-clad female figure on the steps, who now lifts me under the armpit in her hands and dips me in the water. I see the reflection in the water of the sunlight that finds its way in through some of the laths at the far end. This is the only spot of light in the otherwise dark picture. Then I let out a cry of protest and am dipped into the dark, inhospitable water.

Now I no longer scream consciously. My cry that time in the bathhouse has long since joined the tens of thousands of other cries of anxiety that form the bottom layer of a child's unconscious. But I ask myself in wonder: how did that thirty-year-old woman actually function in married life, when she had to wear a bathing costume that so completely concealed her body in the company of her three-year-old son in a cramped island bathhouse, totally shut off from public view?   (Lidman 1952:62)

It was not just from her son that the mother was concealing her body; it was also from herself. She had been taught to regard her own body as attractive and therefore shameful. She had consented to regard herself from a man's viewpoint. Bathing was a critical situation, where rules of modesty about nakedness clashed with the ever-increasing demands for cleanliness. Anyone interested in Victorian prudery will find a fruitful field of study in the ethics and techniques of bathing. We

Clean and Proper

may look at a few examples of the many problems that confronted the women especially.

Ann Margret Holmgren states that it was strictly forbidden for a lady to reveal in the presence of gentlemen that she intended to go bathing. This could arouse improper associations: "Such a strict degree of modesty was observed that we were not allowed to carry the towel draped over one arm; instead we were ordered to roll it up and carry it under the arm as inconspicuously as possible" (Holmgren 1921:65).

The rigid system of taboos designed to protect the female sex also meant that very young children (like Sven Lidman above) were denied insight and information. Alice Quensel explains that the vigilance exercised increased when brothers and sisters bathed together, following and reinforcing their parents' decrees. The nakedness of even the younger sisters had to be concealed from their brothers. Swimming was a highly private affair in those days.

> In the country we used to bathe in a bathhouse that had such a little pool that a child could swim no more than three strokes in it. We were not allowed to swim outside the bathhouse. Nevertheless we were supposed in theory to have learned the art. Some of us schoolfriends went for swimming lessons one winter. . . . My aunt came one day to observe our progress. Since she happened to be looking after my youngest brother, then almost three years old, he came along with her. This shocked my brother Gösta, guardian of morals in the nursery, and when my aunt countered with the defense that the little boy was so young, the answer she got was: "But he can spread what he sees in there!" (Quensel 1958:103f.)

The necessity for bodily hygiene also involved frequent washing of the entire body, a standard of cleanliness that was preached with increasing intensity the further up the social hierarchy one came. "Civ-

Bourgeois Discipline

ilized people bathe daily or at least once a week," according to one dictionary of etiquette (*BVT:s Lexikon* 1930:13). Women had to learn how to wash the upper part of their body with soap, water, and a flannel, without removing their lingerie. This required a certain suppleness and no little patience, but it meant that the ritual wash could be performed without neglecting the rules for decency. Such modesty could even be shown in the women-only department of the heated public baths. It was possible to clean the body without removing the garments closest to it, thus avoiding the inquisitive gaze of the female bath attendant. Bathing was included in the timetable for pupils at the French school in Stockholm from the turn of the century:

> I do not recollect how often this happened, but what I do remember is that when we came in to the bath attendant, we could not undress completely, but entered the water in the lingerie which we were wearing. I have forgotten how the attendant managed the brushing. It probably required great skill, but I do remember that it was only after we got out of the water and dried ourselves in some ingenious way that we were able to put on clean linen.   (Stjernstedt 1953:73)

The Ever Present

An obvious consequence of this secrecy was a heightened interest in what was concealed. Bourgeois society was built like a fortress, the walls of which defended the purity within from the dirt and pollution outside. Paradoxically, this conscious attempt to eliminate sensuality instead implanted it in everything, providing a systematic education of the senses that would have been unthinkable in peasant society, and also making sexuality into a subject for scientific study and inquisitive

Clean and Proper

obfuscation. This repressed sexuality was built into the schools, which were meant to be a focus of learning, a place where the growing generation was to be illuminated by the light of higher moral principles:

> One only has to glance over the architectural layout, the rules of discipline, and their whole internal organization: the question of sex was a constant preoccupation. The builders considered it explicitly. The organizers took it permanently into account. All who held a measure of authority were placed in a state of perpetual alert, which the fixtures, the precautions taken, the interplay of punishments and responsibilities, never ceased to reiterate. The space for classes, the shape of the tables, the planning of the recreation lessons, the distribution of the dormitories (with or without partitions, with or without curtains), the rules for monitoring bedtime and sleep periods—all this referred, in the most prolix manner, to the sexuality of the children. (Foucault 1978:27f.)

The repression of sexuality was thus symbolized in many aspects of culture: in the houses, in their planning and furnishing, and also of course in interpersonal relations. It is obvious that in a culture that felt compelled by decency to drape chair legs with fringes in order to avoid improper associations, there were constant reminders of what was supposed to be concealed.

Sven Lidman's autobiography (1952) is beyond comparison the frankest of the literary works that deal with Oscarian sexual education; accurate in its descriptions of his parents' home, forthright in its recording of the boy's impressions. The numerous fences around nakedness, the concealment of sexuality, and the veiled hints whispered in the home merely served to provoke Sven Lidman's curiosity.

> I want to go no further now. Feelings of shame and modesty try to restrain me from confessing something—a picture, a

Bourgeois Discipline

vision, a conscious act, which stands out in my memory with
repulsive clarity.

I am very curious, very inquisitive to see my father's member. I often sneak into the bedroom when he comes home
from work or from journeys, in order to look on while he
changes, takes off his jacket and waistcoat and trousers and
shirt. I want to see what he has inside his underpants, but my
longing is never satisfied.

But now he is dead—I am not sure now whether it is in his
coffin or on his deathbed, but I seem to remember that he
was in the coffin—and I sneak into the room and pull up the
shirt or the sheet or the shroud—with some difficulty. I see a
little shriveled penis surrounded by gray hair. I am filled with
a terrible disappointment: is that all there is? Is there nothing
more? This was my farewell to and last glimpse of my father,
who sired me. The child takes his revenge on death and the
dead man for concealing for so long the sight of his sex. (Lidman 1952:65f.)

There were peepholes in the fence, cracks in the wall through which
children could satisfy their curiosity, or perhaps increase it. For many
children from bourgeois families, life in the country was a source of
new knowledge. The summer vacation was in many respects a time of
freedom from compulsion and supervision, the constant companions
of town life. Here children could have their own experiences, drawing
their own conclusions from what they observed. In reading the memoirs one is struck by how often the authors remember the insights into
the mysteries of reproduction that they derived from visits to the
country. At home and in school they had acquired theoretical knowledge about the pollination of flowers by bees, but this was anchored in
concrete reality by the firsthand evidence to be observed outside the
stables. The parents naturally did not wish their children to absorb
this sort of knowledge, but there was little practical possibility of pre-

venting it. In any case, prohibitions would only have encouraged the children to try harder to see what was happening. Israel Holmgren spent the summers at Hessle, his relatives' farm in the mining district of Bergslagen:

> At Hessle we had a magnificent life. Nothing was forbidden, with a single exception. We were not allowed to look on while the mare was being covered. This was strictly forbidden, and consequently highly enticing. By means of clever strategic planning and tactical inventiveness we were usually able to observe. The stallion had a curb on his nose with a long rope on either side, so that a man could control the stallion's charge from a safe distance. The stallion reared up on his hind legs with a loud neigh and strode forward to the mare, who submissively bore her fate. Afterward a bucket of water was poured over the mare's rump to make her contract and retain what she had received. This performance was watched with enormous interest.   (Holmgren 1959:18)

Male sexuality was ever present. This was what women had to be protected against, and it was consequently what they were incessantly reminded of. Men of the Victorian era have been characterized as a collection of voyeurs. Women, whether they are treated in science or in art, are considered through a male temperament. It is always the man who is the observer and the actor, the man who defines what is feminine and what is not. It is also the man's suppressed view that is transferred to the women, becoming the filter through which they view themselves. The women had to learn that male sexuality was animal, something natural to which they were forced to be subordinate. The Victorian woman's given role was to "close her eyes and think of the Empire."

Only a deep and lasting love could justify sexual contact, writes Is-

Bourgeois Discipline

rael Holmgren in a section where he describes his mother's attitude to such matters: "Sexual intercourse without love was repulsive, a crime above all crimes. . . . She despised sensuality and anything that could lead the thoughts to sex. It disgusted her. I once heard her in a discussion . . . in the heat of the argument say: 'The natural reaction of a woman to the sight of a naked man is to vomit'" (Holmgren 1959:39f.). Holmgren emphasizes how his mother's outlook on these questions left lasting traces in his development. When seen against this background, the intense interest he showed above for what went on in the stables appears all the more natural. Every taboo makes the forbidden thing at once exciting, highly charged, dirty, and, understandably enough, ever present.

Hands on the Blanket

Male sexuality was successfully disciplined to the extent that men rarely embarked upon sexual relationships with women until quite late in life. Peasants probably made their sexual debut relatively early. The actual age depended on the age when they married. Belonging to the circle of young adults (after confirmation) and participating in the customs of night courtship made sexuality legitimate (Wikman 1937:17ff.).

In bourgeois culture the ideal for young people of both sexes was to "save it for marriage." In desperation over the breakup of his engagement, Israel Holmgren had his first sexual intercourse with a woman at the age of twenty-eight (Holmgren 1959:74). Before this he had never "touched" his fiancée; premarital intercourse was unacceptable.

This inhibition laid the foundation for a double standard of morality, which made prostitution a necessary evil. Whores allowed men to relieve their frustrations at regular intervals with no untoward social consequences. Scientific discourse even emphasized the physiological

Clean and Proper

benefits to be derived from regular evacuations, which for men obviously required either marriage or prostitution.[2] Bourgeois women, who by definition did not have the same urgent drives, could wait until it was time for them to bring children into the world.

Male sexuality was nevertheless a constant threat until it was safely steered into the marital haven. Perhaps the clearest evidence for this caution and fear is the widespread terror provoked by masturbation. It was believed that if parents were not vigilant enough in the nursery, their children could grow into habitual onanists. The mother had to ensure that her sons slept with their hands on the blanket. Young boys were told always to look up, not down, when they were in company.

Sven Lidman grew up in his uncle's home in Västerås. His uncle's greatest fear was that his nephew would become a masturbator, a word with "such a terrible and repulsive sound that it sufficed to deter me from even thinking of such a vice" (Lidman 1952:260f.). The first time the young boy became aware of the significance of the word was in early puberty.

> During the first weeks of my stay in Västerås I was asked in a ruthless and inquisitorial fashion if I was in the habit of "jerking off."
>
> Since the very thought of spending my time fingering the little instrument stuck between my legs, which I used exclusively for "tinkling" with, was so totally foreign to me, I naturally replied no in great embarrassment at this completely unexpected question.
>
> "Don't lie, just tell the truth and you won't get a beating. But if you lie, you're for it. All boys jerk off, all boys lie, all boys steal, but they can be made civilized. Just tell the truth and you'll escape a beating."
>
> I told the truth and therefore got a beating. A severe beat-

Bourgeois Discipline

ing. With a swift and practiced grip of my collar and the skin
of my neck he lifted me like a pup, and the stick danced on
my back and my flaying legs. Never in my life had I been
beaten by an adult. It was a violent, surprising, overwhelming
pain, which caused my whole being to explode in screams. I
screamed until it hurt so much that I was prepared to admit
my guilt of any crime. I lied and confessed that I had occasionally "jerked off." This although I was ignorant of the reality behind the strange and repellent words! So the beating
stopped with the grim admonition: "Right, you won't try to
tell lies again." (Lidman 1952:212f.)

The punishment was administered by a man who was a high school
teacher, and consequently knew what young boys got up to. He was
the founder of a park in Västerås, Djäkneberget, where the educational
mission was proclaimed in the many maxims inscribed in stone: "Remove the secret sins of the early years. Precocious lust destroys the
fruit of years of solicitude." Future generations of schoolchildren could
thus be made to understand that there were rewards awaiting those
with the ability to discipline their instincts.

All weapons were permissible in the war against the solitary vice of
masturbation. Medical books proffered concrete advice to parents
concerning cures for the habit, from diets, water baths, and medicine
to more drastic measures such as spiked cages and plaster casts to
keep boys from fingering their genitals, and even surgery—there are
accounts that show that doctors circumcised young boys and cured
girls of the vice by clitoridectomy or infibulation.[3] The mechanical and
surgical measures were probably rare, however; the best way to pre-
vent children from masturbating was direct parental control. Doctor
Ruff's popular medical encyclopedia describes how young self-
abusers could be detected:

Clean and Proper

For this purpose parents, teachers, and educators must always keep their eyes open. The onanist can be recognized even when he is not caught in the act, by unmistakable signs: when he is absent-minded in class, when he lags behind in his studies despite previous evidence of ability, when he is excessively fond of visiting the lavatory, by his furtive gaze, pale complexion, rings around the eyes, difficulty in breathing in bed, sullenness in the mornings, lack of vigor despite long rest at night. The alpha and omega of the treatment of this sort of onanist is stern discipline. In school the teacher's eye should always be on him; he should be under supervision during the breaks; at home the parents must undertake supervision. He should not sleep alone in his room; one must not shun the trouble of going to his bed several times a night and drawing down the blanket, whether he is asleep or not. When threatened by such visitations, the misled boy will not dare practice his manipulations. Should he nevertheless do so, he must have stout sticks tied tightly to his wrists at night; brothers and sisters should be allowed to see these instruments of punishment, without of course being informed of the meaning or reason behind them; at night he should also be dressed in a one-piece garment fully sealed to the shape of his trunk and limbs; with the aid of this dress even the toughest little sinner can be rendered meek.   (Ruff 1893:553)

Further assistance in the struggle against self-abuse was provided by doctors who could assure masturbators that they were destroying their own body and soul. There was a rich array of notions about the abnormal punishments that awaited the masturbator, from hairs in the palms of the hands to atrophy of the spinal cord, epilepsy, and even total paralysis. August Strindberg tells in *The Son of a Servant* of an encounter with one of the nineteenth century's most important

Bourgeois Discipline

books in the battle against masturbation, *Warning by a Friend of Youth against the Most Dangerous Enemy of Youth*, by the German pietist Karl von Kapff.[4] During a summer vacation in the country, Strindberg's hero, having learned how to masturbate from an older friend, had welcomed the habit as a gift from nature. Back in Stockholm, however, when he read Kapff's book,

> his eyes skipped over the pages without daring to stop. His knees trembled, the blood drained from his face, his pulse froze. It was all too clear: he was condemned to death or lunacy at the age of twenty-five! His spinal marrow and his brain would rot, his face would turn into a death's-head, his hair would fall out, his hands would tremble. Horrible! And the cure? Christ! But Jesus could not heal the body, only the soul. The body was condemned to death at five-and-twenty; the only thing left was to save the soul from everlasting damnation. (Strindberg 1967b:108).

It is important not to blame only the medical profession for the myths about the effects of self-abuse. Of course, their declaration that this moral transgression could lead to physical and mental illness did put a weapon in the hands of anxious parents, giving medical legitimacy to their supervision of the nursery. But the message found an excellent seedbed in the aura of secrecy and feelings of guilt surrounding what was forbidden. In supervising the sexuality of their children, parents were fighting their own sexuality (DeMause 1974:43).

Young people in bourgeois culture were expected to have a healthy mind, a go-ahead spirit, and good carriage. The picture of the onanistic youth was the exact opposite of the ideal—the sinner was apathetic, insecure, and lacking in backbone. In short, he lacked the self-discipline that was the ultimate virtue of his culture. He had given free rein to his natural drives. Sexuality links us to the animals and is con-

Clean and Proper

sequently a threat to civilized life and the rational social order. It was considered an antisocial force that had to be bridled lest it break down the individual and ultimately his society. The stricter the social order, the more repressed is sexuality.

"Disorder is the beginning of all sin" is another of the precepts from Djäkneberget, which urged young people to exercise discipline and self-control. Later on in life the children would make the acquaintance of heterosexual love and in the safe haven of marriage learn to restrict sexual intercourse to the minimum necessary for the reproduction of the species. To give the natural drives a freedom greater than this moderation was to endanger one's health in the same way as with masturbation. In a book of advice for people in love and newlyweds entitled *Tyst!* (Silence!), which appeared in a number of editions, the author writes:

> For a rational person, sexual intercourse should, like every-
> thing else, have its value *not in the pleasure it affords*, but
> more in the fact that our Creator's purpose for it was *the
> preservation of the human race*. If this purpose is to be
> fulfilled, moderation in the enjoyment of intercourse is the
> chief precondition for its attainment, and this applies not just
> to one of the sexes, but to both.   (Becker 1916:17)

When parents ensured that their children slept with their hands on the blanket, it was primarily in the hope that they would one day be able to practice this ordered and controlled form of sexuality.

The Subordinates

The madonnalike bourgeois mother conveyed a stunted feminine ideal to the inhabitants of the nursery. She impressed on her daugh-

Bourgeois Discipline

ters the role of subordination and made her sons suspicious of women in any position other than that of housewife. The children's view of the world was filtered through her care. It is probably true to say, however, that the mother's role in Victorian society has been overestimated. Instead it was the constant presence of the servants that gave children their ideas of how society was structured, how they themselves functioned, and—perhaps most of all—gave them their view of the relations between the sexes (Davidoff 1976).

The home demanded a lot of work, not in the sense that it was a sphere of production, like the peasant farm, but because it required constant cleaning. With the disappearance of practical work from the home, the need for cleanliness—paradoxically—increased.[5] The textiles in the home had to be washed at regular intervals, the house had to be swept every day, and the floor had to be scrubbed frequently. The many ornaments had to be dusted and polished until they shone. Every aspect of daily life in the home was governed by order:

> The first of these duties [of the housewife] is *order*. If a
> housewife lacks a sense of order she must work with all her
> might to attain it, for without order there is not and never can
> be any ability to manage a house properly. Order does not
> merely consist of keeping rooms tidy, so that nothing is "lying
> around"; what is not visible must have its place and *be in its
> place*. But this is just order in one sense. There must be a
> fixed order for the day, according to which all recurrent daily
> tasks are carried out. The servants must know that *first* they
> must light fires in all the rooms, *then* they must sweep up,
> *and then* lay the table, and so on, so that the table is not laid
> in a room with no fire, so that there are no twigs or bark lying
> in front of the fireplace after the room is swept, and so on.
>
> In addition, there must be a definite order for when meals
> are to be had by children, parents, and servants; children
> should have their set times for washing, reading, and the like;

Clean and Proper

clean towels and sheets should be issued at fixed times; porcelain and glass should never be left on the drainboard in the
kitchen; beds must be made, rooms must be aired—in a
word, all household duties must be performed in a certain
order, which should be broken only when absolutely necessary. Every job to be done should be carried in the housewife's mind like a timetable, and when she has attained good
order and can maintain it, it will soon become a habit both
for her and for all in the household, and this will make everything incomparably easier, just as it will spread a sense of
well-being and give a feeling of order to daily life. (Langlet
1884:9).

The responsibility for order in the home rested on the shoulders of
the housewife, but the practical duties were discharged by the subordinates. While the lady of the house planned what was to be done, it
was the servants who were put to work. Naturally, this pattern was varied to suit the economic circumstances of the household and the
phase of the family circle in which they found themselves. Each
household strove to the best of its ability to keep both a housemaid,
who took care of the routine tasks of keeping order, and a cook, whose
job was to buy and prepare the food. Thus it was left to the subordinates to transform raw food into cooked, to transform nature into culture. It was a sign of the elevated position of the housewife in society
that she escaped the tiresome work and all direct contact with organic
processes.

To consider for a moment the actual duties of the servants, the
maids had to exert themselves to keep dirt outside the house. They
had the practical concern of ensuring that order and culture reigned
in the safety of the home. From the contemporary point of view, the
most interesting duty of the maid was to rear the children. Of course,
she did not bear the moral responsibility for their upbringing—which

Bourgeois Discipline

was in the hands of the parents—but she was responsible for the everyday contact with the young children. She ensured that they were clean, changed their diapers and began their toilet training, blew their noses, and wiped the food off their faces at the table. Furthermore, it was usually the maid who ate with the children until they had learned good enough manners to be allowed to graduate to the parents' dining table (Nolan 1979).

All the close, physical processes, all the essentials of life were thus in the care of the domestics. They did the monotonous and dirty manual work of looking after the home. Theirs was the everyday duty of transforming the children into cultured beings. As has been shown, a lower status is attached to such tasks all over the world. It is involved in the question of the subordination of woman—she has traditionally been the one responsible for transforming nature into culture. It is also involved in the role of the servants in a bourgeois household.

There is, however, an important difference between the allocation of labor according to sex and according to social status. Servants in the bourgeois home were recruited from a completely different class of people from the master and mistress of the household. They mostly came from a rural background or from the working class of the towns. Housework was the traditional source of income for young unmarried women well into the 1930s (Moberg 1978).

This circumstance must have been of great importance for the world of the nursery. Children had to learn that the people who cleaned up, who cooked their food, who put them to bed and ensured that they were clean and proper, were actually their subordinates. Such duties were discharged by people over whom both the children and the parents had power and authority.

Children could see clearly that the servants were people of a different sort. While the children were instructed from an early age in the arts of good behavior, correct speech, keeping a dry nose, and not smelling, they had before them people who did not live up to this

Clean and Proper

ideal. Country girls were not so particular about hygiene, they did not speak correctly, often having instead a noticeable dialect or a "coarse" speech of the sort used by the lower classes of society. Education, finesse, class, and refinement, which the children of the nursery were incessantly urged to attain, were qualities that the servants seldom possessed.

Earlier, theories were mentioned about how aversion to other people is built into the individual with the help of physical control (chapter 4, under "The Body as a Bridge.") The cultural basis of such physical disgust finds a classic illustration in the relationship between children and subordinates. Children who learned step by step how to suppress the animal in them, to distance themselves from organic processes, nevertheless saw daily examples of people who represented what they had been taught was improper or unsuitable for people of their own sort. The wonder felt at the behavior of the lower classes was therefore hardly a conscious reaction. Later in life they saw the existence of class barriers as self-evident. They did not distance themselves from the lower classes out of malice or explicit ill-will; it was a feeling that sat in their backbone.

The servants had yet another quality that is frequently found in people in the marginal areas of society who work with transformations from nature to culture: their supposed moral laxity. As soon as they entered the house, their morals had to be supervised by the housewife: "No men in your room." Moreover, they were a living threat to the morality of the whole family. The master of the house saw the maids as easy prey; the children could through them learn many of the things from which their parents sought to shield them (Nolan 1979).

> The parents should watch carefully to ensure that no intimate relationship develops between the children and the servants, since this can quite often be dangerous for the children's morals. Above all, the children should not be left alone

Bourgeois Discipline

with the servants when the parents are away. Even with respect to the relationship between the nanny, or the nurse-
maid as she is now called, and the children entrusted to her
care, a conscientious mother cannot be too attentive. (Norden 1913:196)

These words from a book of advice to the housewife can be juxta-
posed with contemporary accounts in the memoirs of how exciting it
was for children to listen to servants' tales and how unsuitable the
parents found this habit (see chapter 3, under "Invisible Parents"). It
was usually in the kitchen that children in bourgeois homes came to
understand some of the broad outlines of the mysteries of reproduction. It was in the same place that they first learned dirty words (Rehnberg 1969). In his memoirs, the ambassador Fredrik Wrangel looks
back with displeasure on the close relations between himself and the
servants during his childhood. At a mature age he realizes that the
knowledge derived from this association was not of the sort from
which he could benefit later in life. This bridging of class barriers was
undesirable:

We got on well with our servants, of whom some had seen
our birth and that of our mother; but when I think back to
that intimacy, especially with the male servants at a slightly
later period, I must confess that I consider such company
after the very earliest years of childhood to be unsuitable, not
to say downright harmful, for a growing youth. I learned most
of the obscenities and indecent songs and some bad habits
from the younger menservants, whose society appeared
more pleasant to me at that time than that of the more serious teachers. (Wrangel 1924:313)

Philippe Ariès cites similar attitudes about servants from eighteenth-
century France (Ariès 1962:117). Menservants were to be found in the

homes of the Swedish nobility, like that of Fredrik Wrangel, but in ordinary town houses at the turn of the century this was a rare luxury. Instead it was the female help and the nursemaids who were in contact with the children. It was therefore entirely logical that the children associated them with the sphere of the erotic. Maids represented what was close, physical, dirty, and sexual. These properties contrasted particularly strongly with the image of the pure, radiant, distant mother.

There is a pronounced hierarchical aspect in the bourgeois view of sexuality. Men turned to the girls of the lower classes instead of to their own equals. This can be explained in part by the inaccessibility of the daughters of the better classes, but there was also a clearly expressed attraction in lower-class women. This difference must be due in large measure to the conditioning of the nursery (Davidoff 1976).

The Origins of Self-discipline

The same strict rules that directed people's sexual lives were applied throughout the physical register. A cultured person was one who knew how to discriminate the physical from the social. This cultural ideal of prudery has been seen in bourgeois milieus at the turn of the century, and specific examples of it have been identified going back a few decades into the last century. Is it possible to pinpoint the historical period when it started to spread throughout Swedish society?

It is necessary to go no further back than the middle of the nineteenth century to find a human type that differed in significant respects from the moderate and restrained bourgeois ideal. I am referring not to the less-disciplined peasantry but to the upper stratum of society. From Stockholm in the 1840s comes an account by Erik af Edholm, marshal of the court, of a dinner-dance at the home of Fredrik af Klercker, with the following riotous and uninhibited scene:

Bourgeois Discipline

> After the dinner we danced a frantic "Weave the Homespun,"
> in which the gentlemen fling each other against the wall and
> the ladies get bruised arms, sweat pours and trousers rip,
> followed by a *hambo* wild enough to straighten curls as
> heads swung, and skirts flew up to the knee, and finally a
> dance called "Hot Sauna," I think, or at least it justified such a
> name. Last of all, L. danced a *polska* without music with five
> men, so lively that Björkenstam's wig fell down over his nose
> and forced him to rush out into the hall, much to everyone's
> amusement.   (af Edholm 1948:1733)

At this dance there are no cultured people in the sense of the term used hitherto. Men grasp their partners tightly, swing wildly, and are not ashamed to sweat. To what extent the liveliness of this *tableau vivant* was matched by similar abandon in everyday life is uncertain, but it is clear that the reckless enjoyment of physical sensations had not yet been proscribed.

Therefore, it was not until the second half of the nineteenth century that self-discipline as a life-style began its spread through the higher levels of society. Yet it does not mean that these features are found first at this time. The history of prudery goes back much further.

Medieval etiquette books, first written for princes and the nobility, stress basically the same rules of tidiness that applied on the peasant's farm. The ideal was to be clean and wholesome and well-behaved in front of other people, but there was no taboo on what was physical. When a young man blows his nose, for example, he should refrain from holding his nose with the same fingers with which he is going to eat; yet it was perfectly legitimate to use the fingers (Elias 1978:143ff.).

Medieval man was, according to Norbert Elias's theory of the civilizing process, a barbarian. He gave full expression to his drives and his aggressions, not bridling his physical self. Brutal violence was an everyday reality, war and the slaughter of the enemy a pleasure. Man

Clean and Proper

satisfied his sexual instinct without the inhibitions of bad conscience or shame. It is important, of course, not to romanticize the Middle Ages as a time of unbridled sensuality—medieval people did not give totally free rein to their passions (Huizinga 1924:95ff.); yet in their attitude toward the affective ego, they let themselves be guided more by their impulses and emotions. It was a later human type that became more calculating in the matter of what could be revealed and what should be concealed.

The putative barbarism of the feudal lords was gradually eliminated after the Renaissance, as a civilized human ideal began to take shape in the sixteenth and seventeenth centuries. The elimination of barbarism was achieved, according to Elias, by means of hygiene.

Let us return to the ethics of nose-blowing to illustrate this theory. During the seventeenth century the handkerchief made its entry into the courts of European kings. Its use began in the influential court of Louis XIV, from whence the fashion spread to the French nobility and to other European courts. The handkerchief was used not just as a decoration, but also for blowing the nose. It was considered distasteful to get mucus on the fingers.

What applied to the nose was later applied to a broader range of bodily functions. People were expected to cough discreetly, to laugh with restraint, to move in a controlled manner. People began to take an interest in how many hours they should sleep, how they should sleep, and so on. The whole of man's physical self became a focus of interest.

Bodily functions were bridled because giving them free rein was said to be dangerous for the health. Strong emotions not only jeopardized spiritual equilibrium, but could also lead to physical complaints. The sexual instinct had to be disciplined because it cost the body too much to produce semen; the exhaustion that followed the excitement of intercourse was an indication of how much of a man's and a woman's power had been consumed in the act. It also came to

Bourgeois Discipline

be seen that keeping the body clean and well cared for was a decisive factor for general health.

An example of these attitudes is a passage from a Danish medical book from the eighteenth century, warning of the effects of fornication and, once again, masturbation: "It is scarcely conceivable that there is any disease of the body or of any part of it or of the soul that does not have its origin in fornication or self-abuse. This more than any other cause destroys all that is beautiful in a person's figure and appearance. It removes all charm, grace, and beauty from every man's and woman's face, quenches the fire and life of the eyes." Among the most important and ineluctable consequences of this vice are listed:

"fatigue and thinness, an old, pale, cachetic, dirty face, . . . epilepsy, convulsions, and all manner of cramp, . . . a thousand types of stomach disorder, . . . swollen eyelids, total blindness, a sort of scurvy with bleeding and loosening of the gums, which when pressed gently emit a foul-smelling mucus, stinking breath, and ill-smelling, white, thick urine, paralysis of one or more parts of the body. . . . (cited in Hansen 1957:39)

Another medical book says that if a man committed adultery, the health of his whole family suffered. The wife could begin to fret, and this could lead, if she were breast-feeding, to the transfer of her mortification via the mother's milk to the child. The life of the child might thus be sacrificed because of the father's adulterous ways (cited in Hansen 1957:41). If this claim sounds familiar, it is because the same argumentation, with health as the constant point of reference and guardian of norms, is heard again in the bourgeoisie of the turn of the century.

Rules about health are most clearly seen in the many handbooks on child-rearing. The seventeenth and eighteenth centuries were, according to Philippe Ariès, the period of the discovery of childhood and its importance for individual character formation. Children had previously been regarded as miniature adults. Their earliest childhood years were nothing more than a period of growth, after which they could function as full social beings. Less importance was therefore attached to their care and upbringing—they did not need to be molded into adults, but were simply absorbed into the adult world (Ariès 1962).

The insight that childhood was a time of learning increased the efforts made in the sphere of education and upbringing. What is of special importance for us is the major place devoted to the child's training in cleanliness. Children were to be imbued at an early age with their own sense of the desirability and necessity of keeping clean. The ultimate reason for needing to be clean and wholesome was *health*; dirt invited disease. Another result of the concern for health was that children should not masturbate or rouse their emotions or indulge in violent physical motion. The child's world and his sphere of activity was circumscribed by parents and guardians with constant reference to the danger that the child could bring on himself by leaving the playpen, by breaking the norms.

Health was the weapon with which barbarism was eliminated. Civilized man was led to believe that what was undesirable in society and what was condemned by other people or authorities was best refrained from for reasons of health. Breaking the norms brought personal injury. People who worried about their physical health and their spiritual equilibrium had to watch themselves and exert self-discipline. Of course, the princes of the Middle Ages had their own etiquette and their rules of cleanliness and good conduct, but they never imagined that they could come to harm by breaking the norms. It might be dishonorable for them to go against convention, they might offend the people around them by maladroit behavior, but they did

Bourgeois Discipline

not imagine that this could bring illness upon them. Civilized man, by contrast, internalized the social norms and the rules of etiquette because he was convinced that he could come to harm by transgressing them. This pacification of the individual took place simultaneously with a general pacification on the social plane.

If this reasoning (based on Elias 1978) is valid, it would mean that the bourgeois mentality at the turn of the century was the product of a relatively short historical process. The strict self-control that was their main characteristic and which was lacking among contemporary peasants can be dated back to the upper-class world of the seventeenth century.

The function of control that Freud calls the superego is, according to Elias, a product of social and historical events. The superego is, according to Freud, that part of the psyche which restrains aggression and the libido, guaranteeing that the drives are not given the free expression that our nature seeks for them:

> His aggressiveness is introjected, internalized; it is, in point of fact, sent back to where it came from—that is, it is directed towards his own ego. There it is taken over by a portion of the ego, which sets itself over against the rest of the ego as superego, and which now, in the form of "conscience," is ready to put into action against the ego the same harsh aggressiveness that the ego would have liked to satisfy upon other, extraneous individuals. The tension between the harsh super-ego and the ego that is subjected to it, is called by us the sense of guilt; it expresses itself as a need for punishment. Civilization, therefore, obtains mastery over the individual's dangerous desire for aggression by weakening and disarming it and by setting up an agency within him to watch over it, like a garrison in a conquered city.   (Freud 1930:123f.)

Clean and Proper

Elias's contribution to an understanding of the way the bourgeois character was formed would then be his indication of the role played by control over all the physical processes. The individual has molded his instinctual life with reference to his health. The strict morals of bourgeois culture can therefore be derived from ideas of hygiene and health, ideas about the importance of always being clean and wholesome in thought, word, and deed.

Disgust and Compassion

We often had a modest little seamstress in the house—always the same person—and she dined with us. Father was very tolerant toward this simple dinner guest, although she sometimes behaved in a way that was in direct conflict with all the laws and prescriptions of our parents. Among other things, she peeled the potatoes with her nails, and she would sometimes proffer a potato hand-peeled in this way to Father and say in a shy but friendly way:
"Would the doctor like a spud?"
Father's charming smile as he accepted the gift revealed nothing of the horror and disgust which must have made his skin crawl.   (Blumenthal-Engström 1947:45)

Table manners had an important social function. To observe the rituals of behavior at table was to reveal that one had received a good upbringing and came from a good family. Table manners also gave security in society, with no need to hesitate about how to hold the knife, which spoon to use for dessert, how to drink toasts, make conversation, and behave at table. On the other hand, it was immediately obvi-

Bourgeois Discipline

ous if a person had not learned the complex codes and infringed one of the many unwritten rules. The dinner table was the classic scene in which the parvenu gave himself away. Here it was evident who had class and who lacked it.

Servants never participated in meals in the bourgeois home. The housemaid waited on people at the table, but she herself ate in the kitchen. Nor did the servants eat the same food as the people upstairs. Temporary workers from outside the household—gardeners, washerwomen, and others—were naturally fed in the kitchen too. The bourgeois consequently exercised the greatest discretion when choosing the people with whom to dine. The thought of having dinner with people who shoveled in the food, chewed with open mouths, and rested their elbows on the table was not particularly inviting. Physical disgust worked as a barrier here.

Eating in public places, in the streets, might be all right for common people, but it was quite unsuitable for children of better families. It was too closely associated with animality:

> Hasse Z. once observed that a person chewing has a sheep-like appearance, reminiscent of a beast chewing the cud. The observation is perfectly correct, and is confirmed beyond refutation by people chewing gum or with their mouths full of candy. As long as chewing is confined to appropriate situations, at the dinner table or by the picnic basket, it is justified, but when a person eats while walking along the street, sitting on the tram, or behind the steering wheel, the judgment hits the nail on the head. One cannot wander along the street while eating. Little children and common individuals may innocently partake of dinner or refreshments during a walk across town, but if a person of respectable character saunters down Main Street stuffing his face with ham sandwiches, beer, or ice cream, this always causes a certain stir. If a per-

Clean and Proper

son is forced by circumstances to consume his food on the
street in a place where there is no proper outdoor service, he
should do it clandestinely, exactly like the Chinaman who
turns his back in shame over having to discharge the natural
need to eat. (Wingårdh 1937:408)[6]

The complicated etiquette of eating also communicated the message
that at table the physical has been dissociated from the social. Although an organic need—hunger—was being satisfied, it was not
permitted to reveal that one was hungry. Food had to be eaten with
self-control. As far as possible, there should be no reminders of the
place in which the food was prepared; there should be no cooking
fumes in the dining room. The person serving the food must wear ritual dress: black and white on ceremonial occasions, otherwise everyday blue and white.

Cooking fumes led the thoughts to people who lived in closer contact with the primitive stage, and were therefore incompatible with
cultured life:

"It smells of concierge," Grandmother often said on the stair-
case. There was a smell of coffee grounds and cabbage and
wet laundry. A washing pot on the range and cabbage, boiled
cabbage, because it is cheap food. Coffee grounds and boiling
coffee smell of poverty. That is not how it should smell. Every
time Grandmother and Grandfather made coffee in their
enormous apartment in Östermalm, the coffee filter was
thrown into the toilet and flushed away so that there would
be no smell of coffee grounds anywhere.   (Kullenberg
1974:132)

It was generally considered gauche to smell. Excessively strong
perfume was vulgar, and body odors were likewise a sign of the lower
classes. Children were imprinted with these prejudices as moral com-

Bourgeois Discipline

mandments; violations of hygiene were sins. Sven Lidman's daughter Ulla has described how painful it felt for her to be told by a stranger that she smelled:

> An elegant lady came in to say goodnight to the girls. Charlotte had not seen her before. She had hair like fire and was white in the face, with large, burning eyes.
> "It smells good in here," she said in a cheerful voice, sniffing the air. "It smells of newly washed children."
> Charlotte was profoundly embarrassed. It was almost as shameful for people to smell as to tell fibs. (Lidman-Frostenson 1963:78)

Which social groups smelled, ate without manners or discipline in the heat of the range and the cooking fumes? Who had an undisciplined attitude about sex and were quick to anger and sorrow? Naturally it was the coarse and uncultured working class and the churlish, unkempt peasant. (Incidentally, the peasant was never such a figure of fun as at the turn of the century, when stereotyped mockery of the riffraff of town and country was at its height.)

In order to understand the cautious prudery, the well-controlled life-style, the emphasis on the home and its order in contrast to the outside world and its chaos, it is important to see these phenomena for what they really were: a defense mechanism against the social unrest that was plaguing society. The working class was being formed, producing the welfare from which the bourgeoisie generally profited. Through their controlled life-style the bourgeoisie acquired an armor that protected them from mixing with the lower classes. The tabooing of the worker as a physical being erected a clear fence between "us up here and you down there." The economic superiority of the bourgeoisie was justified by their greater refinement and culture; the workers were at a different level.

This message was implicit in the rituals and dress of the dinner ta-

Clean and Proper

ble, perhaps more clearly expressed in dress than in anything else. Clothing emphasized the difference between people who needed to earn their living with their bodies and those who lived solely by the power of their minds. Dress was basically intended to show the distance from physical labor. The ladies' corsets and high heels, the artfully arranged hairstyles and the many-pleated skirts excluded any associations with work. The men's pressed trousers, stiff chokers, and starched shirtfronts were likewise incompatible with hard work. Elegance was synonymous with the absence of any clothing that might suggest work. Moreover, the clothes in themselves were a direct obstacle to physical labor (Veblen 1899:120f.).

It is well to note that this message was often concealed. It seldom happened that the bourgeoisie openly admitted their loathing of people from the lower classes. But the physical aversion was always there, as George Orwell says:

> Here you come to the real secret of class distinction in the West—the real reason why a European of bourgeois upbringing, even when he calls himself a Communist, cannot without a hard effort think of a working man as his equal. It is summed up in four frightful words which people nowadays are chary of uttering, but which were bandied about quite freely in my childhood. The words were: *The lower classes smell.*
>
> That was what we were taught—*the lower classes smell.* And here, obviously, you are at an impossible barrier. For no feeling of like or dislike is quite so fundamental as a *physical* feeling. Race-hatred, religious hatred, differences of education, of temperament, of intellect, even differences of moral code, can be got over; but physical repulsion cannot. You can have an affection for a murderer or a sodomite, but you cannot have an affection for a man whose breath stinks—habit-

Bourgeois Discipline

> ually stinks, I mean. However well you may wish him, how-
> ever much you may admire his mind and character, if his
> breath stinks he is horrible and in your heart of hearts you
> will hate him. It may not greatly matter if the average middle-
> class person is brought up to believe that the working classes
> are ignorant, lazy, drunken, boorish, and dishonest; it is
> when he is brought up to believe that they are dirty that the
> harm is done. And in my childhood we *were* brought up to
> believe that they were dirty.   (Orwell 1937:159f.)

All middle-class children were trained in cleanliness; other people's impurity was a concrete reason to repudiate them. The aversion to contact with working-class people was not due to dislike, but to the fact that they were dirty.

Elna Tenow, a journalist who worked energetically to raise the general level of hygiene among Swedes at the turn of the century, found that the Swedish working class in particular needed hygienic rearmament:

> The unskilled Swedish worker huddles in the darkness and
> the dirt, often sleeps in his clothes and his dirty boots, wears
> woollen clothes steeped in months of sweat, eats a lot of
> flatulent food with rancid butter, American bacon, a multi-
> tude of potatoes, beer, coffee, milk, spirits, anything he comes
> across, badly cooked and greedily swallowed. It is perfectly
> natural that as a result he becomes a stinking animal, swear-
> ing, spitting, quid-chewing, smoking the vilest of tobaccos,
> and hating all those who look at him with furtive looks, full of
> scorn, fear, and compassion all at the same time. In these
> looks he reads class hatred, which arouses the animal in-
> stinct of vengeance in him. If he were able to interpret these
> looks more correctly, he could understand that the fear is

Clean and Proper

only of his stinking body, the scorn is only for his filthy clothing, and the compassion is for his broken escutcheon disfig-
uring the chivalry of the human race. (Törne 1906:57f.)

Class hatred has here been transformed into the feeling that seizes the
cultured person on witnessing this revelation of unhygienic animality.
From this description it is understandable that the bourgeoisie of the
time found it difficult to embrace the working class.

It is rare to find such direct evidence of the feelings provoked in
them by the workers—or the peasants for that matter. It is more usual
to find expressions of compassion, the desire to alleviate the wretch-
edness of the working class and the poor in the towns. The latter half
of the nineteenth century was the time when many charitable organizations were founded and even more private initiatives were made a
reality. These practical gestures of help may seem like an attempt to
bridge the class gulf, perhaps appearing to contradict the claim that
bourgeois culture was a bulwark against the working class. But the
truth is that charity was for the most part aimed at people in genuinely
difficult circumstances, the absolute poorest. Its goal was to help
through isolated gestures, by donating clothes and necessities together with a few wise words about the value of order, cleanliness, and
perhaps the fear of God. Charity could be called missionary work in
the outskirts of society. Poverty was for the benefactors a moral rather
than a social problem. The poor had not seized the opportunities
granted to them; they had failed to show the industry and the capacity
for self-discipline that could have taken them out of the slum.

The charitable movements were kept going by women from the middle class. The aim of their work was no doubt noble, but its effect was
only to emphasize more strongly the difference between the two cultures. On one side of the class barrier were the fine, well-off ladies who
sought to uplift poor, abandoned women to their own level. This relationship was not one of equality, so the result was the opposite—it

Bourgeois Discipline

deepened the gulf (Ehrenreich and English 1973:74f.). The moral message and the proclamation of the blessings of hygiene could not be accepted until the material circumstances had changed. This needed much more than charity.

• CONCLUSION: A CULTURE ON THE MOVE •

This book began with a piece of bourgeois self-representation in the form of a definition of culture from an encyclopedia of 1911. The next edition, from 1930, tries to define culture in a different way, avoiding excessively evolutionistic overtones: it is a much more low-key presentation of a middle-class world view. Such transformations of an encyclopedia definition tell us something about the changing identity of a culture on the move.

In our discussions of the culture building of the Oscarian bourgeoisie, we have examined the ways in which several basic cultural themes —from the organization of time to conceptions of the body—have been developed over time, and also how they have been anchored in everyday life. We have not limited the analysis entirely to the period from about 1880 to 1910, but at times have widened the historical perspective both backward and forward in time. In some ways this study has grown out of an ongoing historical dialogue with the present. This somewhat undisciplined handling of the subject comes from the fact that our chief aim is to discuss processes of cultural dominance, subordination, and resistance. For the same reason, we have contrasted middle-class culture with those of the declining peasantry and the emerging working class. This cross-class comparison has served two ends. First of all, we have used these other milieus as cultural contrasts to sharpen the profile of middle-class life-styles. Second, we have been interested in the process of cultural confrontation. This study is part of a larger research effort to look at the ways in which different Swedish subcultures and class cultures have developed in a dialectical relationship including both dependence on and opposition to other groups and classes, the way social hierarchies may be trans-

Conclusion

formed into cultural ones, and the way class conflicts can be expressed in terms of cultural battles, whether definitions of dirt or of a good home.

This relationship between social change and culture building can be illustrated by summarizing the transformations of nineteenth-century bourgeois culture into the middle-class definitions of the good and proper life in the twentieth century. The culture builder evolved in the prosperous, upward-climbing bourgeoisie of the eighteenth century, and this life-style was consolidated in the course of the following century. Accounts of the formation of this life-style usually stress its original character of a counterculture, challenging the dominant aristocratic elite. Understanding the cultural profile of the bourgeoisie in this early era hinges on a reiteration that its quest for power was a battle waged on two fronts. The new class had to define itself not only vis-à-vis the old aristocracy but also vis-à-vis the peasantry. This structure of cultural warfare is mirrored in the use of key identity symbols, in techniques of symbolic inversion, and in other forms of identity building and boundary maintenance. The bourgeoisie defined itself as a class that was fit to lead because of its many virtues: its high moral standards, its self-discipline and moderation, its thrift and rationality, its firm belief in science and progress. The classes above and below were felt to lack these qualities.

The profile that the bourgeoisie turned up toward the aristocracy deserves examination. They pictured the old elite culture as a degenerate life-style, characterized by loose morals and prodigality in the form of conspicuous consumption and other frivolities, irresponsible when it came to handling both public and private spending. The social life of the court circles was seen as plagued by pretentious rituals and empty etiquette; aristocractic culture was, in short, insincere and shallow. The bourgeoisie, by contrast, saw itself as representing a more responsible and more rational life-style, developing a high degree of intimacy and sensitivity in relationships with other human beings as well

Conclusion

as with the natural world. The stress on intimacy in interpersonal relations, the Romantic cult of friendship, the new interest in the education of children, and the importance of a good family and home life must be seen against this background. The bourgeoisie felt that the artificial and petrified life-style of the aristocracy demanded the contrast of a different human ideal, based on a cultivation of inner qualities and eternal values.

It is important, however, not to oversimplify this relationship between the aristocracy and the bourgeoisie. Interestingly enough, there were groups within the aristocracy who also distanced themselves at this time from the feudal way of life. It was ridiculed, used as a moral example of how not to behave, and set up as a symbolic enemy. The transformation of the nobility and the bourgeoisie involved constant interaction between the two groups. The daughters of the moneyed bourgeoisie, for instance, married into the nobility if they could, thus crowning their economic success by association with the prestige of good birth.

It is also important to stress that the Swedish aristocracy was very closely connected to the civil and military administration. They had long been accustomed to service, whether in the government offices, the universities, or the army. Living off the interest on one's fortune and proceeds from one's lands did not really bring any more prestige than living by service. This circumstance has its roots in older traditions. The period of expansion during the seventeenth century, when Sweden was a great European power, created the nobility that she needed on the battlefield and in the chanceries. Outside of the state sector and the army, the career possibilities were limited. There was thus ample opportunity for contact between bourgeois and aristocratic traditions. In certain respects, it is correct to speak of the gradual embourgeoisement of the members of the feudal stratum of society.

The Swedish bourgeoisie was admittedly not a coherent category in

Conclusion

the eighteenth century and the early industrial phase of the nineteenth. The new professional men and the wielders of economic power were to be found in the countryside as well as in the towns. The many ironworks in central Sweden, for example, saw the growth of a bourgeois culture that took its coloring from local conditions. This meant not only constant contact with people from the other estates, but also that the bourgeoisie did not form its own well-defined society. There is a striking contrast here to contemporary German—and indeed English—conditions. In fact, as close to home as Denmark there could be found a bourgeoisie that was centered to a greater degree on the towns, more fully integrated into public life, and which constituted its own society.

The bourgeois attitude to the peasantry was completely different. This gray mass did not represent a degenerate culture, but rather a lack of culture and civilization, living too close to nature, unable to exercise restraint, moderation, or long-term planning in their lives.

This analysis has centered on the hegemonic process that turned an antagonistic bourgeois subculture into Culture itself during the Oscarian era in Sweden. The new, victorious culture defined itself in evolutionary terms. The Oscarians saw themselves as representing higher forms of cultural refinement and sophistication than other social classes. During this period they were busy creating a cultural charter, constructing ancestor myths and genealogies, rewriting history, and defining a Swedish heritage. The life-style of the Oscarian bourgeoisie came to be defined in terms of a national culture, which also had to do with the sharpened class conflicts of the late nineteenth century. For the new elite, it seemed as if the nation was about to be torn apart, and there was a search for symbolic expressions of national solidarity, above the world of class strife. The love of a common peasant heritage and the Swedish landscape was supposed to bind the nation together. This was the period of the erection of national

Conclusion

monuments, the building of folk museums, the celebration of national jubilees, and the writing of patriotic songs.

In order to understand the bourgeois cultural profile of this period, it is also essential to look at the confrontations with the emerging working class, which, more than the dying peasantry, was the main object of the new elite's reforming zeal. The images of this inferior social class had many complex symbolic traits.

The bourgeoisie of the nineteenth and early twentieth centuries often described the mass of the people as *crude*, especially in the sense that they were not complete, mature people. They were considered cultural raw material that had not been refined and developed to the level of civilization.

The working class thus represented not just chaos and disorder, but also underdevelopment. Against their way of life, the bourgeoisie could parade its sense of order as a mark of its greater sophistication. Order became a cardinal virtue both in the bourgeois world view and in their everyday routines and trivialities.

Bourgeois culture drew clear demarcation lines everywhere. In the home they carefully separated activities and territories. The children's world was kept apart from that of the adults, servants were segregated from the family, public from private. Everything had to be in its place. People who did not observe this sort of order—those who slept and ate in the same room, who did not respect the sanctity of privacy, who mixed potatoes, sauce, and vegetables on their plates—evoked bourgeois distaste and disgust.

The same zeal for order is seen in the organization of public life, in the straight rows of hospital beds and school desks, in the symmetry of the engine rooms and the old people's homes. All these seemingly unimportant details are part of the constant struggle against the threat from chaos and from those who live in chaos: the others, the uncivilized masses, the animal-like workers.

The devaluation of manual labor, the aversion to dirt and animals,

Conclusion

and the taboos imposed on everything physical are all part of the moral superiority of the bourgeoisie and at the same time a definition of the inferiority of the working classes. This picture of the workers is rarely presented consciously, but it is implicit in many contexts, in caricatures of working-class life, in schoolbooks, cartoons, memoirs of childhood, social reform programs, and public debates. The working class is what the middle class is not: uncontrolled, undisciplined, hedonistic, irresponsible, irrational, loud-mouthed, vulgar, careless, dirty, physical. These negative qualities were a symbolic inversion of the positive qualities by which the bourgeoisie defined itself.

The way in which class differences were perceived was associated with notions of cultural development; this perception had consequences for the bourgeois attempts to reform the working class. The basic nature–culture opposition was not complementary but hierarchical. Nature was seen as something to be worked upon and transformed.

If the hierarchical polarities of culture and order versus nature and chaos represented one of the basic themes in the culture of the Oscarians, the emphasis on self-control and self-discipline was another. These basic ideas permeated daily life and were expressed in many cultural registers: the ordering of the body and its functions, the suppression of sensuality, the strict drill of children's table manners, the struggle against the horrors of masturbation, the stress on an economy of time, money, and emotions, the focus on moderation, correctness, and restraint in all areas from the choice of colors in clothes to facial expressions, the fear of and anxiety about "the vulgar," the animalistic, and the uncontrollable. Behind the bewildering multitude of etiquette rules there existed a consistent pattern in the ways people were expected to dress, move the body, choose a topic of conversation, handle a fork, or emit pearly laughter.

Oscarian culture-building represented both a constant elaboration and an integration of such themes. A consistent relationship between

Conclusion

ideology and everyday praxis was developed; most of our attention here has been devoted to the level of everyday praxis rather than the loftier world of proclamations of ideals and norms. In order to understand, for example, how newborn barbarians after a few years' training can be turned into civilized beings, one must look to this type of everyday socialization. The important cultural codes were transmitted more effectively through trivial everyday routines than through cultural preaching and normative statements. Table manners, for example, were not so much a lesson in eating as indirect instruction in the art of self-control. In the same way, an important part of socialization lay embedded in the material structures that surrounded the Oscarian child. The straight-backed chairs in the dining room, the white summer clothes, the austerity of the boys' room, all carried their muted messages.

Sanctions did not have to be verbal or very pronounced; children learned to observe themselves and the reactions of others. Theirs was a cultural training of hints, Father's raised eyebrows, the faint red glow on Mother's cheeks, or the questioning glance of a passing stranger on the street.

The strength of the socialization process also lay in the fact that the Oscarians created their own echo chambers. Everyday experiences were fitted to the messages circulating in the public sphere; the same codes and meanings were encountered in breakfast conversations, lessons at school, newspaper debates, and evening entertainments. The Oscarian middle-class child entered an outside world that felt like home, unlike the working-class children who were constantly confronted with the contradictions between material experiences and the statements about the good and proper life that came from schoolteachers, doctors, welfare workers, and others who carried out the cultural policing of the lower classes.

We have showed the ways in which cultural messages were internalized and turned, as it were, into gut reactions. In creating a cultural

Conclusion

hegemony, the Oscarians slowly made their own culture invisible; it was seen more and more in terms of human nature or plain common sense. Ideas about the way the world ought to be were developed into the unquestionable facts of life. This process also affected the missionary activities directed toward the workers and peasants. Moral arguments increasingly gave way to scientific ones, as in the heightened preoccupation with matters of hygiene. At the same time that bourgeois values were becoming more and more unreflected and unconscious, the different life-styles of others were redefined as social, medical, and cultural deviance (see Frykman 1981; Löfgren in press).

In our discussions of the relations between bourgeois and working-class culture, we have stressed the need to avoid reducing this confrontation to one of subjugation and indoctrination. The one-dimensional concept of embourgeoisement is misleading in many ways. It does not capture the dialectics of this culture clash; both parties change in a cultural confrontation. Moreover, much of the endless bourgeois discourse on working-class life had less to do with a missionary zeal than with an attempt to delineate middle-class identity; it was an ongoing process of self-definition.

· N O T E S ·

Introduction

1. See in particular the discussion in Löfgren in press; Ehn and Löfgren 1982; and, most recently, our conclusions in Frykman and Löfgren 1985:460ff.

1. The Time Keepers

1. The literature on the cultural organization of time has grown rapidly. I have used Edmund Leach's classic cross-cultural discussions of time (1961 and 1976) as a starting point. For more recent research see the encyclopedic survey of Wendorff (1980), as well as Kern's study (1983).
2. The reports on peasant life that Swedish provincial governors and doctors sent to the central administration during the nineteenth century provide numerous examples of similar views of the listlessness and sloth of the peasantry. See, for example, the survey in Arnberg et al. 1972:16, 24.
3. See the discussion in Fridholm, Isacson, and Magnusson 1976, as well as Löfgren 1977:49.
4. Mats Rehnberg has discussed this development (1967:28ff.). See also Sigfrid Svensson's account of the late spread of almanacs and watches during the eighteenth and nineteenth centuries (1967:66ff.).
5. For a discussion of the differences between peasantry and bourgeoisie with respect to the work ethic and time discipline, see

Zerlang 1976:60ff., which also critically examines Max Weber's analysis of the growth of the Protestant ethic (Weber 1930).

6. Asko Vilkuna (1959) has examined Nordic folk beliefs concerning the life cycle in peasant society, showing the view of life as a predictable course of fixed elements. For a discussion of the development of the career mentality see Bledstein 1976. See also Odén's treatment of planning and time horizons (1975).

7. Examples from the memoirs showing the training in time discipline in conjunction with mealtimes can be found in Blumenthal-Engström 1947:44 and Posse 1955:22. Hugo Hamilton recounts in his memoirs (1928:47) how as a four-year-old he was given the duty of meeting his father at a fixed time somewhere on the estate lands.

8. Cf. the discussions of the cult of speed (Kern 1983), future orientation (Dundes 1969), and nostalgia (Davis 1979 and Lowenthal 1985).

9. It was said of Värmland farmhands who lived according to the rhythm of the gruel bell: "The laborers acquired pocket watches and kept track of the right time. It was almost as if they had started to have an idea of their own human dignity" (cited in Rehnberg 1967:30).

2. The Nature Lovers

1. For a detailed analysis of this stereotype as viewed through English eyes see Austin 1968:93ff.

2. See the research survey on leisure habits by Genrup and Nordin 1977.

3. There is a rich literature on the development of these new attitudes toward nature, tracing their cultural roots in the intellectual climate of late eighteenth-century Europe and their development during the following centuries. Raymond Williams's work on *The*

Country and the City (1973) is already a classic, while Keith Thomas in a more recent book (1984) has analyzed the changing perceptions of both the landscape and the animal kingdom in England between 1500 and 1800. An excellent discussion of "the Romantic eye" can be found in the German study by Grossklaus and Oldemeyer (1983). Another recent study by Charlton (1984) deals with the French eighteenth-century debate.

4. See the discussion in Gustavsson 1981 and Eskilsson 1981. There exists, of course, an older tradition of idyllizing the rural landscape and its inhabitants, namely the pastoral idyll with its roots in antiquity (discussed in Olwig 1984), but this is to a large extent a different landscape with different ideological connotations from the nineteenth-century cult of the wilderness.

5. For a discussion of this change in cultural climate among Swedish writers and artists see Björck 1946 and Rapp 1978.

6. This idealization of peasant culture and "the little community" is found in many cultural arenas of the period, for example in the planning of middle-class suburbs; see Stavenow-Hidemark 1971 for Sweden and Davidoff, L'Esperance, and Newby 1976 for England. The peasant village came to represent a utopian type of community, stable and harmonious, where class boundaries were unproblematic because relations were patriarchal and everybody knew his or her proper station in life.

7. The Laurin quotation comes from a review of maritime paintings in *Stockholms-Tidningen* in 1909. Rich empirical material on middle-class perceptions of the inferior ways in which workers and peasants used and experienced nature can be found in an interesting questionnaire from 1929 that dealt with attitudes to nature, among other things. For a discussion of the responses see Dahllöf 1981 and Alsmark 1985.

8. For a more extensive analysis of changing attitudes to the animal

world in Sweden during the past two centuries see Löfgren 1985b, which also discusses current research in the field of animal symbolism.

9. The information on the activity of the society has been taken from its published annual reports, *Sållskapet småfoglarnes vänner, dess verksamhet o. förhandlingar*, 1869–1872.

3. The Home Builders

1. See Bringéus's discussion of the position of old maids in Swedish peasant society (1978b) and the study of widowhood and remarriage in Gaunt and Löfgren 1981 and Gaunt 1983:174ff.

2. I have treated the topics of gender and the division of labor in Löfgren 1975b and 1982. Ivan Illich (1982) has pointed out how difficult it is to compare modern and traditional concepts of male and female identity and authority. He tends, however, in his polemical zeal, to romanticize the traditional world of female collectivity, strength, and identity.

3. The study of the making of Victorian family ideals is a rapidly expanding field. I have drawn on the work of Leonore Davidoff (1976 and 1979) and Davidoff, L'Esperance, and Newby (1976), together with three volumes of American studies (Vicinus 1972 and 1977; and Wohl 1978). For a discussion of more recent research see Halttunen 1982 and Green 1983.

4. This ethnocentric tendency is marked in Edward Shorter's work on *The Making of the Modern Family* (1975) and also, though to a lesser degree, in Lawrence Stone's study of the English family (1977).

5. This quotation comes from the collection of peasant traditions in the Nordic Museum, Stockholm: EU 2739:2. For other examples see EU 2649:13, 2739:2, 3044:64, 3064:93, 3422:267, and 3627:307.

6. Quoted from EU 3627:311 and 12351:240; see also EU 14211:583. For further discussion see Löfgren 1969 and 1972:251ff.

7. Melberg's analysis (1978) of Frederika Bremer's mid-nineteenth-century vision of family and sexuality, for example, reveals a totally different morality and ideology from that found in the preceding century in Carl Linnaeus's exuberant sex-education manual (Linné 1969) or Hallenstierna's diary of his love life (1972).

8. The diary left behind by Nils Strindberg, the youngest member of Andrée's ill-fated polar expedition, gives us a rare insight into erotic play on the limits of what was permitted in bourgeois society at the turn of the century (cited in Sundman 1968:43ff.). See also the discussion in Gay 1984 about the risks of overemphasizing the nonerotic character of Victorian premarital relations.

9. The intimacy of the couple is also met with in medical literature. The nineteenth century saw the development of a range of theories about the married couple as a physical unity and a whole, not least in speculation about how physical and mental characteristics are mixed through copulation. A good example of this can be found in an anonymous work on "the secrets of love" (*Kärlekens hemligheter* 1844:66ff.). See also the discussion in Kern 1974.

10. For a discussion of marrying ages in the different social classes see Carlsson 1977. The declining marriage rate among the aristocracy was a problem treated by Fahlbeck (1898–1902:1.450ff., 2.117ff.) and von Willebrand (1932:57ff.). The precarious position of unmarried bourgeois women in the eighteenth century is studied in Qvist 1960. See also Matovic 1984:229ff.

11. This is, for obvious reasons, a tabooed subject in the memoirs. An exception is Sigfrid Siwertz's autobiography (1949:116ff.). See also the discussion in Frykman 1977:188ff.

12. Cited in Michanek 1962:100. A survey of eight hundred prostitutes in Stockholm at the turn of the century revealed that the women's sexual debuts were to a proportionately high extent with upper-

and middle-class men. Some 30 percent consisted of professional men such as officers, cadets, government officials, merchants, clerks, students, and high-school boys (Statistiska Centralbyrån 1914:53). See also Lundquist 1982.

13. Sex education books were directed mainly toward men, while women had to content themselves with veiled advice on sexuality and femininity in housekeeping manuals such as Grubb 1889. See Michel Foucault's discussion of the development of the scientific discourse on sexuality (1978), together with Peter Gay's counterargument (1984). See also Kern 1974, Barker-Benfield 1976, and Trudgill 1976.

14. The range of variation between different regions is demonstrated by a number of local studies on child-rearing. Those from Norrland emphasize the parental tenderness (Johansson 1934; Borelius 1936; Hedlund 1943–1944). Levander's survey (1946) depicts a harder attitude, partly as a moral message directed to contemporary readers and educators. Måwe's study from Värmland (1958) contains some interesting observations. For an essay dealing with general trends in peasant child rearing and sex-role socialization see Bang 1973.

15. See John Falk's memoirs (1946:15ff.). Other examples of this child-rearing ideology can be found in Edholm 1919:40; Hamilton 1928:44; Holmgren 1959:26; and Aspelin 1968:37; for further discussion see Åström 1979:20ff.

16. The quotations are taken from a collection of pen portraits of the fathers of famous Swedes (Oljelund 1949), which often unconsciously embody this ambiguity. See also Bjerre 1947; Lidman 1952; Hägglöf 1976:188; and the discussion in Åström 1979:20ff.

17. For a discussion of the role of wet nurses in Swedish bourgeois culture see Jacobson 1977. The problematic triangle of children, parents, and domestic maids is discussed from a Swedish angle in

Notes to Pages 124–151

Nolan 1979; see also Davidoff 1979; Martin-Fugier 1979; and Müller 1981.

18. This theme recurs in many memoirs; see, for example, August Strindberg's description of his childhood (1967b:37f.), as well as Edholm 1919:41ff.; Holmgren 1926:107ff.; and Hägglöf 1976:9.

19. Examples can be found in Leche-Löfgren 1949:146; Svedelius 1889:29; Quensel 1958:130ff.; and Lindström 1964:16; see also the discussion in Rehnberg 1969.

20. Interior decoration is discussed in great detail and well illustrated in Paulsson 1950:2.307ff., 326ff., and 523ff. See also Stiernstedt 1946:190ff.; Gejvall 1954; and Thue 1975.

21. For a theoretical analysis of the growth of privacy see Habermas 1965, especially chapter 2. Paulsson 1950 illustrates its concrete results in Swedish homes. Gösta Arvastson has studied this process among the eighteenth-century clergy (1977:106ff.), while its later spread to the larger nineteenth-century farms is discussed in Löfgren 1974:25ff.

22. The pioneer of this new attitude in Sweden was Ellen Key (see Stavenow-Hidemark 1971:192ff.; Ambjörnsson 1978:62f.). See also the discussion of the spread of the nursery in Gejvall 1954.

23. For an extensive study of the interview evidence for working-class conditions in Landskrona see our study of culture and class on the move (Frykman and Löfgren 1985:109ff.).

24. Many scholars have drawn attention to the segregation of the sexes and the relative unimportance of family life in working-class settings: Erixon 1949:135ff.; Paulsson 1953:225ff.; Daun 1974:218; Ek 1982:120ff.

25. The figures are from the 1850s. Only Vienna had a higher rate of illegitimacy, while the percentage of women who were married was 51 percent for Paris and 46 percent for London; see the discussion in Matovic 1984:73.

26. See the changing perspectives on these paradoxes in Lasch 1977; Foucault 1978; Berger and Berger 1983.

4. The Cultural Basis of Physical Aversion

1. Mary Douglas's theories of purity and dirt, on which this study relies heavily, were presented in Douglas 1966 and further developed in Douglas 1973 and 1975. Equally important is Edmund Leach's theory of classification and taboo, especially as outlined in his pioneering essay (Leach 1964); for a later discussion see Leach 1976. The theories were first discussed within the sphere of Scandinavian anthropology in Hastrup et al. 1975.

2. The nature–culture dichotomy has since been the subject of intensive debate. The universality that Ortner claimed for this polarization of the sexes has been discussed in the editors' contributions to MacCormack and Strathern 1980. See also Ardener 1975. My treatment here of the way the woman is bound to her reproductive functions is indebted to Simone de Beauvoir (1952).

5. Peasant Views of Purity and Dirt

1. Erixon 1947:125f.; Sundt [1857]1968:63ff. Bundling is a favorite topic in ethnology. The most detailed survey is Wikman's dissertation (1937). See also Sarmela 1969. Anne Swang (1979) has analyzed night courtship as a "feast," an interesting application of the model in Edmund Leach's essay on "Time and False Noses" in Leach 1961. Orvar Löfgren (1969) examines Swedish courtship patterns from bundling to teenage culture.

2. In southern Sweden, young livestock could be brought into the dwelling house in the coldest weather. Further north, where there were fires in the cowsheds, there was no need to have animals in the house. On the contrary, the young people moved out to the

cowshed during the bundling season. In some cases the shed was carefully cleaned for the summer season, when people moved there out of the house; this was however, in the region where transhumance was the custom. See Szabó 1970b; Erixon 1947: 117ff.; Nyman 1970.

3. The most exhaustive studies of the wall hangings of southern Sweden are by Nils-Arvid Bringéus (especially 1978a and 1982), who has also examined both the interpretation and the use of folk pictorial art (1981). The folk paintings of Dalarna are the subject of Svante Svärdström's doctoral dissertation (1949). For a general Scandinavian survey see the volume edited by Svensson (1972).

4. Eriksson 1970:19f.; Rosén and Wetter 1970. There are excellent photographs of such collective facilities in a recent book on privies published by the pharmaceutical company Ferrosan (1984).

5. In his revision of the great study of *Das Weib* by Ploss, Bartels, and Bartels (1927:2.223ff.), von Reitzenstein aired the view that night courtship was a customary way for young people to find partners with whom they were compatible sexually and otherwise. Once a couple had found each other, they could indulge in uninhibited sex, believing that the time before marriage was intended for testing whether the bride could conceive. The notion is too unreasonable to need refutation. A betrothal was not broken off because a bride did *not* get pregnant. See Frykman 1977:181ff.

6. Bourgeois Discipline

1. See Norbert Elias's classic work from 1939 (English translation, Elias 1978), and the collection of essays for Elias (Gleichmann, Goudsblom, and Korte 1977). The growing research on the history of civilization in Europe stresses repeatedly the way changes in the elite of society function as models for other groups. Elias focuses on the spread of civilization from the court to the nobility

and later the bourgeoisie. The discussion here of the meeting of folk culture and elite culture in Scandinavia would scarcely be possible without the rich corpus of evidence on folklife in the nineteenth century.

2. For an overview of prostitution and sex roles from a sociological point of view see Rita Liljeström's contribution to a volume on prostitution (1981), which also includes a detailed analysis of historical and present-day conditions in Sweden. A rather more quantitatively based study of prostitution in the latter half of the nineteenth century can be found in Lundquist 1982.

3. Evidence of surgery is discussed in DeMause 1974:48f.; one of the gruesome mechanical devices is illustrated in Trudgill 1976, plate 5.

4. Sixt Karl von Kapff's *Warnung eines Jugendfreundes* went through over twenty German editions in the latter half of the nineteenth century, while the Swedish translation went through at least nine. For a more exhaustive analysis of the Swedish debate on masturbation and its risks see Nilsson 1981. It was only toward the turn of the century that some doctors began to argue against the established theories of the destructiveness of the habit, but these notions were by then thoroughly entrenched among the bourgeoisie. It was not until the 1930s and 1940s that a real reorientation could be discerned.

5. Recent years have seen the publication of a large number of works within this field. Feminist culture theory has once again put housework in the center of research on women. The rationalization of housework as it affected Sweden has been analyzed by Lissie Åström (1985), whose doctoral dissertation (1986) studies the way praxis was handed down from generation to generation. Rational housework was a necessity for middle-class women if they were to satisfy their own demands on themselves, their environment, and their work situation.

6. Wingårdh was conscious of the fact that rules for etiquette change

through time and that, as he says in his foreword, "what was customary a hundred years ago is perhaps not applicable now." Despite constant revision through seven editions, however, his condemnation of eating in public remained unchanged.

• BIBLIOGRAPHY •

Archival Sources

EU   Etnologiska Undersökning, Nordiska Museet [Ethno-
logical Survey, Nordic Museum], Stockholm.

IFGH   Institutet för Folklore, Göteborgs Högskola [Folklore
Institute, Gothenburg University].

LUF   Lunds Universitets Folklivsarkiv [Folklife Archive, Department of European Ethnology, Lund University].

NM   Nordiska Museet [Nordic Museum], Stockholm

ULMA   Uppsala, Landsmålsarkivet [Uppsala Institute for Dia-
lectology and Folklore Research].

Literature Cited

Alkman, Annastina. 1965. *När gräset var grönt . . . Minnen från ett
oscariskt barndomshem*. Stockholm: Bonniers.

Alsmark, Gunnar. 1985. "Ljus över bygden." In *Modärna tider: Vision
och vardag i folkhemmet*, ed. Jonas Frykman and Orvar Löfgren,
294–352. Skrifter utgivna av Etnologiska sällskapet i Lund. Lund:
Liber Förlag.

Ambjörnsson, Ronny. 1978. *Familjeporträtt: Essäer om familjen, kvin-
nan, barnet och kärleken i historien*. Stockholm: Gidlunds.

Améen, Louis A. 1889. "Om bergsklättring." *Svenska Turistföreningens
årsskrift* 1889:52–63.

———. 1890. "Kinnekulle." *Svenska Turistföreningens årsskrift*
1890:63–68.

Bibliography

————. 1924. "Tal vid Svenska Turistföreningens 100 000-fest." *Svenska Turistföreningens årsskrift* 1924:ix–xxiv.

Ariès, Philippe. 1962. *Centuries of Childhood: A Social History of Family Life.* Robert Baldick, trans. New York: Vintage.

Ardener, Shirley, ed. 1975. *Perceiving Women.* London: Malady.

Arnberg, Marianne, Ann-Christin Bengtsson, Lena Halldén, Pia Küller, and Carl Svantesson. 1972. "1800-talets bondevardag genom ämbetsmannaögon." Department of European Ethnology, Lund University. Mimeo.

Arvastson, Gösta. 1977. *Skånska prästgårdar: En etnologisk studie av byggnadsskickets förändring 1680–1824.* Skrifter från Folklivsarkivet i Lund 19. Lund: Liber Läromedel.

Aspelin, Gunnar. 1968. *Lek och allvar: Minnesbilder från pojkåren.* Lund: Gleerups.

Aström, Lissie. 1979. "Högreståndskultur contra arbetarkultur i jämförande sekelskiftsperspektiv." Department of European Ethnology, Lund University. Mimeo.

————. 1985. "Husmodern möter folkhemmet." In *Modärna tider: Vision och vardag i folkhemmet,* ed. Jonas Frykman and Orvar Löfgren, 196–255. Skrifter utgivna av Etnologiska sällskapet i Lund. Lund: Liber Förlag.

————. 1986. *I kvinnoled: Om kvinnors liv genom tre generationer.* Malmö: Liberförlag.

Austin, Paul Britten. 1968. *On Being Swedish: Reflections Towards a Better Understanding of the Swedish Character.* London: Martin Secker.

Bang, Aase. 1973. "Det skall tidigt krökas det som krokigt skall bli." Department of European Ethnology, Lund University. Mimeo.

Barker-Benfield, G. J. 1976. *The Horrors of the Half-known Life: Male Attitudes toward Women and Sexuality in Nineteenth-Century America.* New York: Harper & Row.

Bibliography

Barthes, Roland. 1972. *Mythologies*. Annette Lavers, trans. London: Cape.

Bausinger, Hermann. 1961. *Volkskultur in der technischen Welt*. Stuttgart: Kohlhammer Verlag.

de Beauvoir, Simone. 1952. *The Second Sex*. H. M. Parshley, trans. New York: Knopf.

Becker, C. W. 1916. *Tyst! Oumbärlig rådgifvare för älskande och nygifta*. Tomteboda: Kronwalls Förlag.

Berger, Brigitte and Peter Berger. 1983. *The War over the Family: Capturing the Middle Ground*. New York: Doubleday.

Bergh, Richard. 1900. "Svenskt konstnärskynne." *Ord och bild* 9:129–141.

Beskow, Natanael. 1946. "Löjtnantsfrun som blev prostinna." In *Min Mor*, 19–25. (*See* Oljelund 1946.)

Bjerre, Poul. 1947. "Min faders verk." In *Barndomshemmet*, 9–19. (*See* Söderberg 1947.)

Björck, Staffan. 1946. *Heidenstam och sekelskiftets Sverige: Studier i hans nationella och sociala författarskap*. Stockholm: Natur och Kultur.

Björkman, Eva. 1975. "Den goda tonen och den sanna belevenheten: En studie av etikettbokslitteraturens förändring under 1800- och 1900-talet." Department of European Ethnology, Lund University. Mimeo.

Bledstein, Burton J. 1976. *The Culture of Professionalism: The Middle Class and the Development of Higher Education in America*. New York: Norton.

Blom, Tarras. 1969. "Carl G. Laurin: Minnen 1868–1888." Department of Ethnology, Stockholm University. Mimeo.

Blumenthal-Engström, Inga. 1947. "Barnläkaren som var en krutdurk." In *Barndomshemmet*, 41–48. (*See* Söderberg 1947.)

Boberg, Torsten. 1949. "Dalkarl, gruvkarl, jägare." In *Min Far*, 29–36. (*See* Oljelund 1949.)

Bibliography

Bock, Philip K. 1980. *Continuities in Psychological Anthropology: A Historical Introduction*. San Francisco: Freeman.

Boon, James A. 1974. "Anthropology and Nannies." *Man* 9:137–140.

Boqvist, Agneta. 1978. *Den dolda ekonomin: En etnologisk studie av näringsstrukturen i Bollebygd 1850–1950*. Skrifter från Folklivsarkivet i Lund 21. Lund: Gleerups.

Borelius, Fredrik. 1936. *Där forntiden lever: Tornedalsstudier*. Uppsala: Lindblads Förlag.

Bringéus, Nils-Arvid. 1970. "Människan, maten och miljön." In *Mat och miljö: En bok om svenska kostvanor*, ed. Nils-Arvid Bringéus, 9–22. Handböcker i etnologi. Lund: Gleerups.

————. 1975. "Food and Folk-Beliefs: On Prophylactic Measures Connected with the Boiling of Blood-Sausage." In *Ethnological Food Research: Reports from the Second International Symposium for Ethnological Food Research, Helsinki, August 1973*, ed. Toivo Vuorela et al., 29–53. Kansatieteellinen Arkisto 26. Helsinki: Suomen muinaismuistoyhdistys.

————. 1978a. *Sydsvenskt bonadsmåleri*. Lund: Lunds Konsthall.

————. 1978b. "Gammelpigorna på glasberget." *Norveg* 21:273–288.

————. 1981. *Bildlore: Studiet av folkliga bildbudskap*. Stockholm: Gidlunds.

————. 1982. *Sydsvenska bonadsmålningar*. Lund: Bokförlaget Signum.

Bruzelius, Nils G. 1876. *Allmogelivet i Ingelstads härad i Skåne under slutet av förra och början av detta århundrade*. 3d ed. reissued by Sigfrid Svensson. Lund: Ekstrand Bokförlag, 1978.

BVT:s Lexikon för etikett och god ton. 1930. Compiled by D. af H. 4th ed. Stockholm: Bonniers.

Campbell, Åke. 1936. *Kulturlandskapet*. Studentföreningen Verdandis småskrifter 387. Stockholm: Bonniers.

Carlsson, Sten. 1977. *Fröknar, mamseller, jungfrur och pigor: Ogifta kvinnor i det svenska ståndssamhället*. Acta Universitatis Upsalien-

289

Bibliography

sis, Studia Historica Upsaliensia 90. Uppsala: Almqvist & Wiksell International.

Cederblom, Elin. *Handledning i sexuell undervisning och uppfostran.* 2 vols. Stockholm: Norstedt & Söners Förlag.

Charlton, D. G. 1984. *New Images of the Natural in France: A Study in European Cultural History 1750–1800.* Cambridge: Cambridge University Press.

Cominos, Peter T. 1972. "Innocent Femina Sensualis in Unconscious Conflict." In *Suffer and Be Still: Women in the Victorian Age,* ed. Martha Vicinus, 155–172. Bloomington: Indiana University Press.

Dahllöf, Tordis. 1981. *Folkbildning och livsmiljö på 1920-talet: En presentation av ett bildningsprojekt och dess upphovsman Carl Cederblad.* Stockholm: LTs Förlag.

Danver, Karin. 1942. "Födelsedag och namnsdag särskilt med hänsyn till deras firande hos vår allmoge." *Folkkultur* 2:5–71.

Daun, Åke. 1974. *Förortsliv: En etnologisk studie av kulturell förändring.* Stockholm: Bokförlaget Prisma.

Daun, Åke and Orvar Löfgren, eds. 1971. *Ekologi och kultur.* Copenhagen: NEFA's Forlag.

Davidoff, Leonore. 1976. "The Rationalization of Housework." In *Dependence and Exploitation in Work and Marriage,* ed. Diana Leonard Barker and Sheila Allen, 121–151. London: Longman.

———. 1979. "Class and Gender in Victorian England: The Diaries of Arthur J. Munby and Hannah Cullwick." *Feminist Studies* 5:87–141.

Davidoff, Leonore, Jean L'Esperance, and Howard Newby. 1976. "Landscape with Figures: Home and Community in English Society." In *The Rights and Wrongs of Women,* ed. Juliet Mitchell and Ann Oakley, 139–175. Harmondsworth: Penguin.

Davis, Fred. 1979. *Yearning for Yesterday: A Sociology of Nostalgia.* New York: Free Press.

DeMause, Lloyd. 1974. "The Evolution of Childhood." In *The History of*

Bibliography

Childhood: The Evolution of Parent–Child Relationships as a Factor in History, ed. Lloyd DeMause, 1–73. New York: Psychohistory Press.

Douglas, Mary. 1966. Purity and Danger: An Analysis of Concepts of Pollution and Taboo. London: Routledge & Kegan Paul.

———. 1973. Natural Symbols: Explorations in Cosmology. 2d ed. London: Barrie & Jenkins.

———. 1975. Implicit Meanings: Essays in Anthropology. London: Routledge & Kegan Paul.

Dundes, Alan. 1969. "Thinking Ahead: A Folkloristic Reflection on the Future Orientation in American Worldview." Anthropological Quarterly 42:53–72.

af Edholm, Erik. 1948. "På hovbaler och societetstillställningar." In Det glada Sverige: Våra fester och högtider genom tiderna, vol. 3, ed. Gösta Berg, Birger Beckman, Bengt Idestam-Almquist, and Gustaf Munthe, 1727–1767. Stockholm: Natur och Kultur.

Edholm, Lotten. 1919. Från barndom till ålderdom: Minnesteckning. Stockholm: privately published.

Egardt, Brita. 1962. Hästslakt och rackarskam: En etnologisk undersökning av folkliga fördomar. Nordiska Museets handlingar 57. Stockholm: Nordiska Museet.

Egnahemskomitén. 1901. Betänkande af den utaf Kongl. Maj:t den 10 juli 1899 tillsatta Egnahemskomitén. Vol. 1, Förslag och motivering. Stockholm: Ivar Hæggströms Boktryckeri.

Ehn, Billy and Orvar Löfgren. 1982. Kulturanalys: Ett etnologiskt perspektiv. Lund: Liber Förlag.

Ehrenreich, Barbara and Deirdre English. 1973. Complaints and Disorders: The Sexual Politics of Sickness. Old Westbury, N.Y.: Feminist Press.

Ejder, Bertil. 1969. Dagens tider och måltider. Skrifter utgivna genom Landsmålsarkivet i Lund 19. Lund: Gleerups.

Bibliography

Ek, Sven B. 1982. *Nöden i Lund: En etnologisk stadsstudie.* 2d ed. Skrifter från Folklivsarkivet i Lund 11. Lund: Liber Förlag.

Elias, Norbert. 1978. *The Civilizing Process.* Vol. 1, *The History of Manners.* New York: Urizen Books.

Eriksson, Marianne. 1970. "Personlig hygien." *Fataburen* 1970:9–22.

Erixon, Sigurd. 1947. *Svensk byggnadskultur: Studier och skildringar belysande den svenska byggnadskulturens historia.* Reprinted Lund: Ekstrand Bokförlag, 1982.

————. 1949. *Stockholms hamnarbetare före fackföreningsrörelsens genombrott: En etnologisk studie.* Skrifter utgivna av Samfundet för svensk folklivsforskning 6, Liv och Folkkultur 2. Stockholm: Nordisk Rotogravyr.

Eskeröd, Albert. 1947. *Årets äring: Etnologiska studier i skördens och julens tro och sed.* Nordiska Museets handlingar 26. Stockholm: Nordiska Museet.

Eskilsson, Lena. 1981. "Från fjäll till hembygd: Några kommentarer kring det svenska turistlivets utveckling med utgångspunkt från STF:s årsskrifter." In *Naturligtvis: Uppsatser om natur och samhället tillägnade Gunnar Eriksson,* 136–151. Skrifter från Institutionen för idéhistoria, Umeå universitet 14. Umeå: Institutionen för idéhistoria.

Fahlbeck, Pontus E. 1898–1902. *Sveriges adel: Statistisk undersökning öfver de å Riddarhuset introducerade ätterna.* 2 vols. Lund: Gleerups.

Falk, John. 1946. *Från livets färdvägar.* Stockholm: Norstedt & Söners Förlag.

Ferrosan. 1984. *En bok om avträden.* Malmö: AB Ferrosan.

Foucault, Michel. 1977. *Discipline and Punish: The Birth of the Prison.* Alan Sheridan, trans. Harmondsworth: Allen Lane.

————. 1978. *The History of Sexuality.* Robert Hurley, trans. Vol. 1, *An Introduction.* New York: Pantheon.

Bibliography

Freud, Sigmund. 1930. *Civilization and Its Discontents.* James Strachey, trans. In *Standard Edition* 21:59–145. London: Hogarth, 1963.

Fridholm, Merike, Maths Isacson, and Lars Magnusson. 1976. *Industrialismens rötter: Om förutsättningarna för den industriella revolutionen i Sverige.* Verdandi-debatt 80. Stockholm and Uppsala: Bokförlaget Prisma/Föringen Verdandi.

Frode-Kristensen, Selma. 1966. *Vid brunnen: En kulturbild från sekelskiftet.* Skrifter från Folklivsarkivet i Lund utgivna genom Sällskapet Folkkultur 8. Lund: Gleerups.

Frykman, Jonas. 1977. *Horan i bondesamhället.* Lund: Liber Förlag.

———. 1979. "Ideologikritik av arkivsystemen." *Norveg* 22: 231–242.

———. 1981. "Pure and Rational: The Hygienic Vision, a Study of Cultural Transformation in the 1930's." *Ethnologia Scandinavica* 1981:36–62.

———. 1984. "Ur medelklassens familjeliv." In *Familjebilder: Myter, verklighet, visioner,* ed. Bengt-Erik Andersson, 103–127. Stockholm: Studieförbundet Näringsliv och samhälle.

Frykman, Jonas and Orvar Löfgren, eds. 1985. *Modärna tider: Vision och vardag i folkhemmet.* Skrifter utgivna av Etnologiska sällskapet i Lund. Lund: Liber Förlag.

Gårdlund, Torsten. 1942. *Industrialismens samhälle.* Stockholm: Tidens Förlag.

Gathorne-Hardy, Jonathan. 1972. *The Rise and Fall of the British Nanny.* London: Hodder and Stoughton.

Gaunt, David. 1977. "I slottets skugga: Om frälsebönders sociala problem i Borgeby och Löddeköpinge under 1700-talet." *Ale* 1977(2): 15–30.

———. 1983. *Familjeliv i Norden.* Stockholm: Gidlunds.

Gaunt, David and Orvar Löfgren. 1981. "Remarriage in the Nordic Countries: The Cultural and Socio-economic Background." In *Marriage and Remarriage in Populations of the Past,* ed. J. Dupâquier, E. Hélin, P. Laslett, et al., 49–60. New York: Academic Press.

Bibliography

Gawell-Blumenthal, Ida. 1946. "Hon hade ingen ovän." In *Min Mor*, 41–44. (*See* Oljelund 1946.)

Gay, Peter. 1984. *The Bourgeois Experience: Victoria to Freud*. Vol. 1, *The Education of the Senses*. New York: Oxford University Press.

af Geijerstam, Gustaf. 1894. *Anteckningar om arbetarförhållanden i Stockholm*. Reprinted with comments by Edmund Dahlström, Folke Isaksson, Joachim Israel, and Birgitta Odén. Samhälle i utveckling 5. Lund: Studentlitteratur, 1973.

Gejvall, Birgit. 1954. *1800-talets Stockholmsbostad: En studie över den borgerliga bostadens planlösning i hyreshusen*. Monografier utgivna av Stockholms kommunalförvaltning 16. Stockholm: Almqvist & Wiksell.

Genrup, Kurt and Urban Nordin. 1977. *Fritidsboendevanor: Kunskapsöversikt rörande vissa sociala och kulturhistoriska aspekter*. Fysisk riksplanering, underlagsmaterial 10. Stockholm: Bostadsdepartementet.

Giddens, Anthony. 1981. *A Contemporary Critique of Historical Materialism*. Berkeley: University of California Press.

Gleichmann, Peter R., Johan Goudsblom, and Hermann Korte, eds. 1977. *Human Figurations: Essays for Norbert Elias*. Amsterdam: Sociologisch Tijdschrift.

Göransson, K. F. 1946. "En bruksvärdinna." In *Min Mor*, 87–89. (*See* Oljelund 1946.)

Green, Harvey. 1983. *The Light of Home: An Intimate View of the Lives of Women in Victorian America*. New York: Pantheon.

Grossklaus, Götz and Ernst Oldemeyer, eds. 1983. *Natur als Gegenwelt: Beiträge zur Kulturgeschichte de Natur*. Karlsruhe: von Loeper Verlag.

[Grubb, Laura, née Fåhraeus] (L. G. Fr.). 1889. *Oumbärlig rådgifvare för hvarje hem: En lättfattlig handbok för hvarje husmoder att rådfråga samt en fullständig kokbok*. Malmö: Kyhns Förlag.

Gustafsson, Berndt. 1956. *Manligt-kvinnligt-kyrkligt i 1800–talets*

Bibliography

svenska folkliv. Stockholm: Svenska Kyrkans Diakonistyrelsens Bokförlag.

Gustavsson, Anders. 1981. *Sommargäster och bofasta: Kulturmöte och motsättningar vid bohuskusten*. Skrifter utgivna av etnologiska sällskapet i Lund. Lund: Liber Läromedel.

Habermas, Jürgen. 1965. *Strukturwandel der Öffentlichkeit: Untersuchungen zu einer Kategorie der bürgerlichen Gesellschaft*. 2d ed. Berlin: Luchterhand Verlag.

Hägglöf, Gunnar. 1976. *Porträtt av en familj*. Stockholm, Norstedt & Söners Förlag.

Hallenstierna, Gustaf. 1972. *Mina kärleksäventyr: En dagbok från sjuttonhundratalet redigerad och med inledning av Gardar Sahlberg*. Stockholm: Rabén & Sjögren.

Halttunen, Karen. 1982. *Confidence Men and Painted Women: A Study of Middle-Class Culture in America, 1830–1870*. New Haven: Yale University Press.

Hamenius, Barbro. 1972. "Minnestavlor." In *Nordisk folkkonst*, ed. Sigfrid Svensson, 274–285. Handböcker i etnologi. Lund: Gleerups.

Hamilton, Hugo. 1928. *Hågkomster: Strödda anteckningar*. Stockholm: Bonniers.

Hansen, Georg. 1957. *Sædelighedsforhold blandt landbefolkningen i Danmark i det 18. århundrede*. Copenhagen: Det danske forlag.

Hanssen, Börje. 1952. *Österlen: En studie över social-antropologiska sammanhang under 1600-och 1700-talen i sydöstra Skåne*. Reprinted as *Österlen: Allmoge, köpstafolk & kultursammanhang vid slutet av 1700-talet i sydöstra Skåne*. Stockholm: Gidlunds, 1977.

————. 1978. *Familj, hushåll, släkt: En punktundersökning av miljö och gruppaktivitet i en stockholmsk förort 1952 och 1972 enligt hypoteser, som utformats efter kulturhistoriska studier*. Stockholm: Gidlunds.

Hastrup, Kirsten, Jan Ovesen, Knud-Erik Jensen, Jacob Clemmesen, and Kirsten Ramløv. 1975. *Den ny antropologi*. Copenhagen: Borgen/Basis.

Bibliography

Hedlund, Märta. 1943–1944. "Barnets uppfostran och utbildning i en storfamilj." *Folk-Liv* 7–8:72–90.

Hedström, Gerda, ed. 1947. *Vårt svenska hem: 33 författare ser på hemmets problem.* Stockholm: Lindqvists Förlag.

Holmgren, Ann Margret. 1926. *Minnen och tidsbilder.* Vol. 1. Stockholm: Wahlström & Widstrand.

Holmgren, Israel. 1959. *Mitt liv.* Vol. 1. Stockholm: Natur och Kultur.

Holmgren, Thorbjörn. 1983. *På upptäcktsfärd i bohusländska skärgården.* Kattegat–Skagerrak-projektet, Meddelelser 3. Aalborg: Kattegat–Skagerrak-projektet.

Huizinga, Johan. 1924. *The Waning of the Middle Ages: A Study of the Forms of Life, Thought and Art in France and the Netherlands in the XIVth and XVth Centuries.* F. Hopman, trans. London: Arnold.

Illich, Ivan. 1982. *Gender.* New York: Pantheon.

Jacobson, Bjarne. 1977. "Vem var den gamla amman?" *Fataburen* 1977:89–106.

Jirvén, Karin. 1971. "Badgästerna." In *Så minns jag 10-talet,* ed. Märta de Laval, 86–88. Stockholm: Proprius Förlag.

Johansson, Levi. 1927. "Om renlighetsförhållanden i Frostviken (Jämtland)." *Svenska landsmål och svenskt folkliv* 1927:119–138.

————. 1934. "Barnauppfostran i det gamla Frostviken." *Jämten* 28: 209–220.

Kärlekens hemligheter, en gåfva för älskande och nygifta, eller parktisk rådgifvare före och under äktenskapet: En hjelpreda i sådane fall, der blygsamheten förbjuder at muntligen förfråga sig. 1844. Gothenburg: Ekbohrn.

Kern, Stephen. 1974. "Explosive Intimacy: Psychodynamics of the Victorian Family," *History of Childhood Quarterly: Journal of Psychohistory* 1(3):437–462.

————. 1983. *The Culture of Time and Space 1880–1918.* Cambridge, Mass.: Harvard University Press.

Kiechel, Samuel. 1866. *Die Reisen des Samuel Kiechel,* ed. K. D. Haszler.

Bibliography

Bibliothek des litterarischen Vereins in Stuttgart 86. Stuttgart: Litterarischer Verein.

af Klintberg, Bengt. 1975. "När djuren kunde tala." In *Sista lasset in. Studier tillägnade Albert Eskeröd 9 maj 1974*, 269–298. Stockholm: Nordiska Museet.

Konsumentverket. 1978. *Rent till varje pris? En debattbok om städning.* Stockholm: Konsumentverket.

Krook, Oscar. 1946. "Hemmet var hennes borg." In *Min Mor*, 113–119. (*See* Oljelund 1946.)

Kullenberg, Annette. 1974. *Överklassen i Sverige.* Stockholm: Tidens Förlag.

Lagercrantz, Herman. 1944. *I skilda världar.* Stockholm: Norstedt & Söners Förlag.

Langlet, Mathilda. 1884. *Husmodern i staden och på landet: En fullständig handbok i hushållningens alla grenar.* Stockholm: Bonniers.

Lasch, Christopher. 1977. *Haven in a Heartless World: The Family Besieged.* New York: Basic Books.

Läsebok för folkskolan. 1901. 9th ed. Facsimile ed. Köping: Civiltryckeriet, 1968.

Laurin, Carl G. 1916. *Kvinnolynnen.* Stockholm: Norstedt & Söners Förlag.

Leach, Edmund R. 1961. *Rethinking Anthropology.* London School of Economics Monographs in Social Anthropology 22. London: Athlone Press.

———. 1964. "Anthropological Aspects of Language: Animal Categories and Verbal Abuse." In *New Directions in the Study of Language*, ed. Eric H. Lennenberg, 23–63. Cambridge, Mass.: M.I.T. Press.

———. 1976. *Culture and Communication: The Logic by Which Symbols Are Connected.* Themes in the Social Sciences. Cambridge: Cambridge University Press.

Leche-Löfgren, Mia. 1949. "Darwinisten, folkbildaren, radikalen." In *Min Mor*, 144–155. (*See* Oljelund 1949.)

297

Bibliography

Le Goff, Jacques. 1980. *Time, Work, and Culture in the Middle Ages.* Chicago: University of Chicago Press.

Leijonhufvud, Åke. 1978. *Anna och Christian.* Stockholm: Wahlström & Widstrand.

Leman, Karin. 1961. *Dagboken berättar för barn och barnbarn.* Gothenburg: privately published.

Levander, Lars. 1946. *Barnuppfostran på svenska landsbygden i äldre tid.* K. Gustav Adolfs Akademiens småskrifter 4. Stockholm: Lantbruksförbundets Tidskrifts AB.

Lidman, Sara. 1977. *Din tjänare hör.* Stockholm: Bonniers.

Lidman, Sven. 1952. *Gossen i grottan.* Stockholm: Natur och Kultur.

Lidman-Frostenson, Ulla. 1963. *Tidigt kallad.* Stockholm: Gummessons Bokförlag.

Liljeström, Rita. 1979. *Kultur och arbete.* Framtidsbilder. Stockholm: Liber Förlag and Sekretariatet för framtidsstudier.

———. 1981. "Könsroller och sexualitet." In *Prostitution: Beskrivning, Analys, Förslag till åtgärder,* by Arne Borg, Folke Elwien, Michael Frühling, Lars Grönwall, Rita Liljeström, Sven Axel Månsson, Anders Nelin, Hanna Olsson, and Tage Sjöberg, 172–279. Stockholm: Liber Förlag.

Lindhagen-Kihlblom, Brita. 1949. " I kamp för rättvisa och humanitet." In *Min Mor,* 156–162. (*See* Oljelund 1949.)

Lindroth, L. 1903. "Kortfattade badresor för turister." *Svenska Turistföreningens årsskrift* 1903:116–147.

Lindström, Margareta. 1964. *Jag var en herrgårdsflicka.* Stockholm: Bonniers.

———. 1966. *En herrgårdsflicka bryter upp.* Stockholm: Bonniers.

Lindström, Ulla. 1970. "Renlighetsuppfostran." *Fataburen* 1970:23–32.

Linné, Carl von. 1969. *Collegium medicum: Om sättet at tillhopa gå. Sexualföreläsningar av Carl von Linné,* ed. Nils Isberg. Gothenburg: Zindermans.

Löfgren, Orvar. 1969. "Från nattfrieri till tonårskultur." *Fataburen* 1969:25–52.

298

Bibliography

_____. 1972. "Familj och hushåll—släkt och äktenskap." In *Land och stad: Svenska samhällstyper och livsformer från medeltid till nutid*, ed. Mats Hellspong and Orvar Löfgren, 227–284. Handböcker i etnologi. Lund: Gleerups.

_____. 1973. "Arbetsgillen bland skånska bönder." *Skånes hembygdsförenings årsbok* 1973:75–92.

_____. 1974. "Family and Household among Scandinavian Peasants: An Exploratory Essay." *Ethnologia Scandinavica* 1974:17–52.

_____. 1975a. "Fetströmming och lusmörtar: Folktro och kognitiva system i två kustbygder." In *Sista lasset in. Studier tillägnade Albert Eskeröd 9 maj 1974*, 321–342. Stockholm: Nordiska Museet.

_____. 1975b. "Arbeitsteilung und Geschlechterrollen in Schweden." *Ethnologia Scandinavica* 1975:17–52.

_____. 1976. "Peasant Ecotypes: Problems in the Comparative Study of Ecological Adaptation." *Ethnologia Scandinavica* 1976: 100–115.

_____. 1977. *Fångstmän i industrisamhället: En halländsk kustbygds omvandling 1800–1970.* Skrifter utgivna av Etnologiska sällskapet i Lund. Lund: Liber Läromedel.

_____. 1978. "The Potato People: Household Economy and Family Patterns among the Rural Proletariat in Nineteenth-Century Sweden." In *Chance and Change: Social and Economic Studies in Historical Demography in the Baltic Area*, ed. Sune Åkerman, Hans Chr. Johansen, and David Gaunt, 95–106. Odense: Odense University Press.

_____. 1980. "Historical Perspectives on Scandinavian Peasantries." *Annual Review of Anthropology* 9:187–215.

_____. 1981a. "On the Anatomy of Culture." *Ethnologia Europaea* 12:26–46.

_____. 1981b. "De vidskepliga fångstmännen—magi, ekologi och ekonomi i svenska fiskarmiljöer." In *Tradition och miljö: Ett kulturekologiskt perspektiv*, ed. Lauri Honko and Orvar Löfgren,

64–94. Skrifter utgivna av Etnologiska sällskapet i Lund. Lund: Liber Läromedel.

————. 1981c. "Människan i landskapet—landskapet i människan." In *Tradition och miljö: Ett kulturekologiskt perspektiv*, ed. Lauri Honko and Orvar Löfgren, 235–260. Skrifter utgivna av Etnologiska sällskapet i Lund. Lund: Liber Läromedel.

————. 1982. "Kvinnfolksgöra: Om arbetsdelning i bondesamhället." *Kvinnovetenskaplig tidskrift* 3(3):6–14.

————. 1984a. "The Sweetness of Home: Class, Culture and Family Life in Sweden." *Ethnologia Europaea* 14:44–64.

————. 1984b. "Family and Household; Images and Realities: Cultural Change in Swedish Society." In *Households: Comparative and Historical Studies of the Domestic Group*, ed. Robert McC. Netting, Richard R. Wilk, and Eric J. Arnould, 446–471. Berkeley: University of California Press.

————. 1985a. "Wish You Were Here! Holiday Images and Picture Postcards." *Ethnologia Scandinavica* 1985:90–107.

————. 1985b. "Our Friends in Nature: Class and Animal Symbolism." *Ethnos* 50:184–213.

————. In press. "Deconstructing Swedishness: Class and Culture in Modern Sweden." In *Anthropology at Home*, ed. Anthony Jackson, ASA Monographs 25. London: Tavistock Publications.

Lönqvist, Niclas Olof. 1924. *Berättelse om Bara härad 1775*. Ed. Gunnar Carlquist. Bidrag till Bara härads beskrivning 2. Lund: Bara härads hembygdsförenings förlag.

Lowenthal, David. 1985. *The Past Is a Foreign Country*. Cambridge: Cambridge University Press.

Lundquist, Tommie. 1982. *Den disciplinerade dubbelmoralen: Studier i den reglementerade prostitutionens historia i Sverige 1859–1918*. Meddelanden från Historiska institutionen i Göteborg 23. Gothenburg: Skriv-City.

Lundwall, Sten. 1946. "Barnbalerna och deras bakgrund." In *Sverige i*

Bibliography

fest och glädje, ed. Mats Rehnberg, 169–184. Stockhold: Wahlström & Widstrand.

MacCormack, Carol P. and Marilyn Strathern, eds. 1980. *Nature, Culture and Gender*. Cambridge: Cambridge University Press.

Martin-Fugier, Anne. 1979. *La place des bonnes: La domesticité à Paris en 1900*. Paris: Grasset.

Martinson, Harry. 1935. *Nässlorna blomma*. Stockholm: Bonniers.

Matovic, Margareta R. 1984. *Stockholmsäktenskap: Familjebildning och partnerval i Stockholm 1850–1890*. Monografier utgivna av Stockholms kommun 57. Stockholm: Liber Förlag.

Måwe, Carl-Erik. 1958. *Studier i den sociala kontrollen i Östmark*. Uppsala: Appelbergs Boktryckeri.

Merlberg, Arne. 1978. *Realitet och utopi: Utkast till en dialektisk förståelse av litteraturens roll i det borgerliga samhällets genombrott*. Stockholm: Rabén & Sjögren.

Michanek, Germund. 1962. *En morgondröm: Studier kring Frödings ariska dikt*. Stockholm: Bonniers.

Moberg, Kerstin. 1978. *Från tjänstehjon till hembiträde: En kvinnlig låglönegrupp i den fackliga kampen 1903–1946*. Acta Universitatis Upsaliensis, Studia Historica Upsaliensia 101. Uppsala: Almqvist & Wiksell International.

Müller, Heidi. 1981. *Dienstbare Geister: Leben und Arbeitswelt städtischer Dienstboten*. Schriften des Museums für deutsche Volkskunde 6. Berlin: Museum für deutsche Volkskunde.

Näsström, Gustaf. 1937. *Dalarna som svenskt ideal*. Stockholm: Wahlström & Widstrand.

Nicolovius [Nils Lovèn]. [1847] 1957. *Folklivet i Skytts härad i Skåne vid början av 1880-talet: Barndomsminnen*. Stockholm: Bonniers.

Nilsson, Martin P:n. 1934. "Folklig tideräkning." In *Tideräkning*, ed. Martin P:n. Nilsson, 95–121. Nordisk kultur 21. Stockholm: Bonniers.

Nilsson, Monica. 1981. "Självbefläckelse och självtukt: En studie i re-

Bibliography

pressionen av onani." Department of European Ethnology, Lund University. Mimeo.

Nolan, Ann. 1979. "Veta sin plats." Department of European Ethnology, Lund University. Mimeo.

Norden, Ingrid, ed. 1913. *Illustrerad handbok för hemmet: Av fackbildade på olika områden*. Stockholm: Kvinnans Bokskatt.

Nordisk familjebok: Konversationslexikon och realencyklopedi. 2d ed. 38 vols. Stockholm: Nordisk Familjeboks Förlag, 1904–1926.

Nordström, Ludvig. 1907. *Fiskare*. Stockholm: Bonniers.

———. 1938. *Lort-Sverige*. Reprinted Sundsvall: Tidsspegeln, 1984.

Nyblom, Elsa. 1946. *När hjärtat var ungt*. Stockholm: Ljus.

Nyman, Anders. 1970. "Folk och fä: Samboendets renlighet och hygien." *Fataburen* 1970:143–154.

Nyman, Åsa. 1972. "Fäbodarnas osynliga invånare." In *Nordiskt Fäbodväsen: Förhandlingar vid fäbodseminarium i Älvdalen, Dalarna, 1–3 sept 1976*, ed. Göran Rosander, 58–67. Stockholm: Nordiska Museet.

Nystedt, Olle. 1972. "Tyst, pojke!" In *Jag minns min barndom*, vol. 2, ed. Allan Hofgren, 67–73. Stockholm: EFS-förlaget.

Odén, Birgitta. 1975. "Individuella tidshorisonter." In *Forskare om befolkningsfrågor: Blandvetenskaplig bilaga till Ett folks biografi*, ed. Torsten Hägerstrand and Anders Karlqvist, 87–153. Stockholm: Samarbetskommittén för långtidsmotiverad forskning.

Ödmann, Samuel. [1830] 1957. *Ett prästhus i Småland från förra århundradet*. In his *Hågkomster*, 5–32. Stockholm: Ljus.

Oljelund, Ivan, ed. 1946. *Min Mor: Fyrtiofem svenska män och kvinnor om sina mödrar*. Uppsala: Lindblads Förlag.

———, ed. 1949. *Min Far: Ny samling: Trettioen svenska män och kvinnor om sina fäder*. Uppsala: Lindblads Förlag.

Öller, Jöran Johan. 1800. *Beskrifning öfwer Jemshögs Sochen i Blekinge*. Facsimile ed. Olofström: Erik Jeppson, 1967.

Olwig, Kenneth. 1984. *Nature's Ideological Landscape: A Literary and*

Bibliography

Geographical Perspective on Its Development and Preservation on Denmark's Jutland Heath. London Research Series in Geography 5. London: Allen & Unwin.

Ortner, Sherry B. 1974. "Is Female to Male as Nature Is to Culture?" In Woman, Culture, and Society, ed. Michelle Zimbalist Rosaldo and Louise Lamphere, 67–87. Stanford: Stanford University Press.

Orwell, George. 1937. The Road to Wigan Pier. London: Gollancz.

Ottesen-Jensen, Elise. 1945. Säg barnet sanningen. Stockholm: Liber Förlag.

Palm, Göran. 1974. Bokslut från LM. Gothenburg: Författarförlaget.

Panduro, Elna. 1922. Det seksuelle Spørgsmaal i Hjem og Skole: En Vejledning for Mødre og Lærerinder. 3d ed. Copenhagen: Nordisk Sundhedsforlag.

Paulsson, Gregor. 1950. Svensk stad: Liv och stil i svenska städer under 1800-talet. 2 vols. Reprinted Lund: Studentlitteratur, 1973.

————. 1953. Svensk stad: Från bruksby till trädgårdsstad. Reprinted Lund: Studentlitteratur, 1973.

Pernö, Ulf. 1979. "Att upptäcka världen: Två hem, två världar, i sekelskiftets Sverige." Department of European Ethnology, Lund University. Mimeo.

Persson, Eva. 1977. Maskin, makt: Teknikens utveckling och arbetets förändring under industrialismen med vävningen som exempel. Stockholm: Riksutställningar.

Ploss, Heinrich, Max Bartels, and Paul Bartels. 1927. Das Weib in der Natur- und Völkerkunde: Anthropologische Studien. 3 vols. 11th ed. by Ferdinand Frh. von Reitzenstein. Berlin: Neufeld & Henius.

Posse, Margaretha. 1955. Herrgårdsliv vid Vättern. Stockholm: Wahlström & Widstrand.

Quensel, Alice. 1958. Äldsta dotter: Minnen av Stockholm och ämbetsmannafamilj. Stockholm: Wahlström & Widstrand.

Qvist, Gunnar. 1960. Kvinnofrågan i Sverige 1809–1846: Studier rörande

303

Bibliography

kvinnans näringsfrihet inom de borgerliga yrkena. Kvinnohistoriskt arkiv 2. Gothenburg: Akademiförlaget-Gumperts.

Rapp, Birgitta. 1978. *Richard Bergh—konstnär och kulturpolitiker 1890–1915*. Stockholm: Rabén & Sjögren.

Rehnberg, Mats, ed. 1953. *Verkstadsminnen. Svenskt liv och arbete 19*. Stockholm: Nordiska Museet.

———. 1967. *Blå välling—sur sill: Vällingklockor och vällingklocksramsor*. Reprinted Stockholm: LTs Förlag, 1978.

———. 1969. *Utredning rörande ämnet den borgerliga kulturen*. Humanistiska forskningsrådet, Stockholm. Mimeo.

Robertson, Priscilla. 1974. "Home as a Nest: Middle Class Childhood in Nineteenth-Century Europe." In *The History of Childhood: The Evolution of Parent–Child Relationships as a Factor in History*, ed. Lloyd DeMause, 407–431. New York: Psychohistory Press.

Rooth, Anna Birgitta. 1969. "Etnocentricitet." In her *Lokalt och globalt*, 2:178–211. Lund: Studentlitteratur.

Rosaldo, Michelle Zimbalist. 1974. "Woman, Culture, and Society: A Theoretical Overview." In *Woman, Culture, and Society*, ed. Michelle Zimbalist Rosaldo and Louise Lamphere, 17–42. Stanford: Stanford University Press.

Rosander, Göran. 1976. "Turismen och den folkliga kulturen." In *Turisternas Dalarna*, ed. Göran Rosander, 213–225. Dalarnas hembygdsbok 1976. Falun: Dalarnas fornminnes och hembygdsförbund, Dalarnas Museum.

Rosén, Sander and Bertil Wetter. 1970. "Ett bidrag till hemlighusets historia." *Fataburen* 1970:169–186.

Ruff, Josef. 1889–1893. *Illustreradt Helsovårds-Lexikon: En populär handbok för alla*. Stockholm: Blixten.

Sällskapet småfoglarnes vänner, dess verksamhet o. förhandl:r. Gothenburg: Zetterström, 1869–1872.

Sarmela, Matti. 1969. *Reciprocity Systems of the Rural Society in the*

Bibliography

Finnish–Karelian Culture Area. FF Communications 207. Helsinki: Suomalainen Tiedeakatemia.

Schivelbusch, Wolfgang. 1977. *Geschichte der Eisenbahnreise: Zur Industrialisierung von Raum und Zeit im 19. Jahrhundert.* Munich: Hanser.

Sennett, Richard. 1977. *The Fall of Public Man.* New York: Knopf.

Sennett, Richard and Jonathan Cobb. 1972. *The Hidden Injuries of Class.* New York: Knopf.

Shorter, Edward. 1975. *The Making of the Modern Family.* New York: Basic Books.

Siwertz, Sigfrid. 1949. *Att vara ung: Minnen.* Stockholm: Bonniers.

Sjöqvist, Kerstin. 1970. "Att skura golv." *Fataburen* 1970:131–142.

Söderberg, Sten, ed. 1947. *Barndomshemmet: Kända män och kvinnor berätta om sitt barndomshem.* Stockholm: Wahlström & Widstrand.

SOU 1933:14. *Undersökning rörande behovet av en utvidgning av bostadsstatistiken jämte vissa därmed förbundna bostadspolitiska frågor.* Statens offentliga utredningar 1933:14. Finansdepartementet. Stockholm: Isaac Marcus.

Statistiska Centralbyrån. 1914. *Utom äktenskapet födda barn.* Statistiska meddelanden, serie A, vol. 1:4. Stockholm: Norstedt & Söners Förlag.

Stattin, Jochum. 1984. *Näcken: Spelman eller gränsvakt?* Skrifter utgivna av Etnologiska sällskapet i Lund. Lund: Liber Förlag.

Stavenow-Hidemark, Elisabet. 1970. "Hygienism kring sekelskiftet." *Fataburen* 1970:47–54.

———. 1971. *Villabebyggelse i Sverige 1900–1925: Inflytande från utlandet, idéer, förverkligande.* Nordiska Museets handlingar 76. Stockholm: Nordiska Museet.

STF:s årsskrift. Svenska Turistföreningens årsskrift (Yearbook of the Swedish Touring Club). 1886–

Stiernstedt, Marika. 1946. "Borgerligt liv i 1800-talets slutskede." In

Bibliography

Sverige i fest och glädje, ed. Mats Rehnberg, 185–213. Stockholm: Wahlström & Widstrand.

————. 1947. "Ett officershem." In *Barndomshemmet,* 167–177. (*See* Söderberg 1947.)

Stjernstedt, Ruth. 1953. *Ocensurerad.* Stockholm: Fritzes Bokförlag.

Stone, Lawrence. 1977. *The Family, Sex and Marriage in England 1500– 1800.* London: Weidenfeld and Nicolson.

Sträng, Gunnar. 1979. "Man känner fattigdomens lukter." *Vi* 1:10–11.

Strindberg, August. [1902] 1962. *Fagervik och Skamsund.* In *Skrifter* 5:1–136. Stockholm: Bonniers.

————. 1967a. *The Red Room: Scenes of Artistic and Literary Life.* Everyman's Library 348. London: Dent.

————. 1967b. *The Son of a Servant: The Story of the Evolution of a Human Being.* London: Cape.

Sundbärg, Gustav. 1910. *Det svenska folklynnet.* Stockholm: Norstedt & Söners Förlag.

Sundin, Bo. 1981. "Från rikspark till hembygdsmuseum: Om djur- skydds-, naturskydds- och hembygdsrörelserna i sekelskiftets Sverige." In *Naturligtvis: Uppsatser om natur och samhälle tilläg- nade Gunnar Eriksson,* 152–194. Skrifter från Institutionen för idé- historia, Umeå universitet 14. Umeå: Institutionen för idéhistoria.

————. 1984. "Ljus och jord! Natur och kultur på Storgården." In *Paradiset och vildmarken: Studier kring synen på naturen och naturresurserna,* ed. Tore Frängsmyr, 320–360. Stockholm: Liber Förlag.

Sundman, Per Olof. 1968. *Ingen fruktan, intet hopp: Ett collage kring S. A. Andrée, hans följeslagare och hans expedition.* Stockholm: Bonniers.

Sundt, Eilert. [1857] 1968. *Om sœdelighetstilstanden i Norge.* Vol. 1. Oslo: Pax Forlag.

————. [1869] 1975. *Om renligheds-stellet i Norge.* Vol. 9 of *Verker i utvalg.* Oslo: Gyldendal Norsk Forlag.

Bibliography

Svärdström, Svante. 1949. *Dalmålningar och deras förlagor: En studie i folklig bildgestaltning 1770–1870.* Nordiska Museets handlingar 33. Stockholm: Nordiska Museet.

Svedelius, Wilhelm Erik. 1889. *Anteckningar om mitt förflutna lif.* Stockholm: Fahlcrantz.

Svenonius, Fredr. 1892. "Om lappkåtar samt Turistföreningens lappska fjällhyddor." *Svenska Turistföreningens årsskrift* 1892:3–41.

Svensson, Sigfrid. 1967. *Bondens år: Kalender, märkesdagar, hushållsregler, väderleksmärken.* 2d ed. Reprinted Stockholm: LT:s Förlag, 1972.

———, ed. 1972. *Nordisk folkkonst.* Handböcker i etnologi. Lund: Gleerups.

Swahn, Jan-Öjvind. 1963. *Jubelfest: Några notiser till guld- och silverbröllopsfirandets historia.* Lund: Cygnus Förlag.

Swang, Anne. 1979. "Ungdomens festbruk: Nattefrieriet." In *Studiet af fester: Seminar over teori og metode i nyere folkloristik afholdt i København 9.–11. marts 1978,* ed. Flemming Hemmersam and Bjarne Hodne, 105–119. Unifol Årsberetning 1978. Copenhagen: Institut for Folkemindevidenskab, Københavns Universitet.

Swensson, Hugo. 1947. "Bergsgatan och Solöfjärden." In *Barndomshemmet,* 178–184. (*See* Söderberg 1947.)

Szabó, Mátyás. 1970a. "Rena djur." *Fataburen* 1970:155–168.

———. 1970b. *Herdar och husdjur: En etnologisk studie över Skandinaviens och Mellaneuropas beteskultur och vallningsorganisation.* Nordiska Museets handlingar 73. Stockholm: Nordiska Museet.

Talve, Ilmar. 1970. "Bastu och badstugor." *Fataburen* 1970:55–68.

Tegnér, Torsten. 1947. "Bland tonerna på Tegnabo." In *Barndomshemmet,* 193–205. (*See* Söderberg 1947).

———. 1963. *Uppväxt: "Minnen från medeltiden."* Stockholm: Tidens Förlag.

Tenow, Elna. (*See* Törne.)

Bibliography

Therkildsen, Marianne. 1974. "Bondens børn: Om studiet af opdragelse og kulturel indlæring i 1800-årenes danske bondesamfund." *Folk og Kultur* 1974:90–116.

Thomas, Keith. 1984. *Man and the Natural World: Changing Attitudes in England 1500–1800.* New ed. Harmondsworth: Penguin.

Thomas, William Widgery, Jr. 1892. *Sweden and the Swedes.* Chicago: Rand McNally.

Thompson, E. P. 1967. "Time, Work-Discipline, and Industrial Capitalism." *Past and Present* 38:56–97.

Thue, Anniken. 1975. "Interiører og holdninger: Historisme og klunkestil ca. 1850–1900." *Gamle Bergen Årbok* 1975:5–30.

Tilander, Gunnar. 1968. *Stång i vägg och hemlighus: Kulturhistoriska glimtar från mänsklighetens bakgårdar.* 3d ed. Gothenburg: Fabel.

Tingsten, Herbert. 1961. *Mitt liv: Ungdomsåren.* Stockholm: Wahlström & Widstrand.

Törne, Elsa [Elna Tenow]. 1906. *Renhet: En häfstång för den enskilde och samhället.* Vol. 2 of *Solidar.* 2d ed. Stockholm: Sandbergs Bokhandel.

———. 1910. *Kärlek och lycka.* Stockholm: Bonniers.

Trudgill, Eric. 1976. *Madonnas and Magdalens: The Origins and Development of Victorian Sexual Attitudes.* London: Heinemann.

Veblen, Thorstein. 1899. *The Theory of the Leisure Class: An Economic Study of Institutions.* New York: Macmillan.

Vendelfelt, Erik. 1962. *Den unge Bengt Lidforss: En biografisk studie med särskild hänsyn till hans litterära utveckling.* Lund: Gleerups.

Vicinus, Martha, ed. 1972. *Suffer and Be Still: Women in the Victorian Age.* Bloomington: Indiana University Press.

———. ed. 1977. *A Widening Sphere: Changing Roles of Victorian Women.* Bloomington: Indiana University Press.

Vilkuna, Asko. 1959. *Die Ausrüstung des Menschen für seinen Lebensweg.* FF Communications 179. Helsinki: Suomalainen Tiedeakatemia.

Bibliography

Wahlman, L. J. 1902. "En gård och dess trefnad." *Ord och bild* 11:17–34.

Wahlström, Lydia. 1946. "Fyra flickors mor." In *Min Mor*, 237–244. (*See* Oljelund 1946.)

Wallquist, Einar. 1947. "Bruksgården på Dal." In *Barndomshemmet*, 215–222. (*See* Söderberg 1947).

Weber, Max. 1930. *The Protestant Ethic and the Spirit of Capitalism.* Talcott Parsons, trans. Reprinted with an introduction by Anthony Giddens. London: Allen & Unwin, 1976.

Wendorff, Rudolf. 1980. *Zeit und Kultur: Geschichte des Zeitbewusstseins in Europa.* Opladen: Westdeutscher Verlag.

Wikdahl, Magnus and Marianne Ekenbjörn. 1980, "Kultur- och klassgränser i den självbiografiska litteraturen: Ett diskussionsunderlag kring memoaranalys." Department of European Ethnology, Lund University. Mimeo.

Wikman, K. Rob. V. 1937. *Die Einleitung der Ehe: Eine vergleichend ethno-soziologische Untersuchung über die Vorstufe der Ehe in den Sitten des Schwedischen Volkstums.* Sonderdruck der Acta Academia Aboensis, Humaniora 11:1. Turku: Åbo Akademi.

Wikmark, Gunnar. 1979. *Pehr Högström: en storman i Norrlands kulturliv.* Bidrag till Kungl. Svenska Vetenskapsakademiens historia 15. Stockholm: Kungl. Vetenskapsakademien.

von Willebrand, B. M. 1932. *Den svenska adeln: En demografisk-kulturhistorisk undersökning av Sveriges och Finlands adel.* Stockholm: Bonniers.

Williams, Raymond. 1973. *The Country and the City.* Reprinted London: Hogarth Press, 1985.

Wingårdh, Marius. 1937. *Så går det till i umgänge och sällskapsliv.* Stockholm: Natur och Kultur.

Wohl, Anthony S. 1978. "Sex and the Single Room: Incest among the Victorian Working Classes." In *The Victorian Family: Structure and Stresses*, ed. Anthony S. Wohl, 197–216. London: Croom Helm.

Bibliography

Wrangel, F. U. 1924. *Barndomsminnen från stad och land 1853–1870.* Stockholm: Norstedt & Söners Förlag.

Zerlang, Martin. 1976. *Bøndernes klassekamp i Danmark—agrarsmåborgerskabets sociale og ideologiske udvikling fra landboreformernes tid til systemskiftet.* Copenhagen: Medusa.

Zetterberg, Hans. 1969. *Om sexuallivet i Sverige: Värderingar, normer, beteenden i sociologisk tolkning.* Statens offentliga utredningar 1969:2. Utbildningsdepartementet. Stockholm: Esselte.

· INDEX ·

Italic page numbers refer to illustrations.

Index

Index

Index

Index